STUART BUTLER, ANNA KAMINSKI,
JOHN NOBLE, ZORA O'NEILL

Contents

PLAN YOUR TRIP

- Highlights 6
- Best For 12
- With Kids 14
- Accessible Trails 16
- Essentials 18
- Walking in Spain 20

BY REGION

THE PYRENEES 27
- Punta del Pacino 30
- Alto & Bajo Sestrales 32
- Plan de Aigualluts 34
- Ibón de Anayet 36
- Valle de Otal 38
- Cañón de Añisclo 40
- Circo de Gurrundué 42
- Ibón Gran de Baticielles 46
- Estanh de Rius & Estanh Tort de Rius 48
- Estanys de Siscaró Loop 50
- Ordesa Canyon via the Faja de Pelay 52
- Puerto de Barrosa 56
- Circ de Colomèrs 58

PICOS & NORTHERN SPAIN 65
- Puertos de Áliva 68
- San Sebastián to Pasai Donibane 70
- Ruta del Cares 72
- Vega de Ario 74

- Mirador de Ordiales 76
- Horcados Rojos 78
- Picu Pierzu 80
- Costa Naviega 82
- Picu Urriellu 84
- Somiedo Lakes 86
- Arantzazu, Aizkorri, San Adrián 90
- Anboto 92

GALICIA 97
- Illas Cíes 100
- Parada de Sil Circuit 102
- Castro Caldelas Magical Forests 104
- O Vicedo to Porto de Espasante 106
- Muxía to Lires 108
- Lires to Cabo Fisterra 110

CENTRAL SPAIN 117
- Laguna Grande de Gredos 120
- San Lorenzo de El Escorial to Machota Baja 122
- Peñalara 124
- Siete Picos 126
- La Mira 130
- El Morezón 134
- Ruta de Carlos V 136

ANDALUCÍA 143
- Castaño del Robledo & Alájar Loop 146
- Río Borosa 148
- Sierra de Cazorla 150
- Cómpeta to El Acebuchal 152

- Las Negras to Agua Amarga 154
- La Tahá 156
- Mulhacén 158
- Acequias del Poqueira 162

MEDITERRANEAN COAST 169
- Montserrat 172
- Camí dels Molins 174
- Peña Cortada Loop 176
- Serra de Bèrnia Loop 180
- Cadaqués to Cap de Creus 182
- Volcanoes of Garrotxa 184
- Costa Brava Magic 186

MALLORCA & MENORCA 193
- Platja de Cavalleria to Platja de Binimel·là 196
- Cala Morell to Ciutadella 198
- Sant Tomàs to Son Xoriguer 200
- La Trapa Monastery 204
- Valldemossa a Deià 206
- Mirador de ses Barques to Sa Calobra 208
- Alcúdia Peninsula 212

- LANGUAGE 216
- BEHIND THE SCENES 218
- BY DIFFICULTY 219
- INDEX 220
- OUR WRITERS 224

As Europe's second-most mountainous country, Spain is a land of cinematic landscapes. From the snowy majesty of the Pyrenees to rugged coastal cliffs lashed by Atlantic storms and rural landscapes painted with white-washed, silent-at-noon villages, Spain inspires with its natural diversity.

In this book, we lead you along trails that will take you high into the Picos, Pyrenees and Sierra Nevada, through wild-flower meadows in Andalucía and to lofty coastal viewpoints in Mallorca and Menorca. We also point you towards off-the-beaten-path routes in Celtic-flavoured Galicia, semi-desert wilderness trails just back from the Mediterranean and the forgotten mountains of the Basque Country.

Throughout these hills, mountains, fields, beaches and cliffs there is an extensive and well-maintained network of walking trails, as well as numerous mountain lodges and village guesthouses, all of which help to make Spain a walker's dream. So, lace up your boots and hit the Spanish trail.

Highlights

CIRC DE COLOMÈRS, THE PYRENEES
A roller-coaster loop over a high, rocky pass and past dozens of glimmering lakes set in flower meadows and glacial bowls. p58

PICU URRIELLU, PICOS & NORTHERN SPAIN

Hike up to the awe-inspiring 500m-high rock pillar at the heart of the Picos de Europa, arguably the greatest concentration of mountain drama in the country. **p84**

LIRES TO CABO FISTERRA, GALICIA

An unforgettable coastal hike of long, wild beaches, high cliffs and capes and many a jagged, ocean-battered rock, to the lighthouse at the 'end of the Earth'. **p110**

MIRADOR DE SES BARQUES TO SA CALOBRA, MALLORCA & MENORCA

One of Mallorca's finest walks, this day hike comprises rambles through olive groves to gorgeous viewpoints, forested cliff stretches and the west coast's finest beaches. **p208**

EL MOREZÓN, CENTRAL SPAIN

Climb to a dramatic high peak with unrivalled views of the stunning glacial cirque and lake at the heart of the Sierra de Gredos. **p134**

COSTA BRAVA MAGIC, MEDITERRANEAN COAST
A journey of mesmerising beauty along the best of Catalonia's 'Rugged Coast' – sandy coves, clifftop pine woods, quaint fishing villages and turquoise waters. p186

ORDESA CANYON VIA THE FAJA DE PELAY, THE PYRENEES

Glacial mountain peaks, soaring canyon walls and a palette of colours. Every step you take through the 'Grand Canyon' of Europe will have you gasping in wonder. p52

RÍO BOROSA, ANDALUCÍA

Walk up beside a tumbling mountain river with countless waterfalls through scenery that progresses from the pretty to the majestic. p148

RUTA DEL CARES, PICOS & NORTHERN SPAIN

Breathtaking walk along a 1000m-deep Picos de Europa canyon, with pinnacle peaks piercing the sky and a mountain river tumbling along far below. **p72**

ACEQUIAS DEL POQUEIRA, ANDALUCÍA

Hike up a beautiful valley from a postcard-perfect white Andalucian village and return by a high-level path with vistas of the Sierra Nevada's highest peaks. **p162.**

Best For...

PATJO/SHUTTERSTOCK ©
JOSERPIZARRO/SHUTTERSTOCK ©

🔭 WILDLIFE

Spain is blessed with an incredibly rich diversity of plants and animals, and observant walkers have a good chance of spotting some exotic creatures.

CIRCO DE GURRUNDUÉ
Watch for bones falling from the sky as the mighty, and endangered, bearded vulture soars overhead. **p42**

PICU URRIELLU
There's a high chance of seeing chamois (and plenty of vultures) on this walk deep in the upper reaches of the Picos de Europa. **p84**

LAGUNA GRANDE DE GREDOS
With enormous sweeping horns, the ibex (pictured above) is a seriously impressive creature, and on this walk you're almost guaranteed a close-up sighting. **p120**

ILLAS CÍES
Pack binoculars to see nesting colonies of shag and yellow-legged gulls on this coastal walk. **p100**

CAMÍ DELS MOLINS
Spot hawks and wild goats on this quiet route through wild and remote country. **p174**

🧭 OFF-THE-BEATEN PATH

Clear the mind on these walks that take you far from the madding crowd.

CASTRO CALDELAS MAGICAL FORESTS
Dive deep into the dense woodlands, lost-in-time hamlets and medieval monasteries of the Ribeira Sacra. **p104**

ALTO & BAJO SESTRALES
Contemplate the scenery in peaceful solitude from this awe-inspiring Pyrenean viewpoint. **p32**

CASTAÑO DEL ROBLEDO & ALÁJAR LOOP
Beautiful inter-village walk through wooded hills in the little-visited Sierra de Aracena (pictured above). **p146**

CALA MORELL TO CIUTADELLA
Ponder over mysterious stone pyramids and shipwreck monuments in Menorca's uninhabited northwestern corner. **p198**

IBÓN GRAN DE BATISIELLES
Relish the beauty of the glowing, mountain-ringed Baticielles lakes. **p46**

12/PLAN YOUR TRIP

PAWEL KAZMIERCZAK/SHUTTERSTOCK ©

ARRIETAPHOTO/SHUTTERSTOCK ©

JORDICARRIO/SHUTTERSTOCK ©

COASTAL VIEWS
Some of the best walks in Spain are those that take you to the seaside.

COSTA BRAVA MAGIC
Everything from plunging cliffs and turquoise coves to white-painted fishing villages (pictured above). **p186**

SERRA DE BERNIA LOOP
On a clear day, you can see across a glittering Mediterranean to faraway Ibiza. **p180**

COSTA NAVIEGA
Twenty kilometres of roaring seas, cliffs, beaches and coves. **p82**

SANT TOMÀS TO SON XORIGUER
White-sand coves and precipitous cliffs await along Menorca's south coast. **p200**

LAS NEGRAS TO AGUA AMARGA
The dramatic beauty of Cabo de Gata's cliffs, coves and beaches. **p154**

BRINGING THE PAST TO LIFE
Walk with the spirit of history on these routes.

VALLDEMOSSA TO DEIÀ
Check out Chopin's winter retreat in pretty Valldemossa. **p206**

PEÑA CORTADA LOOP
March like a legionnaire on a Roman aqueduct and through an old fortress town. **p176**

ARANTZAZU, AIZKORRI, SAN ADRIÁN
An art-laden monastery (pictured above), prehistoric monoliths and part of the medieval Camino de Santiago. **p90**

LA TAHÁ
Sense the Moorish ambience of the villages of Las Alpujarras. **p156**

PARADA DE SIL CIRCUIT
Enjoy centuries-old watermills, vineyards and a monastery. **p102**

PRETTY VILLAGES
Mother Nature is a great artist, but some Spanish villages can give her a run for her money.

CADAQUÉS TO CAP DE CREUS
Admire a tumble of white houses ringing up from a superb natural harbour (pictured above). **p182**

ACEQUIAS DEL POQUEIRA
Capileira, a delightful mountain village on the slopes of the plunging Poqueira Gorge. **p162**

CAMI DELS MOLINS
Enjoy Ares del Maestrat, with its lovely mountaintop castle. **p174**

PICU URRIELLU
Sotres is a huddle of red-tile-roofed houses in a green valley among high limestone crags. **p84**

VALLDEMOSSA TO DEIÀ
Walk from one Tramuntana artists' village to another. **p206**

With Kids

Walking with children can be incredibly rewarding for both you and your kids. It's time together as a family without the distractions and pressures that day-to-day life brings.

TRAILS & TRIBULATIONS

As wonderful as walking with children can be, it does bring challenges and requires careful planning. The most important thing is to pick your route wisely, and not be overly ambitious.

If your child consistently finds the walks you choose too difficult, they'll quickly be put off walking for good. But, on the other hand, the shortest and easiest walks are not always the best ones to do with children either. If it's too easy then many a child loses interest. Throw in some boulders to climb, summits (achievable ones) to conquer and streams to jump across, and you'll probably find your kids can't get enough.

It's a good idea to go through the different trail options with your children the night before and let them decide if they think they can do it or not. When it comes to walk times, keep in mind that the times written in this book are for walking only and don't include stops. With children you'll stop more often than if you were only with adults, so it's best to double all walk times. For most children under the age of 12, a walk we list as taking five hours (for adults) will take most of the day with children. Start early and have a torch just in case it takes more than all day!

Don't take a risk with the weather. Trudging up the side of a mountain in sheets of rain will not endear you to your children. Ideally, choose only dry, sunny days but ones that aren't too hot either. If it is hot, choose a walk that involves a lake, stream or beach and let them cool off in the water.

BEST WALKING REGIONS

There are good walks for children in every corner of Spain, but the coastal regions are the king of the (sand) castle when it comes to family-friendly walks. Mallorca and Menorca are probably the overall best bet with some easy-going coastal walks but also a few more child-challenging mountain walks to keep

Walking with Babies & Toddlers

Walking with children below the age of about four or five presents a unique set of issues. If your child is still a baby and hasn't yet found their feet, walking with them is generally pretty easy. You just need to wrap them up warm and put them in a baby backpack (on most walking trails you can forget about pushchairs) and off you go.

Toddlers and young children are a different matter. Chances are they're not likely to want to spend all that long strapped to your back, but they can't generally walk very far either. You might find that getting more than a few hundred metres from the car park is something of a struggle. Don't let that put you off entirely though. Instead, find a walk that has interest within the first kilometre (such as a beach or a river). If children start associating walking with fun outdoor activities, you'll have them hooked for life.

 ## Best Family Walks

Platja de Cavalleria to Platja de Binimel·là, Mallorca & Menorca Short and gentle walk with the promise of beaches. p196

Peña Cortada Loop, Mediterranean Coast Roman aqueduct tunnels and a high bridge bring history to life. p176

Río Borosa, Andalucía Children will be thrilled by the tunnels through the Cerrada de Elias gorge. p148

Plan de Aiguallots, The Pyrenees Fall in love with the Pyrenees on this wonderful family hike. p34

Illas Cíes, Galicia Beaches + lighthouses + birdwatching hides + clifftop viewpoints = happy children. p100

interest levels up. Andalucía and the Mediterranean Coast also have some superb options, and the coastal walks in Galicia are perfect in high summer.

For higher altitudes, both the Pyrenees and the Picos have some wonderful family-friendly options. In fact, most of the valley walks in these two areas are busy with walking families between late spring and early autumn.

WHAT TO PACK

Make sure your children have good-quality, comfortable walking shoes – you really don't want them getting blisters due to ill-fitting shoes. Bring plenty of warm clothes as well as spare clothes (because if there's a stream there's a good chance they'll get wet!). Most importantly, bring lots of food, snacks and water – at least twice as much as you think they might want. You'll be amazed at how much they can eat while walking.

TOP TIPS

Make things a little easier for all of you by following these tried and tested tips.

• Let the kids map-read or use a compass (but keep an eye on progress yourself!).

• Take a plastic container for collecting wild blueberries, raspberries and other identifiable berries. In many mountain areas there are other cool things for kids to collect: unusual stones, feathers etc.

• Ask them to find their own walking stick.

• Bring or download a field guide to the animals, birds and flowers of an area and see how many they can identify.

• Searching for animal footprints is also a good way of keeping children interested.

Accessible Trails

ACCESSIBLE TRAVEL IN SPAIN

Generally, Spain is not overly accommodating for travellers with disabilities, but things are slowly changing. For example, disabled access to official buildings and hotels represents a change in local thinking. In major cities, more is slowly being done to facilitate disabled access to public transport and taxis; in some cities, wheelchair-adapted taxis are called 'Eurotaxis'. Newly constructed hotels in most areas of Spain are required to have wheelchair-adapted rooms. With older places, you need to be a little wary of hotels that advertise themselves as being 'disabled-friendly', as this can mean as little as wide doors to rooms and bathrooms, or other token efforts.

Further information on accessible travel in Spain is available from these sites and organisations:

COCEMFE (www.cocemfe.es) Spanish NGO offering a wide range of services and support to people with physical disabilities.

Accessible Spain Travel (www.accessiblespaintravel.com) Organises accessible tours, transport and accommodation throughout Spain for travellers with limited mobility, although there's nothing really aimed at those wanting to get out on the trails.

Lonely Planet Download Lonely Planet's free Accessible Travel guide from https://shop.lonelyplanet.com/categories/accessible-travel.com.

Rutas Movilidad Reducida en España (https://es.wikiloc.com/rutas/sendero-accesible/espana)

Around 500 reduced-mobility routes are listed on this Wiki Loc page. Unfortunately, they're not organised in any logical manner.

CHOOSE YOUR REGION WISELY

Although many trails in Spain are challenging for people with reduced mobility or for the older or less fit walker, there are some routes that are at least partially accessible, and highly rewarding, to everyone.

Throughout this book, any of the walks given an 'Easy' walk rating can be conquered by almost anyone, although some are still on partially uneven paths or involve gentle climbs and descents. Note that a walk marked as 'Easy' in the Picos or Pyrenees is not the same as a walk marked 'Easy' in a flat coastal region. Less fit walkers

Illas Cíes

The Illas Cíes, a small group of protected islands off the coast of Galicia, are a fantastic destination for wheelchair users and those who are less mobile.

Wheelchairs, amphibious crutches, information materials in braille and a Joëlette chair are available for use free of charge from the national park information kiosk 170m along a wooden boardwalk from the boat jetty. The first three items are normally available on the spot, but can also be reserved in advance (email iatlanticas@xunta.gal for a reservation form). The Joëlette chair is only available by advance reservation.

Several paths on the islands, including those to the Faro de Cíes lighthouse and Praia de Figueiras beach, are wheelchair-accessible.

Ferries to the islands are accessed by wheelchair-accessible boardwalks.

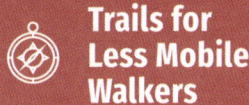

Trails for Less Mobile Walkers

Illas Cíes, Galicia p100

Sant Tomàs to Basílica de Son Bou, Mallorca & Menorca p215

Volcanoes of Garrotxa, Mediterranean Coast p184

O Vicedo to Porto de Espasante, Galicia p106

Valle de Otal, The Pyrenees p38

---

should add plenty of rest time onto the standard walk times we have listed (the walk times in this book do not include any stoppage time).

It's always worth contacting the local tourist board of your chosen region and asking their advice on accessible trails. The following gives a rundown on the plus and minus points for every region of Spain included in this book.

THE PYRENEES

High mountains, steep inclines and rocky trails don't exactly lend themselves to being wheelchair accessible. Less fit walkers should find pleasure strolling the first part of the Cañón de Añisclo and Valle de Otal trails. It should also be possible to explore lower parts of the Ordesa canyon.

PICOS & NORTHERN SPAIN

The vertically inclined Picos are similar to the Pyrenees in being not very wheelchair friendly. Elsewhere along the north coast of Spain are a few other options that have some sections that should be passable. The Costa Naviega and Somiedo Lakes walks are fairly flat and would be good bets for less fit walkers.

GALICIA

Galicia has some interesting trails for both wheelchair users and the less fit walker; although many follow the convoluted coastline and aren't great for wheelchairs, they are fine for otherwise less mobile walkers.

CENTRAL SPAIN

Central Spain is also an area of mountain peaks with trails that aren't really suitable to the less mobile. The Silla de Felipe II, which is a stop on the San Lorenzo de El Escorial to Machota Baja walk, can be reached via a 1km wheelchair-friendly trail called the Senda Ecológica. For more information, check www.sanlorenzoturismo.es.

ANDALUCÍA

Perhaps surprisingly, Andalucía doesn't have many options for less mobile walkers, although the first half of the Río Borosa route is fairly flat and good for the less fit.

MEDITERRANEAN COAST

The Mediterranean Coast has plenty of wheelchair-friendly short coastal routes in and around the resorts and towns, but if you want to get into wilder country then things are considerably more challenging.

MALLORCA & MENORCA

Although Mallorca and Menorca have good general holiday facilities for less mobile visitors, there are fewer options when it comes to walking. Trails on Menorca are generally flatter and easier going than those on rugged Mallorca.

Essentials

WHEN TO WALK

There is some form of walking available year-round in Spain. In lower-altitude, hotter southern parts of the country, the best walking periods are autumn through to late spring. Galicia and the northern coast is best from late spring through to autumn. Throughout the country, winter in the high mountains is universally cold and snowy, with many trails being blocked by snow from late November through to early April. Summer is the most popular walking period for the high mountains. Overall then, by far the best periods for a general walking holiday in Spain are spring (late March to mid-May) and autumn (September to October).

Further details on the best time to walk in each area are given in the relevant chapters.

RESPONSIBLE WALKING

By its very nature, walking is an activity with a low environmental footprint. The following points should always be kept in mind.

Park regulations National parks and other protected areas often have very strict regulations that are clearly marked on signboards near parking areas. Stick to these rules.

Camping Wild camping is generally forbidden in protected areas except at designated spots (often in the immediate vicinity of mountain refuges). Bivouacking though is normally allowed for a night. Outside of protected areas the rules can be a little hazier. Camping is always forbidden on beaches, but in rural areas putting up a small tent for the night well away from houses is often tolerated. Make sure you obtain the permission of landowners if you are wanting to camp on private land.

Trails Always stick to marked trails – never try to create your own shortcut, as this is potentially dangerous and leads to erosion.

Fire Campfires are prohibited in protected areas, on beaches and on almost all other public lands. In some regions (the Mediterranean and Andalucía), walk areas can be closed in summer due to the high risk of forest fires.

Water Avoid buying bottles of mineral water and instead invest in a portable water filtration system. There are many different types on the market.

Disturbance Don't pick wild flowers and avoid disturbing wildlife.

Rubbish Remove all of your rubbish. It's a good idea to bring a small waste bag.

Safety Tips

- Check the weather forecast before you go (www.aemet.es) and be prepared for it to change suddenly for the worse.
- Inform someone of your intended route and when you expect to be back.
- Set your pace and objective to suit the slowest member of the party.
- Carry a mobile phone for emergencies, but don't rely on it for navigation.
- Pack for all weather even if the forecast is fine.
- Bring enough food to get you through a night. And always have a torch.
- Dial 112 in case of an emergency. Operators speak English.
- Spain's hunting season is October to early February: if you see signs reading *coto deportivo de caza* or *escenario de caza*, enter the area with caution.

Resources

Federación Española de Deportes de Montaña y Escalada (FEDME; Spanish mountain sports federation; www.fedme.es) Top resource for mountain sports and hiking routes. In Spanish.

Sendero de Gran Recorrido (www.senderosgr.es) Official site for all of Spain's long-distance trails. In Spanish.

Misenda (https://misenda fedme.es/buscador-de-senderos) Extensive listings, descriptions and route maps for thousands of official PR trails across Spain. In Spanish.

Walks in Spain (www.walksin spain.org) User-generated, countrywide walk routes.

WHAT TO PACK

The number one rule when it comes to packing for a Spanish walking holiday is to bring less than you think you might need. Bring too much and half your gear will remain unused at the bottom of your bag.

Some essentials that nobody should come without include the following:

- Quality hiking boots
- Comfortable backpack
- Walking poles
- Sun cream
- Sunglasses and hat
- Relevant maps (Alpina produces superb hiking maps to almost every corner of Spain)
- Torch (flashlight)
- Wet-weather gear (including waterproof trousers)
- Water filtration system and bottle (tap water is fine to drink, but it's sensible to filter water you pull out of a lake passed on a trail)
- Fleece and other warm clothing (nights in the mountains can be cold even in high summer and snow can fall as early as September and as late as May).

WAYMARKERS

Official walking trails almost always have some kind of waymarker to help with route finding. These waymarkers come in a confusion of styles.

Long-distance (more than 50km) walking tracks across Spain are called Sendero de Gran Recorrido (GRs) and have red-and-white waymarkers. Such routes are invariably very well marked throughout their length. Important shorter trails (10km to 50km) are called Sendero de Pequeño Recorrido (PRs) and have yellow-and-white waymarkers. These are also normally very clearly marked.

Important local trails are called Sendero local and are normally marked in green and white; however, waymarkers on these trails can sometimes be a bit hit-and-miss. You might also encounter local walking trails around, for example, a village, which can be marked in whatever paint colours the local council had lying around (yellow is common). In mountain areas you should also keep an eye out for rock cairns (small piles of rocks) that serve the same purpose.

On very popular routes there are often also destination signs, which can include the remaining distance too.

Walking in Spain

Spain is a natural wonder. The Pyrenees and Picos de Europa are as beautiful as any mountain range on the continent, while the snowcapped Sierra Nevada rises up improbably from the sun-baked plains of Andalucía; these are hiking destinations of the highest order. The wildly beautiful cliffs of Spain's Atlantic northwest are offset by the charming coves of the Mediterranean. And all across the interior, wild Spain survives, from the wolves and bears that inhabit remote mountain valleys to the central *meseta* (high plateau) that rolls out beyond the horizon like one of Don Quijote's visions.

NATURAL WALKERS

With so many diverse landscapes and so many quality walking trails, it won't come as a surprise to learn that the Spanish are natural walker, and that hiking is one of the most popular activities in the country with people of all ages. It's not at all unusual to see people aged over 70 striding up the side of a Pyrenean mountain slope as if they were just taking a quick stroll around the park. There are walking clubs and groups in most towns, and at weekends it's common to see large groups of club members out walking together.

There are also numerous walking magazines, and an endless number of websites, blogs and apps covering walking in Spain. Many Spanish people travel, both within the country and further afield, solely for the purpose of hiking, and there are numerous walking-holiday companies to cater to this demand.

All of these are fairly new developments that have occurred over the past few decades. But many of Spain's thousands of kilometres of walking trails are actually ancient paths that, before the invention of the car, were once the main routes between villages, towns and cities. Vestiges of days past are often visible alongside these trails: old water fountains that still spurt forth delicious cool, clear water, ancient drystone walls lining the paths, stone route markers with distances carved by hand into the rock. Sometimes you may even find yourself walking along an old cobbled or paved road laid by Roman hands. If you know where to look, then it would be fair to say that any countryside walk in Spain is a walk through history.

WHERE TO WALK

With so many options to choose from it can be very hard to know where to begin when planning a Spanish walking holiday. Take our advice and don't try to be too ambitious. Instead of rushing here, there and everywhere across the country and spending more time in a car or on a train than out on the trail, focus on just one or two parts of the country. It would be simple enough to combine a week of walking in the Pyrenees with a week of walking in the Picos and the north coast, for example, or to combine Andalucía and central Spain.

THE PYRENEES

For good reason, the Pyrenees, separating Spain from France, are Spain's premier walking destination. The range is prim and chocolate-box pretty on the lower slopes, wild and bleak at higher elevations, and relatively unspoiled compared to many European mountain ranges.

The Pyrenees contain two outstanding national parks: Aigüestortes i Estany de Sant Maurici and Ordesa y Monte Perdido.

PICOS & NORTHERN SPAIN
Breathtaking, accessible limestone ranges with distinctive craggy peaks (usually hot rock-climbing destinations too) dominate Spain's first national park, the Picos de Europa, which straddles Cantabria, Asturias and León provinces. It's one of Spain's best hiking areas.

Elsewhere in northern Spain, a network of trails bounds up and down coastal cliffs and links timeless inland villages.

GALICIA
In summer, when great swathes of southern and central Spain are broiling and walking can be more endurance than pleasure, Galicia comes to the rescue. Lush, damp and startlingly green, Spain's northwestern corner is a convulsion of twisting coastline, old stone villages and hills piled upon hills. There's superb walking throughout and, except for on the world-famous Camino de Santiago, you'll encounter very few foreign walkers on the trails.

CENTRAL SPAIN
There's more to central Spain than Don Quijote, windmills and vast wheat fields. A spine of rocky and rugged 2200m-plus mountains called the Sistema Central rise up from the *meseta,* providing an oasis of delightful alpine wilderness. The mountain trails here are popular with *madrileños* (people from Madrid), but are chronically overlooked by foreign walkers.

ANDALUCÍA
The hot southern region of Andalucía is an area of striking contrast. Here you can slink between whitewashed villages in the Alpujarras valleys and the Sierras de Cazorla and Sierra de Grazalema mountain ranges, scale snowy peaks and splash from one outstanding beach to the next along Andalucía's unexpectedly wild Mediterranean coast. This variety makes Andalucía a great year-round hiking destination.

PREVIOUS PAGE: WALKING THE SENDA DE LOS CAZADORES (P53)
THIS PAGE: TOP: STREETS OF CADAQUÉS (P182)
BOTTOM: WAYMARKER, CAMINO DE SANTIAGO

MEDITERRANEAN COAST

While Spain's Mediterranean coastline might be better known for sprawling sangria-and-sunlounger resorts, in-between and beyond the concrete jungles are vast areas of wild lands. The walking trails of the Mediterranean coast cover the gamut of hiking experiences: cliffside coastal trails to idyllic beaches, pilgrimage trails and hardy mountain walks where silence will be your lone companion. Although Spain's Mediterranean coastline is one of the worlds biggest tourist destinations, out on the trail you can go for hours without meeting another soul.

The region's warm and dry coastal trails are a great autumn-to-spring walking destination, whereas the cooler mountainous interior is better from spring to autumn.

MALLORCA & MENORCA

Mallorca and Menorca welcome visitors with a varied kaleidoscope of landscapes: pristine coves with turquoise waters, forested ravines, rocky canyons, precipitous cliffs, pine and holm-oak forests, remnants of ancient cultures and long stretches of white-sand beach. Though some trails are well-trodden, you may have the rest entirely to yourself.

CAMINO DE SANTIAGO

One of the world's most famous long-distance trails, the Camino de Santiago (Way of St James) originated as a medieval pilgrimage and, for more than 1000 years, people have taken up the Camino's age-old symbols – the scallop shell and staff – and set off on the adventure of a lifetime to the tomb of St James the Apostle in Santiago de Compostela, in the Iberian Peninsula's far northwest.

There are several *caminos* (paths) to Santiago de Compostela in Galicia, passing through a number of Spanish regions, including Navarra, Cantabria and Asturias, Castilla y León and Galicia. The most popular is the **Camino Francés**, which spans 770km of Spain's north, starting on the French side of the Pyrenees and attracting walkers of all backgrounds and ages from across the world. Its list of assets (cultural, historical and natural) is impressive, as are its accolades. Not only is it the Council of Europe's first Cultural Itinerary and the centrepiece of the Camino's Unesco World Heritage listing but, for believers, it's a pilgrimage equal to visiting Jerusalem, and by finishing it you're guaranteed a healthy chunk of time off purgatory.

To feel, absorb, smell and taste northern Spain's diversity, for a great physical challenge, for a unique perspective on rural and urban communities, and to meet intriguing travel companions, this is an incomparable walk.

SNOW SHOEING

If you're in the snowbound mountains of Spain in winter then you might think that any form of mountain hiking is out of the question. But then along came snow shoeing (known as *raqueta de nieve* in Spanish), and suddenly mountain hiking became a year-round activity. Snow shoes aren't shoes at all, but are more akin to tennis-racquet-shaped 'skis' that strap onto hiking boots and allow you to walk through deep snow that you'd otherwise sink into. For your first attempts, start by renting gear at a ski station and walking one of the clearly marked snow-shoe trails found in many ski resorts.

REFUGIOS

If you're walking in the mountains of Spain then you'll likely see and hear much mention of *refugios*. A *refugio* is a mountain hut or lodge that can be used for overnight accommodation by walkers. Some *refugios* are staffed from about June to October and meals are often available for guests (nonguests can almost always get

Rock Climbing

Spain offers plenty of opportunities to see the mountains and gorges from a more vertical perspective. Vie ferrate are growing fast in number and popularity around the country. A good source of info is the excellent (but Spanish-only) site http://deandar.com.

For an overview of Spanish rock climbing, check out Rockfax (www.rockfax.com) and Climb Europe (www.climb-europe.com). Both include details on the country's best climbs. Rockfax also publishes various climbing guidebooks covering Spain.

Bears & Wolves

The charismatic *oso pardo* (brown bear) inhabits the Cordillera Cantábrica (in Cantabria, Asturias and northern Castilla y León) with a further, tiny population in the Pyrenees – close to 250 bears survive, spread across the two populations. The last known native Pyrenean bear died in October 2010. The current population in the Pyrenees is entirely made up of introduced bears from Slovenia and their offspring.

Spain's population of *lobo ibérico* (Iberian wolf; pictured right) has been stable at between 2000 and 2500 for a few years now, up from a low of around 500 in 1970. Though officially protected, wolves are still considered an enemy by many country people and the hunting of wolves is permitted in some areas. The species is found in small populations across the north, including the Picos de Europa. But Europe's densest and most easily accessible wild wolf population is in the Sierra de la Culebra, close to Zamora.

---

a hot drink and snack and sometimes even a meal at lunchtime). At unstaffed *refugios*, you'll need to bring your own food and cooking gear.

Although often very basic (expect dorm-style accommodation and shared, cold-water bathrooms), *refugios* are invariably very social places where you'll quickly fall into conversation with other walkers.

In summer, if a *refugio* is staffed, you should always try and book a bed in advance (nowadays, most staffed *refugios* have their own websites) – otherwise you'll likely find them full. With unstaffed *refugios* it's a case of first come, first served. Always have some camping or bivouacking gear with you in case you miss out on a bed.

Refugio staff are usually highly knowledgeable about all the walking trails spinning away from the hut and will be fully aware of any changes to the route or other potential dangers.

In non-mountainous areas *refugios* are rare, but campsites are common and there are sometimes other forms of cheaper accommodation aimed specifically at walkers, such as cheap guesthouses and hostels. Along the Camino de Santiago there are loads of very cheap pilgrim accommodation options. To use them you must be able to prove that you're a genuine pilgrim with a Credencial del Peregrino (Pilgrim's Credential/passport).

WILD SPAIN

Spain is one of Europe's best destinations for wildlife. Most of the excitement surrounds the three flagship species – the Iberian lynx, the Iberian wolf and the brown bear, but while you're very unlikely to encounter any of these three hanging out by the side of a walking trail, you are likely to encounter plenty of other wildlife.

One of Spain's most eye-catching species is the *cabra montés* (ibex), a stocky mountain goat species whose males have distinctive long horns. Almost hunted to extinction by 1900, the ibex was protected by royal decree a few years later (though it's still subject to controlled hunting today). There may now be 50,000 ibex in the country, chiefly in the Sierra de Gredos and in the mountains of Andalucía.

Other common mammals include the *jabalí* (wild boar); the *ciervo, corzo* and *gamo* (red, roe and fallow deer); the *gineta* (genet), a catlike creature with a white-and-black coat; and the *ardilla* (red squirrel). The chamois (*rebeco, sarrio, isard* or *gamuza*), a small antelope, lives mainly above the tree line in the Pyrenees and Cordillera Cantábrica. Southwestern Spain is home to the Egyptian *meloncillo* (mongoose). Gibraltar's 'apes' – actually Barbary macaques – are the only wild monkeys in Europe.

With around 500 species Spain has easily the biggest and most varied bird population in Europe. Around 25 species of birds of prey, including the *águila real* (golden eagle), *buitre leonado* (griffon vulture) and *alimoche* (Egyptian vulture), breed here. Although the white stork is everywhere (its large and ungainly nests rest atop electricity pylons, trees and towers), much rarer is the *cigüeña negra* (black stork), which is down to about 200 pairs in Spain.

NATIONAL & NATURAL PARKS

Much of Spain's most spectacular and ecologically important terrain – about 40,000 sq km or 8% of the entire country, if you include national hunting reserves – is under some kind of official protection. Most of these areas are at least partly open to walkers, naturalists and other outdoor enthusiasts, but degrees of conservation and access vary.

The *parques nacionales* (national parks) are areas of exceptional importance and are the country's most strictly controlled protected areas.

Spain has 15 national parks: 10 on the mainland, four in the Canary Islands and one in the Balearic Islands. The hundreds of other protected areas fall into at least 16 classifications and range in size from 100-sq-metre rocks off the Balearics to Andalucía's 2099-sq-km Parque Natural Sierras de Cazorla. For more information, visit www.mapama.gob.es/es/red-parques-nacionales/nuestros-parques.

WILDLIFE RESOURCES

The following online and book resources will help guide your steps and provide fascinating background information when watching wildlife in Spain.

Fundación Oso Pardo (www.fundacionosopardo.org) Spain's main resource for brown bears.

Iberlince (www.iberlince.eu) Up-to-the-minute news on the Iberian lynx.

Iberia Nature (www.iberianature.com) An excellent English-language source of information on Spanish fauna and flora, although some sections need an update.

Wild Spain (Teresa Farino; 2009) Useful practical guide to Spain's wilderness and wildlife areas.

Collins Bird Guide: The Most Complete Guide to the Birds of Britain & Europe (Lars Svensson *et al*; 2010) Considered the classic field guide to the birds of Europe.

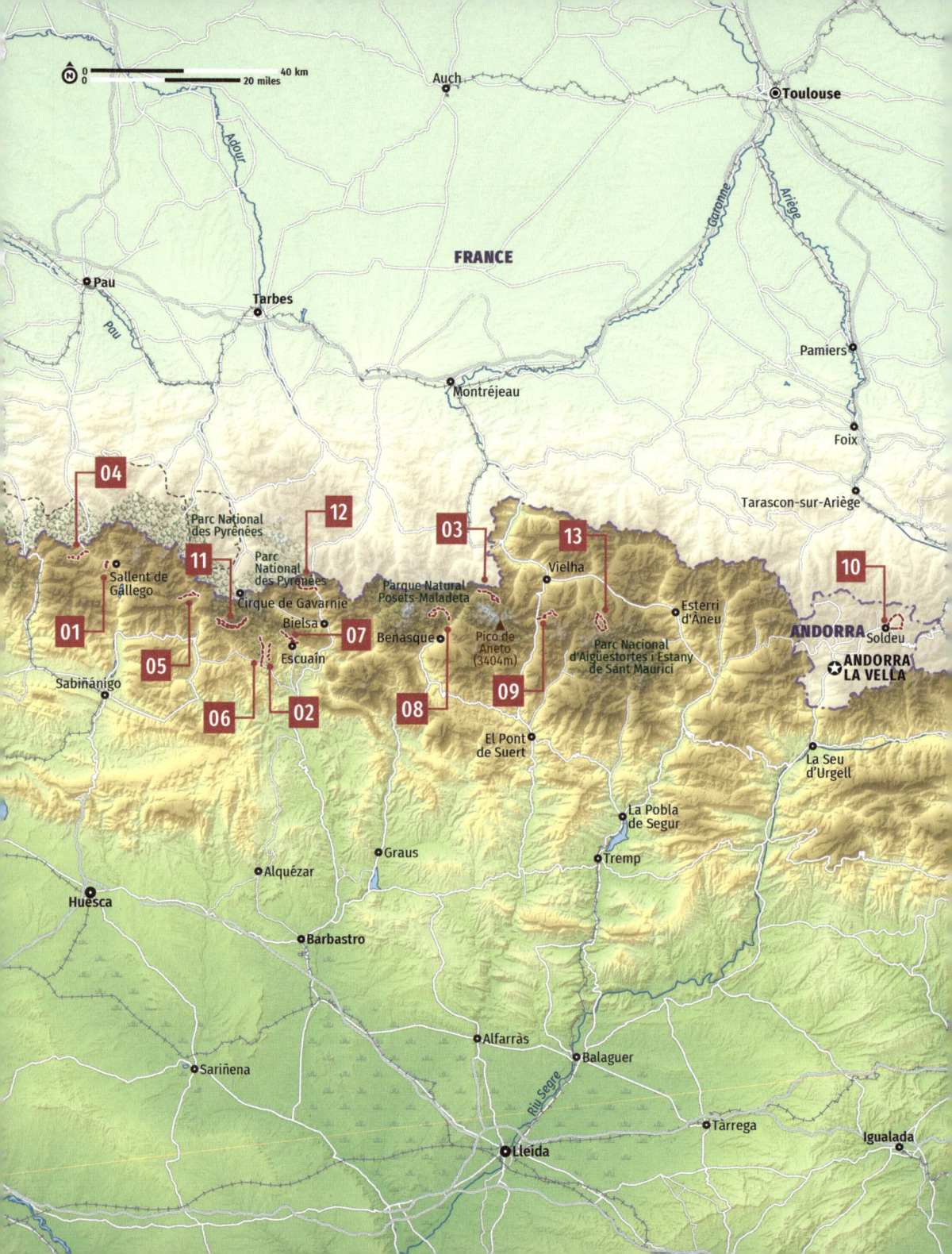

THE PYRENEES

01 **Punta del Pacino** Admire the 360-degree views from this easily reached summit. **p30**

02 **Alto & Bajo Sestrales** Peer gingerly over the edge of these soaring cliffs. **p32**

03 **Plan de Aigualluts** Fall in love with the Pyrenees on this wonderful family hike. **p34**

04 **Ibón de Anayet** Escape the world by walking to this upland plateau and lake. **p36**

05 **Valle de Otal** Stroll through the flower meadows of this picture-perfect valley. **p38**

06 **Cañón de Añisclo** Fawn over Mother Nature's artwork on this beautiful canyon walk. **p40**

07 **Circo de Gurrundué** See lammergeier on the walk to this forgotten mountain cirque. **p42**

08 **Ibón Gran de Batisielles** Enjoy the the tranquil, green-tinged Batisielles lakes. **p46**

09 **Estanh de Rius & Estanh Tort de Rius** Discover these two glorious lakes in the Pyrenees. **p48**

10 **Estanys de Siscaró Loop** Hit the high passes and loll by the lakes on Andorra's finest. **p50**

11 **Ordesa Canyon via the Faja de Pelay** Explore the magnificent 'Grand Canyon' of Europe. **p52**

12 **Puerto de Barrosa** Stand atop this breezy pass and peer down into France. **p56**

13 **Circ de Colomèrs** Lose count of how many lakes you've passed on this epic hike. **p58**

THE PYRENEES/27

Explore
THE PYRENEES

They might not be the biggest of mountains, but the Pyrenees have an unsurpassed beauty. Mirror-glass lakes, spring-flower meadows, snow-dusted summits, neat stone villages and orange-tinted beech forests. It's all here. And with every valley offering something new, it's hardly a surprise that many seasoned walkers rate the Pyrenees as their favourite mountain range.

SALLENT DE GÁLLEGO

This attractive ski-resort and hiking town of grey stone houses sits at the northern end of a large lake and is surrounded by the giants of the western Pyrenees. There's plentiful accommodation and places to eat and a buzzy year-round atmosphere.

TORLA

Torla's stone houses are gathered tightly around the village church and behind rise the sheer, multi-hued walls of one of Europe's greatest canyons: Ordesa. The village setting is unforgettable, as are the numerous walks that start from near here. With heaps of accommodation and places to eat it's the perfect base for the western and southern parts of the famed Parque Nacional de Ordesa y Monte Perdido (Ordesa and Mont Perdido National Park).

BIELSA

The village of Bielsa is a popular base camp for hikers wanting to tackle walking routes on the eastern and southern sides of the Parque Nacional de Ordesa y Monte Perdido. There's a good range of facilities.

BENASQUE

Gateway to the central Pyrenees and the stunning Parque Natural Posets-Maladeta, Benasque is surrounded by the highest peaks in all the Pyrenees. You could spend weeks walking the trails fanning out from this little town and, fortunately, there are lots of hotels, guesthouses, campgrounds and other facilities that will help you do just that.

VIELHA

The large ski resort and summer hiking town of Vielha is the eastern gateway to the lake-splotched Parc Nacional d'Aigüestortes i Estany de Sant Maurici (Aigüestortes i Estany de Saint Maurici National Park). Of all the gateway towns listed here, it's the only one that is a real town and so has plentiful tourist facilities.

SOLDEU

In the north of Andorra this is a classic ski and hiking resort. There's good access to the rest of Andorra (and Spain and France) and very good facilities.

☼ WHEN TO GO

Summer (June to August) is the most popular time to walk in the Pyrenees. The weather is at its most stable, most days are sunny and hot, and snow will have melted everywhere but on the highest summits. There are some negatives to walking in high summer though. Trails

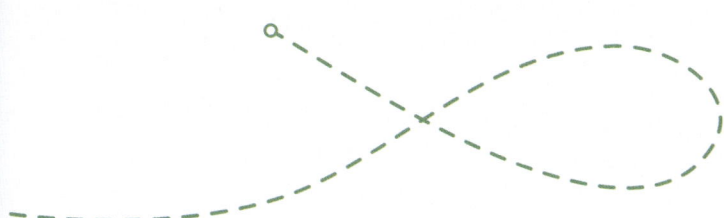

can be busy, it can be too hot to truly be comfortable and heat haze can mess with the views. Afternoon thunderstorms are common.

Spring (April to May) can be good, but late snow may block even fairly low-level routes. Autumn (September to October) is normally fantastic. The weather is often perfect, temperatures are lower than in summer, the haze has cleared, fresh snow covers the summits and, in October, the trees put on an unforgettable colour change as the leaves fall.

 **TRANSPORT**

There are generally no big cities or towns with reliable transport connections to other parts of Spain actually within the mountains themselves. The Pyrenees are not an easy place to explore by public transport, and getting to most of the trailheads (which are invariably outside of towns or villages) is near enough a no-go without your own car. That said, walks around Andorra and the small village of Torla can be accessed by public transport without too much effort.

 **WHERE TO STAY**

Many of the walking base towns are also winter ski resorts and, as such, most have plenty of accommodation. This tends to consist of fairly unmemorable studios and apartments. Formal hotels are not as commonly found. On the plus side, many villages have lovely little guesthouse-style accommodation and there's a growing range of Airbnb options. There are plenty of summertime campgrounds around most Pyrenean villages.

There's a superb network of *refugios* (mountain huts or lodges) buried deep within the peaks. Most are summer-only and, for day walkers, are more useful as places to get a drink rather than for accommodation.

Note, camping is officially forbidden within any of the area's national or natural parks.

 **WHAT'S ON**

Pirineos Sur (www.pirineos-sur.es; ◷Jul) Brilliant world music festival held in Sallent de Gállego.

Resources

The following websites are full of information about each of the region's national and natural parks.

Parque Nacional de Ordesa y Monte Perdido (www.ordesa.net)

Parque Natural Posets-Maladeta (www.rednaturaldearagon.com)

Parc Nacional d'Aigüestortes i Estany de Sant Maurici (parcsnaturals.gencat.cat)

Aragon Tourist Board (www.turismodearagon.com)

Catalonia Tourist Board (www.catalunya.com)

Andorra Tourist Board (www.visitandorra.com)

You should never attempt any of the more ambitious walks in the Pyrenees without a proper walking map and compass. The maps produced by **Editorial Alpina** (www.editorialalpina.com) are by far the best for any of the trails in this chapter.

Ski season (◷Dec-Apr) Put away your hiking boots and hit the powder at one of the region's ski resorts. Formigal near Sallent de Gállego is the biggest ski resort in the Pyrenees.

Transhumance (◷20 Jul) Join the shepherds as they march from San Nicolás de Bujaruelo over the Puerto de Bernatuara and into France with thousands of cows.

01

PUNTA DEL PACINO

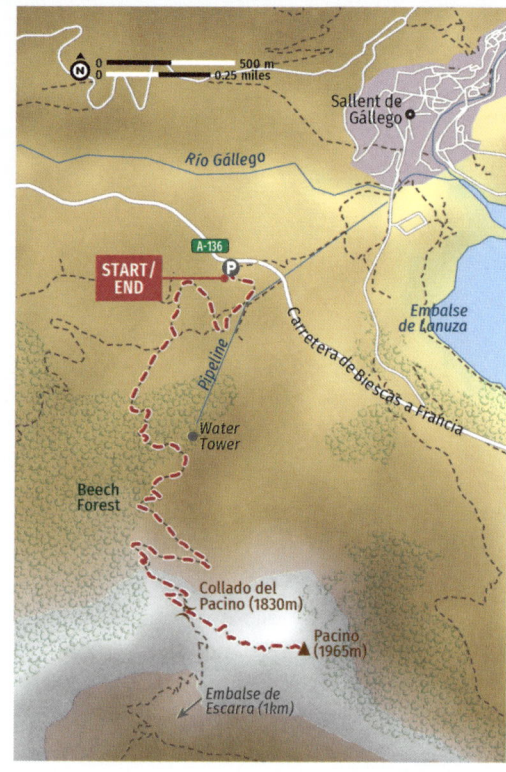

DURATION	DIFFICULTY	DISTANCE	START/END
3½hr return	Easy	8.5km	Parking area off A136, near Sallent de Gállego
TERRAIN	Mountain trail		

Whistle in wonder from this domed summit, which offers one of the best viewpoints in the western Pyrenees. This superb – though at times quite steep – family walk (min/max altitude 1390/1965m) rewards with atmospheric forests and incredible vistas. Less prone to being blocked with snow, it can be walked earlier and later in the season than many other nearby routes.

The trickiest part of this walk is finding where it begins. Take the main exit road out of Sallent de Gállego and turn north along the A136 towards the French border. On the right, after around 900m, is a dirt track and parking area. The walk starts here.

Follow the yellow waymarkers uphill along a forestry track. You will see a large water pipeline coming down the hillside to your south. After 10 minutes, at the junction, turn right (south). A few minutes later, turn onto the signed walking track. Cut across a small pasture, and then lose yourself in a thick **beech forest**, which is a magnificent palate of autumnal colours in October. The trail zigzags very steeply upwards.

The path emerges out of the forest onto a ridge with a large **water tower**, then continues to the **Collado del Pacino** (1830m) pass. Pant upwards to the obvious domed summit to the east; all the time the views open up to the west to reveal a big reservoir, the **Embalse de Escarra**. After a good 20 minutes, you'll come to the summit (1965m) and a view of roughed-up ridges of mountains and serrated sierras.

Return by the same route.

02
ALTO & BAJO SESTRALES

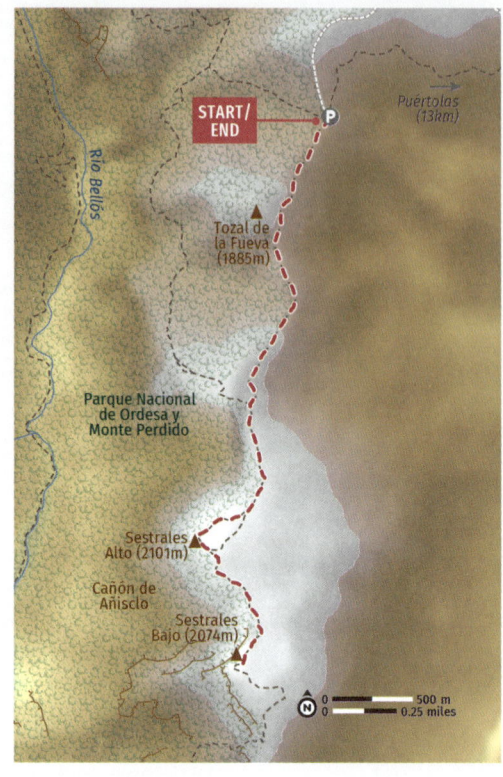

DURATION	DIFFICULTY	DISTANCE	START/END
3½hr return	Easy	9.5km	Parking Plana Canal

TERRAIN	Partially waymarked grassy trail

Crossing gorgeous summer-flower meadows grazed by herds of semi-wild sheep and cattle, this walk takes you to a lofty vantage point with views of Monte Perdido and nerve-tingling glimpses hundreds of vertical metres downwards into the Cañón de Añisclo.

Despite a few short, steep climbs (min/max altitude 1738/2101m), this is a good family walk (but keep hold of children near cliff edges). There's no shade, so avoid very hot days.

You can see the goal of your walk – the great cliffs and plateau immediately to the south of the parking area – throughout this walk. To get to the parking area, drive 2.5km from the village of Puertolas, then take the forest track signed Mt Sesa for 9km to the Plana Canal car park. The route begins by the signpost reading 'Sestrales Alto y Bajo'. Follow the direction of the arrow up and around the **green hill** directly south and then continue up and over another couple of ridges tinged yellow by **broom flowers** in early summer. After 1½ hours, you'll come to an enormous figure-eight-shaped grassy plateau covered in strange **limestone rock formations**. This first part of the plateau is the **Sestrales Alto** (2101m).

Carry on to the second part of the figure-eight plateau. This is the **Sestrales Bajo** (2074m) – although it's slightly lower, the views are better. The cliffs here fall absolutely sheer away for hundreds of metres. You're so high above the Cañón de Añisclo that **eagles** and **vultures** are likely to be soaring on the thermals below.

To return, simply retrace your steps.

Best for

OFF THE BEATEN PATH

03

PLAN DE AIGUALLUTS

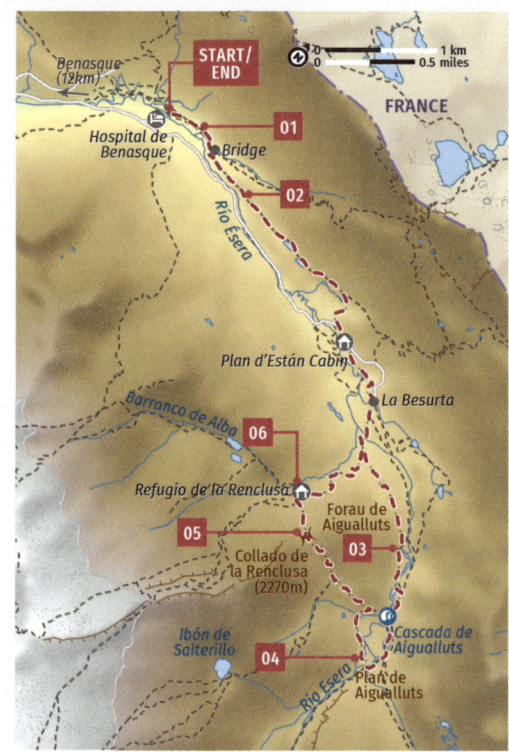

DURATION	DIFFICULTY	DISTANCE	START/END
4½hr return	Easy	16km	Hospital de Benasque

TERRAIN	Easy mountain trail

This family-friendly walk (min/max altitude 1740/2270m) through the glorious Parque Natural Posets-Maladeta just keeps on giving. Idyllic meadows, jewel-blue lakes and streams, glacier views, beautiful waterfalls, an unusual canyon wall and crossing a pass. It's all here! The path is clear and well-indicated and the views are stunning.

GETTING HERE
The walk starts from the large Hospital de Benasque, a former pilgrim and travellers' inn that dates back to the 12th century. From Benasque town it's 13km along the A139.

STARTING POINT
There's a large car park at the Hospital de Benasque and the place continues to serve its age-old purpose of providing beds and food to foot-weary walkers.

01 From the Hospital de Benasque, walk north and cross the bridge over the Río Ésera. The trail is clearly signed in yellow and white from here and the path is obvious. Bend to the east and follow the line of a low **stone wall** through flat grazing pastures with forested peaks piled up on all sides of the valley. After a short distance, cross back over the river via a small **wooden bridge**.

02 The trail wiggles southeast through scattered conifer woodland and comes to a junction. Take the trail marked 'Besurta, Forau de Aiguallut'. Working gently uphill for 10 minutes, you'll come to a number of **sparkling lakelets** and pass a signpost explaining the geology of the valley. A wet prairie opens up in front of you in which you'll find the **Plan d'Están cabin** (a basic unstaffed refuge). Here, another signboard reveals the glacial past of this valley. Continuing over the prairie (an hour from the start), you cross a wooden bridge and come to an important junction known as **La Besurta** (1890m). There's a small car park here, but in summer vehicle access is limited. The path leading south is signed for the **Refugio de la Renclusa** (we will return this way). For now, continue straight ahead (southeast) towards Forau de Aigualluts.

03 The trail is now partially paved with rough stone slabs and the waymarkers change to green. A slightly more ruthless, 45-minute climb follows. Eventually, you'll arrive at the **Forau de Aigualluts** (2000m), a high canyon wall. Just beyond this are the **Cascada de Aigualluts**, one of the more picturesque waterfalls in the Pyrenees (pictured). This sheet of water tumbles down a cliff face at the head of a rocky valley.

04 Continue for another 15 minutes to **Plan de Aigualluts** (2020m), which has views back along the valley and over towards the shimmering glaciers of **Aneto** (3404m), the highest mountain in the Pyrenees.

05 Retrace your footsteps a couple of hundred metres until you reach a side trail heading west and signed for Refugio de la Renclusa. The path climbs upwards through grasslands, conifer trees and boulders. After around 40 minutes, you'll reach the **Collado de la Renclusa** (2270m), a pass with stunning views of the meandering streams of the Plan de Aigualluts.

06 The path drops through more wooded country to the **Refugio de la Renclusa** (2140m). From here, it's a simple half-hour walk back to the trail junction at La Besurta. Then, return to the car by the same route you walked up.

TAKE A BREAK

The **Hospital de Benasque** (☏ 0608 536 053; www.llanosdelhospital.com; Llanos del Hospital; ⊘ closed May & Nov; P 🛜) serves pasta and steaks, and drinks from 1.30pm to 10pm. The Refugio de la Renclusa also serves light meals.

04

IBÓN DE ANAYET

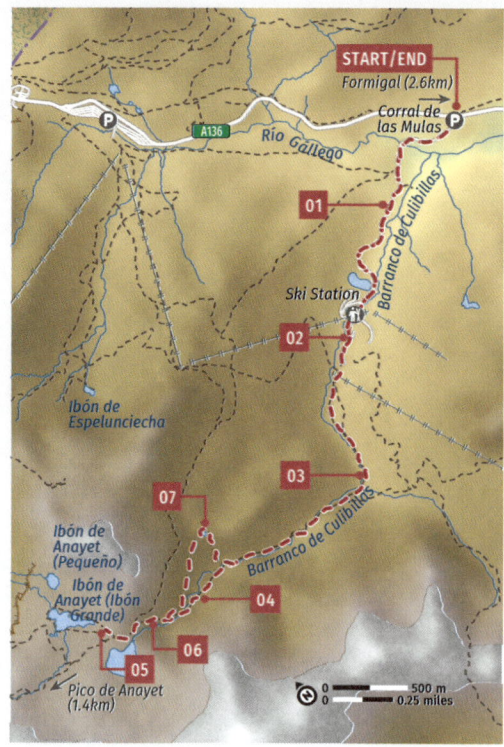

DURATION	DIFFICULTY	DISTANCE	START/END
4hr return	Moderate	11km	Corral de las Mulas

TERRAIN	Mountain trail

When streaks of spring snow lie on the ground around the high-altitude lake of Ibón de Anayet and eagles whirl with the winds, it's easy to imagine that you've been transported to the vast Tibetan plateau. Yes, this is a very special corner of the Pyrenees and what's more, this upland paradise is reached via a clear and easy trail (min/max altitude 1625/2225m) that's accessible even to (energetic) families.

GETTING HERE

From the ski resort of Formigal take the N136 north towards the French border. North of Formigal (2.6km) is a small parking area on the left known as Corral de las Mulas. The walk starts here. However, a minor road runs from Corral de las Mulas to the upper ski station. If the gate is open you could drive along this road and park at the ski station. This would cut 3km (return) of road walking off your hike but, if it's out of season, there's a very real risk that workers at the site might lock the access gate and leave you trapped!

STARTING POINT

There are no facilities at Corral de las Mulas.

01 From Corral de las Mulas either follow the minor road west to the upper car park and **ski station**, or the trail that runs between the road and the **Barranco de Culibillas** stream. Either way, it's a 25-minute, 1.5km gentle uphill walk.

02 The route to the lake is signed from the ski station. Simply follow the red-and-white **GR11 waymarkers** uphill under the ski lifts. The stream will be on your right. After a few hundred metres, the trail veers southwest away from the ski installations, still following the course of the stream.

03 Around 20 minutes from the ski station, the trail veers right (west) and heads up a side valley. All signs of the ski station are now out of sight behind you, replaced by the art of nature. Climb up steadily through the **rocky valley**, with big peaks rising on either side.

04 After a 25-minute climb, the path levels out on a small plateau and crosses the stream. As you approach the head of the valley, the trail begins to zigzag up towards a wide **waterfall**. After 30 minutes more of steady climbing (during which you pass the waterfall), the trail creeps up over a ridge and onto the huge plateau.

05 The **Ibón de Anayet** lake fills the heart of the boggy plateau. The distinctive, fish-head-shaped mountain to the north is the **Pic du Midi d'Ossau** (2884m) in France. The imposing, fang-shaped peak immediately to the northwest of the lake is the **Pico de Anayet** (2545m). To the south lies a wall of often snow-dusted mountains.

06 Return by the same route as far as the fork in the trail just after you pass the waterfall. Instead of sticking to the GR11, carry on straight ahead on a minor trail marked with a few rock cairns. The trail works its way around the eastern flank of a low mountain and goes gently uphill to a low ridge a few hundred metres away. Keep an eye out for **marmots**.

07 There is a small depression on top of this ridge containing a **lakelet**. Circumnavigate it and enjoy the views northwards over a horizon rippled in mountains. Descend in a southerly direction steeply downhill (there's no set trail) to meet up with the GR11. Retrace your steps back to the car park.

TAKE A BREAK

There are plenty of cafes at the upper ski station, but they're only open during the ski season. Enjoy a picnic with a view from the edge of the Ibón de Anayet.

05

VALLE DE OTAL

DURATION	DIFFICULTY	DISTANCE	START/END
4hr return	Moderate	16km	San Nicolás de Bujaruelo
TERRAIN	Clear footpath		

If you had to conjure up an image of the picture-perfect mountain valley, then the Valle de Otal is probably the kind of thing you'd imagine. It has the wild-flower meadows with a backdrop of cloud-scraping mountains, fluorescent turquoise streams, and immense beech and aspen forests. But more than anything, it has a sense of quiet calm and secret discovery that make this family-friendly walk (min/max altitude 1350/1690m) one of the finest leg stretchers in the Pyrenees.

GETTING HERE
The walk begins from San Nicolás de Bujaruelo, a 12th-century religious-run hostel for pilgrims. Today, it's still a hostel and campground, but most of the guests are eager hikers. San Nicolás de Bujaruelo is a 30-minute drive along a rough stone track northwest of Torla and Ordesa.

STARTING POINT
There's a huge car park here, plus basic accommodation and camping available at the **Refugio de Bujaruelo** (the former pilgrim hostel).

01 From the Refugio de Bujaruelo cross over the **Río Ara** via the much-photographed, humpbacked **medieval bridge**. Then swing left (northwest) following the sign to the **Puente de Oncins** (Oncins Bridge), which is 30 gentle minutes away through patches of woodland and open ground.

02 Cross back over the river at the **Puente de Oncins** and 200m later swing right at the sign reading **Otal por Pista** (Otal by track). The trail then sweeps in great serpentine curls

Knights, Pilgrims & Cows

Dating from the 12th century, San Nicolás de Bujaruelo was established by the Knights Templar as a rest house for Santiago-bound pilgrims who'd just crossed the harrowing **Puerto de Bujaruelo** (2275m; Bujaruelo pass) from Gavarnie in France.

Shepherds, taking their cattle to and from higher pastures on both sides of the international border, were also frequent visitors to San Nìcolás de Bujaruelo. It's a tradition that continues today and if you're in the area over the night of 20 July you can join the shepherds taking their cows over the nearby **Puerto de Bernatuara** (2305m; Bernatuara pass) and into France.

uphill for around 50 minutes. Although the going can be hard, the views back down to the river and across towards the **Monte Perdido** massif will keep you smiling.

03 The Valle de Otal is entered after passing through a **farm gate**. The trail is now pretty much flat and the scenery utterly different to what you've just walked through. Instead of vertical slopes and thick forests, there lies in front of you a vast meadow lit by spring flowers and grazed by docile cows. The corners of the valley rise up steeply to the north and south and a wall of frozen summits

blocks off the western end of the valley. Through it all runs a clear mountain brook, which you now follow for a lazy 45 minutes until you get to the **Cabin de Otal** (1640m).

04 Carry on west a couple of hundred metres to a set of small **waterfalls**. From here, you can scramble uphill for a few minutes to a **low rise** (1690m) from where there are stellar views back down the valley.

05 Return the way you came until the junction just before the Puente de Oncins. Instead of crossing the bridge, follow the **signed trail** directly south down the west bank of the river. It should take about 20 minutes to get from here to the car park at San Nìcolás de Bujaruelo.

TAKE A BREAK

The **Refugio de Bujaruelo** (974 48 64 12; www.refugiodebujaruelo.com; San Nìcolás de Bujaruelo; mid-Mar–Oct; P) sizzles up grilled meats, burgers and pasta (mains €8 to €15). Reservations are advised. Plenty of day-trippers picnic by the medieval bridge, but we'd suggest holding out until you reach the Valle de Otal and enjoying your lunch on the peaceful, sunny riverbank.

06
CAÑÓN DE AÑISCLO

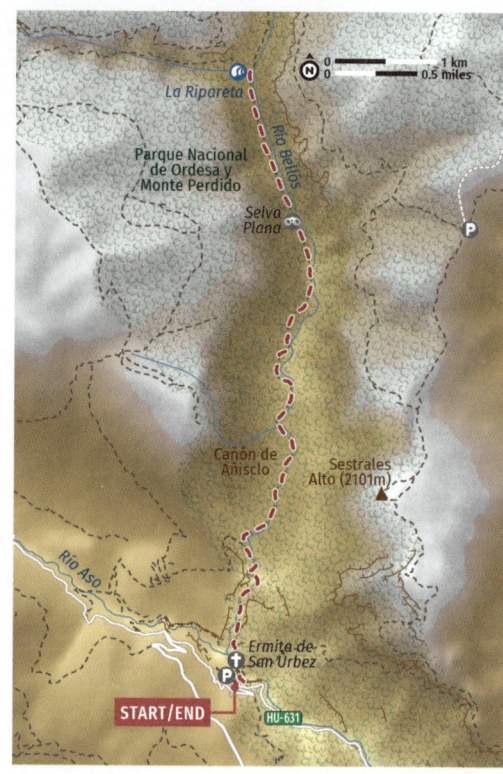

DURATION	DIFFICULTY	DISTANCE	START/END
5hr return	Moderate	14.5km	Car park, Ermita de San Úrbez
TERRAIN	Wide, clear mountain trail		

The second largest of the Ordesa region canyons, the celebrated Cañón de Añisclo is a narrower, more intimate affair than its more famous twin, Ordesa, and the scenery here is less about soaring mountain views and more about the delicate beauty of the river and the extensive beech forests. If you can, do this walk (min/max altitude 900/1410m) in October when the forests shimmer with autumnal shades.

A good family walk would involve going to the point (two hours from the start) at which the path starts climbing steeply up the canyon walls.

From the car park, take the trail heading right (east) down the steps towards the river. At the bottom follow the signs for La Ripareta (three hours).

Within moments, you'll pass the **Ermita de San Úrbez** (San Úrbez Hermitage), a tiny cliff-side retreat that's normally locked. A few minutes later, at the trail junction, carry on straight ahead. It's then simply a case of following a well-maintained and very obvious trail north along the river for three hours.

The route criss-crosses the river a couple of times. At times the gin-blue waters are only metres from the path, but at others the trail wanders into thick **beech forests**. Around two hours from the start, the path begins to climb much more steeply up the **western canyon walls** to reach the **Selva Plana** viewpoint with views over warped walls of rock.

The remainder of the walk is a virtually flat amble through cool, damp woodland. Finally, three hours from the start, the river rises up to meet the path at **La Ripareta**, a beautiful set of low waterfalls and tumbling, clear rapids. Return by the same route.

07

CIRCO DE GURRUNDUÉ

Best for

WILDLIFE

DURATION	DIFFICULTY	DISTANCE	START/END
5hr return	Moderate	15km	Revilla

TERRAIN	Mountain trail

One of the great forgotten trails of the Parque Nacional de Ordesa y Monte Perdido, the hike (min/max altitude 1205/1990m) to the imposing Circo (Cirque) de Gurrundué is a superb option for those looking to escape the crowds of busier nearby trails.

This is also one of the best corners of the Spanish Pyrenees for wildlife. With huge lammergeier (bearded vultrues) commonly seen along the upper levels of this walk, as well as numerous griffon vultures, izard and wild boar, this is an excellent walk for birdwatchers and naturalists. There's also a short two-hour circuit that's a good bet for families.

GETTING HERE

You need a good road map to get to Revilla (also known as Rebilla). It's a tiny semi-abandoned place and even Google Maps can lead you astray! If coming from Escalona near the entrance to the Cañón de Añisclo, carry on north up the A138 towards the Spanish-French border. In the small village of Hospital turn left (west) along a very minor road and follow it for 12.5km to Revilla. Park your car a couple of hundred metres before the village (where the road dead ends anyway), at the point where the road turns very sharply right.

STARTING POINT

There are a couple of walk and wildlife information panels at the start point and space for a dozen or so cars to park.

01 Walk into the village and up the cobbled road following the signs to **Foratarruego**. A few minutes later at the trail junction, take the left trail. The trail zigzags sharply upwards and, after five minutes, this bends right back on itself and starts heading northwest and uphill. You will come to a signpost a moment or so later. Carry on straight ahead here. The trail soon buries itself in mixed woodland.

02 The rocky, but clear trail climbs gently uphill. After 30 minutes, you'll reach a junction. A sign points left for the miradors (viewpoints) and Revilla. Ignore this for the moment (we will head this way on the way back), and carry on straight ahead (northwest). The woodland gets thicker and the trail runs between **drystone walls** and passes signs announcing your arrival in the national park. Emerging out of the forest, you will be greeted by a view down into the **Escuaín gorge**. An hour from the start, a small bridge crosses over a waterfall at the head of the **Barranco de Angonés** (1400m) gorge. Immediately afterwards, at the signed trail junction, turn right and head uphill along the stone path.

03 For the next hour, you will be walking through dense mixed woodland and you'll likely see where **wild boar** have been foraging all along the edge of the trail. Two hours from the start, you'll reach the often dry riverbed of the **Barranco Garganta** (1600m) gorge. At the trail junction and signpost just after this, turn right and start to climb very steeply. The reward for all the exertion is some wonderful views southwards over tabletop escarpments and deep valleys.

The Lammergeier

With a wingspan of 3m, the lammergeier (*Gypaetus barbatus*), is not a bird you can easily miss. A member of the vulture family, it has dark upper wings and a tawny body. It feeds on carrion and spends most of its days soaring on mountain thermals searching for carcasses. But, size aside, what really separates this avian monster from all other birds is that its favourite delicacy is bone marrow. Of course, for an animal without any hands, breaking bones open to get to the marrow isn't easy, but the lammergeier (pictured) has a trick up its wing. Picking up a bone in its bill, it soars into the sky and drops the bone onto rocks from heights of up to 80m in order to crack it open.

To learn more visit the **Eco Museo** (974 50 05 97; www.quebrantahuesos.org; €4; 10.30am-2.30pm & 3.30-8pm Jul-Sep, 11am-7pm Oct-Jun;) in nearby Aínsa.

04 A little under three hours from the start, you'll come to a rocky shale slope. Climb up this and emerge out of the forest onto flatter ground. You will spot the tiny, unstaffed **Refugio de Foratarruego** on a spur of rock above you to your right.

Head across the open pastures to the end of the giant, rocky, **arrow-shaped headland** (1990m) you will have found yourself on, and enjoy the extraordinary 270-degree views all around you – including, to your north, the giant vertical walls of the **Circo de Gurrundué** (pictured) and to your southwest the soaring Sestrales Alto (see walk 02, p32). This is also perhaps the best place in all the Pyrenees to watch rare **lammergeiers** and other raptors, including lots of bulky **griffon vultures**. Izard (chamois) are also commonly seen scrambling around the cliff face of the cirque. It's worth scrambling 10 minutes uphill to the northeast for even better views down into the cirque.

05 Return the way you came until you get to the signed junction for the miradors and Revilla, 30 minutes from the car. Here, leave the trail you walked up and head right (southwest) towards the miradors. After a few minutes, the trail bends sharp right (west) and ambles through woodland to reach the cliff face and some **steps** leading downwards. Note that the signage can be a little confusing here as there are

STUART BUTLER/LONELY PLANET ©

multiple side trails, but in the end most go to the same place. At the bottom of the steps, turn left and onto flatter ground.

After a few minutes, you will come to a sign pointing right to the **mirador**, which is worth the very short detour. Afterwards, walk east along the edge of the cliff face for 10 minutes; there are some stomach-turning drop-offs here, so keep a good hold of children. You will pass another viewpoint and the tiny **Ermita de San Lorién**, which is half-buried into the cliff face.

06 Shortly afterwards, the trail moves away from the cliff edge, crosses over an often **dry stream** and climbs slightly before arriving back at the parking area. The loop via these viewpoints makes for a popular two-hour **family walk**.

TAKE A BREAK

There's nowhere selling food and drink on or near this route. Bring a picnic and munch away with a view of the cirque.

08

IBÓN GRAN DE BATISIELLES

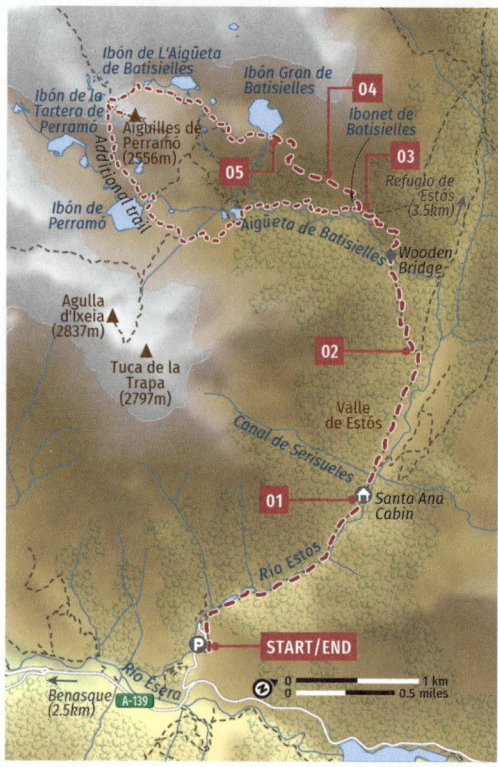

DURATION	DIFFICULTY	DISTANCE	START/END
5½hr return	Moderate	14.5km	Parking Estós

TERRAIN	Mountain trail

Mother Nature let all her creative juices run free when she created the Valle de Estós and Circo (Cirque) de Batisielles with its serene green-tinted lakes. And this walk (min/max altitude 1300/2200m), which is one of the finest in the Spanish Pyrenees, takes you through the best of it all.

GETTING HERE
The walk begins from the Parking Estós, which is 4.3km north of Benasque. To get there take the A139 northbound for 3.8km, then take the small turn-off on the left signed for the Valle de Estós.

STARTING POINT
There are no facilities at the car park.

01 Leaving the car park, saunter along the dirt track signed **Valle de Estós**. A couple of minutes later, at the first bend in the road, take the trail on the left (rocks across the track prevent cars driving any further). The trail starts to climb quite quickly and passes a waterworks. Winding now through dense mixed woodland with the Río Estós to your right (true left), you'll pass through a farm gate (close it after you), cross back over the river and then continue on to the small **Santa Ana cabin**.

02 Continuing in the same easy upwards pattern, you will come to a junction after an hour. The main route continues northwest up the Valle de Estós (it's an easy and delightful five-hour return walk from the parking area to the **Refugio de Estós** (pictured) at the head of this valley). Our adventure though takes the trail leading off left (west), which is signed for the Ibón de Batisielles.

🥾 Keep on Walking

The scenery on this walk is so impressive that some find it hard to resist the temptation to keep on walking. If that's you, you're in luck. It's possible to extend the walk by completing a big loop from the Ibón Gran de Batisielles past a dozen other lakes and pools (the biggest of which is the **Ibón de Perramó**) and over the impressive **Perramó Pass** (2500m) to rejoin the main trail back at Ibonet de Batisielles. Add more excitement to the mix by summiting the Aiguilles de Perramó (2556m) for a view of a slew of Pyrenean giants. The entire walk to and from the Parking Estós takes around 7½ hours without stops. It's not especially difficult but isn't a route for mountain walking newbies.

Best for
OFF THE BEATEN PATH

03 The trail sweeps upwards fairly steeply through forest to a small **wooden bridge** over the crystal-clear, icy-cold **Aigüeta de Batisielles** stream. Around 2½ hours' walk from the car park, the trail bursts triumphantly out of the forest and onto a gentle grassy meadow, at the heart of which sits the small, round lakelet **Ibonet de Batisielles** (1860m). It's a beautiful, quiet spot for a break.

04 It's an energy-sapping 50-minute, very steep haul upwards to the Ibón Gran de Batisielles. Leave the Ibonet de Batisielles and pass to the left of the tiny shepherd cabin near the lakeshore. The path sails upwards in a southwest direction and is marked with small **rock cairns**. By now, the trees have peeled back and stupendous views back down the valley and across to other ranges improve with every strained step.

05 You'll cross through an area of big granite boulders before swinging left and climbing a little more and then, finally, the trail flattens out and skips across a high **flower meadow** to the serene silence of the **Ibón Gran de Batisielles**. On a still day, the surrounding saw-toothed mountains of the Circo de Batisielles will reflect beautifully in the mossy-green lake waters. Return by the same route.

☕ TAKE A BREAK

There are no facilities anywhere along the actual trail but plenty of enticing picnic spots. The banks of the Ibón Gran de Batisielles offer the best rest spot.

09
ESTANH DE RIUS & ESTANH TORT DE RIUS

DURATION	DIFFICULTY	DISTANCE	START/END
5hr return	Moderate	15km	Hospital de Vielha

TERRAIN	Mountain trail

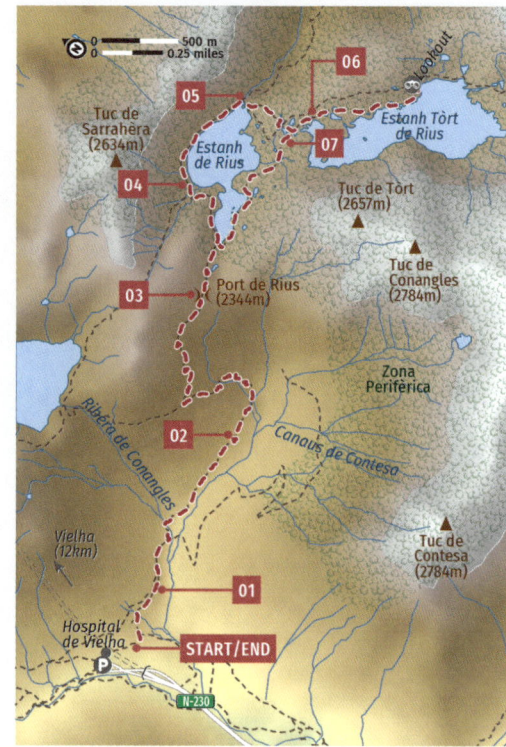

After a long haul up the mountain slopes the reward is a delightful amble around a couple of the most stunning lakes in the Catalan Pyrenees. Children might struggle on the climb upwards, but otherwise this is a good family walk (min/max altitude 1630/2344m).

GETTING HERE
The ski town of Vielha offers the closest accommodation. From Vielha drive south on the N230. Go through the long Túnel de Vielha. Immediately after exiting the tunnel turn off for the Hospital de Vielha (not a hospital at all but an ancient travellers' inn). It's also called the Hospice de Vielha. Park in the big (free) car park here.

STARTING POINT
There are some hiking information panels, but no other facilities.

01 Much of this walk is clearly waymarked with red-and-white GR11 paint slashes. Start by following the track in-between the two buildings of the Hospital de Vielha. The trail heads gently uphill through **flower meadows** that buzz with cicadas and crickets. There are butterflies everywhere. After around 10 minutes, you'll hit an old 4x4 forestry track. Turn right (northeast) and follow it. A short distance later, the forestry track turns back into a footpath and enters the shade of open **woodland**.

02 After around 45 minutes, you'll come to a small plateau carpeted in **wild flowers**. Turn around to admire the **snow-dusted peaks** behind you. The path starts to rise more steeply and slowly bends around towards the northwest. After walking for around one hour 40 minutes, you'll reach a **fork**. Turn sharply right (northeast) here. It can be quite easy to miss this fork. If you stop seeing GR11 trail markers, go back and check you haven't gone the wrong way.

03 Two hours from the start, the path rides up over the **Port de Rius** (Rius Pass; 2344m). In front of you, a large **lake** welcomes you to a delightful, rocky upland plateau.

04 Walk around the northern edge of the **Estanh de Rius** (Rius Lake; pictured). The trail is flat and easy, and gives views of the colours of the lake.

05 At the far eastern tip of the lake, the path splits. The GR11 that you've been following continues straight ahead (east) and is signed for the Refugi dera Restamca. Instead, take the minor southbound trail (stick to the lakeshore) signed for the Estanh de Mar. The trail meanders through rocky terrain with **small pools** – just aim southeast.

06 A few minutes later, you'll reach the tip of the huge **Estanh Tort de Rius** (Tort de Rius Lake). There's no set place to turn around here. The path makes its way along the northern shore of the lake – eventually, it goes to the Estanh de Mar, but visiting that lake and returning is too much for most people in one day. Walk at least halfway along the lakeshore to a small rocky rise that affords the best views.

07 When you've seen enough, turn around and retrace your steps towards the Estanh de Rius. When you get back to this lake, instead of backtracking along its northern shore, take a very minor and unsigned trail along the southern shore. There are frequent rock cairns to guide you. The path rejoins the main route just before the Port de Rius. From here retrace your steps back to the car.

TAKE A BREAK

There's no food or drink available. Bring a picnic and enjoy it snuggled into the silence of the quieter eastern end of the Estanh de Rius.

10

ESTANYS DE SISCARÓ LOOP

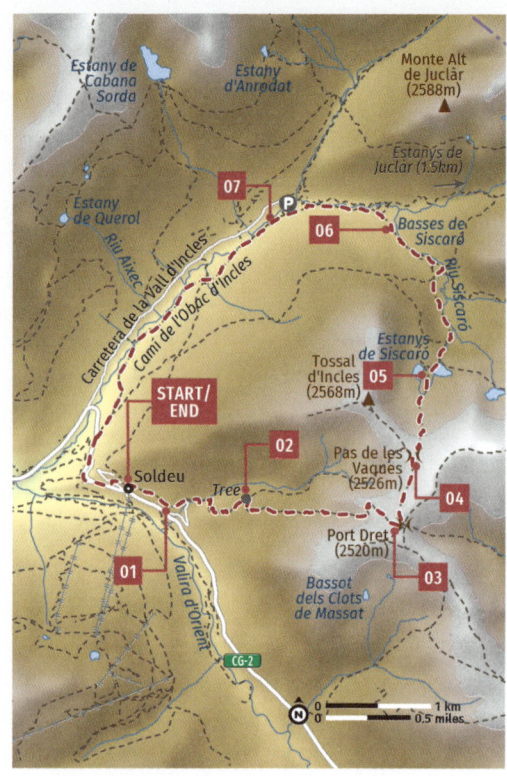

DURATION	DIFFICULTY	DISTANCE	START/END
4½-5hr return	Moderate	14km	Soldeu
TERRAIN	Mountain trail/gravel road		

The Principality of Andorra might be better known for its tax-free shopping, but creased-up folds of mountains hide some remarkable walking routes. The Estanys de Siscaró Loop (min/max altitude 1705/2528m) is unquestionably one of the best. The quiet trail heaves up to a breezy ridge, enters an idyllic valley with the Estanys (lake) de Siscaró at its heart and then drops back to Soldeu through woodlands. This is a good walk with older children, although the initial climb is long and taxing.

GETTING HERE

This is one of the few Pyrenean walks in this book that starts from a town and can be entirely accessed by public transport. The walk begins from the ski town of Soldeu. Buses (40 minutes) run hourly from Andorra's capital city, Andorra la Vella, to Soldeu.

STARTING POINT

Start on Soldeu's main street, 20m downhill from the Hotel Piolets. Look for the walking sign (opposite an ATM) for Clots de los Port Dret and La Portella.

01 Follow the yellow arrows leading to a clear walking trail heading east. Fork left 10 minutes from the start, pass the water treatment centre and cross the **wooden bridge**.

02 After 30 minutes, you'll come to a **tree with walking signs** attached. Head right for Port Dret (Dret Pass). The trail goes up steeply through **dwarf woodlands** and then across bouncy turf pastures.

03 Two hours from the start, you'll crawl up onto the **Port Dret** (2520m), which is marked by a big rock cairn and has vulture-eye views over ridge after mountain ridge. You're now on a well-marked (red and white) HRP trail.

Estanys de Juclàr

The Estanys de Juclàr trail is the most popular walking route in Andorra. From the car park where the road ends in the Inclès Valley, it's a 9km (four-hour) return walk to the twin lakes. Signage is excellent and the track is wide and in good condition. It's best avoided in high summer, however, when crowds can be overwhelming. Also, at this time, road access to the upper car park is often restricted and you'll either have to begin the walk much lower down the trail or take an electric train further up the valley to the upper car park. With plenty of opportunity to stop and splash about in water, this is a good family walk.

MARTIN SILVA COSENTINO/SHUTTERSTOCK ©

04 Amble northwards along a flat ridge following the HRP markers. It only takes a few minutes to reach the **Pas de les Vaques** (2526m). This pass offers a view sharp down the valley to the **Estanys de Siscaró** (Siscaró Lakes), which sit within a glacial bowl framed by a bevy of high peaks. In winter and spring, there are two lakes, but by late summer the most westerly one has normally dried up.

05 For 20 minutes, the trail drops very steeply downwards to the **lakeshore**. From a **ridge** at the far end of the lake, you'll be rewarded with a view of a lush green floodplain, known as the Basses de Siscaró, with a meandering stream and the tiny, unstaffed *refugio* of the same name. Climb down steeply to the floodplain and cross to the furthest side.

06 At the end of the **Basses de Siscaró**, you'll come to a series of **signposts**. Turn left (west) and drop down alongside the now-frothing stream. The path re-enters forest and, 20 minutes later, meets the **trail for the Estanys de Juclàr**. The peace and quiet is now at an end. The Juclàr route is very popular and, in summer, you can expect supermarket crowds. Turn left (west) and follow the trail to the car park. Just by the wall here is a sign reading **Cami de l'Obac d'Incles**. Follow this quieter trail.

07 After 45 minutes, you'll reach a **tarmac road**. Take the trail leading off left and uphill into the forest. Ten minutes later the trail emerges onto the main road at the northwest end of **Soldeu**. Follow this back into town.

 **TAKE A BREAK**

There's nowhere to eat on the walk. For a picnic with a view, saddle up to the Pas de les Vaques. In Soldeu itself, there are numerous places to get a meal. The town has a buzzing après-ski scene in winter.

11

ORDESA CANYON VIA THE FAJA DE PELAY

DURATION	DIFFICULTY	DISTANCE	START/END
6½hr return	Hard	20km	Car park, Pradera de Ordesa
TERRAIN	Clear mountain paths, partially along a steep, narrow cliff path		

Touted as the Grand Canyon of Europe, the walk up the enormous Ordesa Canyon is *the* classic walk of the Spanish Pyrenees. Created long ago by giant glaciers peeling off the sides of Monte Perdido (3355m), every step of this long walk will have you gasping in wonder. The walls of the canyon, which in places soar to around a thousand vertical metres above the canyon floor, are an extraordinary palette of colours and contrasts. Overlooked by glaciers and bleak, grey rockscapes, the head of the canyon runs to an abrupt halt at the Circo de Soaso, which is one of the most impressive glacial cirques in the whole of the Pyrenees. Meanwhile, down on the valley floor, surreal blue waterfalls and an ancient beech forest add the magic touch. Taken together, the whole ensemble is simply visual poetry.

There are a couple of route options along the canyon. Some are reserved for fearless mountaineers with a head for crazy heights, while the standard route simply runs up and down the valley floor. The route we describe here (min/max altitude 1300/1950m) falls somewhere in-between the two. It takes you along the Faja de Pelay, a near-vertical 600m-high ledge that tiptoes along the southern canyon wall before slowly descending to the valley floor at the Circo de Soaso. It then returns to the car park along the standard valley floor route. Although not technically difficult, this is a very long and tiring walk.

There is a limit of 1800 people allowed within the canyon at any one time. Get going early to ensure you are one of them.

GETTING HERE

The start point for this walk is the stone town of Torla. The walk starts at the Pradera de Ordesa car park. However, over Easter, and throughout July and August, cars are banned from parking here. Instead, park in Torla and take one of the park buses (€4.50 return) that run roughly every 15 to 20 minutes. The first bus leaves Torla at 6am and the last returns between 8.30pm and 9pm.

STARTING POINT

There's a small park information office, various information panels and a bar-restaurant.

Refugio de Góriz

You can turn the walk up the Ordesa Canyon into a brilliant overnight trek by continuing up and over the headwall at the end of the canyon to the large and well-equipped **Refugio de Góriz** (974 34 12 01; www.goriz.es; dm €18.10). From the Cola de Caballo waterfall, the clear trail rises up the cirque walls. There are some short, fixed chains to help you up the steeper parts but they're not usually needed. Afterwards, it's a gentle upwards rise to the refuge, which is set on a barren rocky plateau. The next day either return the way you came or spend another night at the refuge and head out on any of a number of challenging walks that depart from here. Although the staffed refuge is large, it's important to make reservations in advance.

01 This is an exceptionally well-marked route and for the most part is easy (but long). Thanks to an extremely steep ascent, the real hard work is done in the first 1½ hours. From the eastern end of the car park, cross the river on the small bridge and follow the sign for the Faja de Pelay and **Senda de los Cazadores** (Trail of the Hunters). The trail enters a beech forest and passes a sign that states that you are now on a very **dangerous path**. (Most of the time there's nothing at all dangerous about this route. However, if it's wet, icy or there's snow, then the Faja de Pelay route can be treacherous and you should not attempt it. Stick instead to the standard valley floor route.)

The trail then starts to climb up. And up. And up a bit more. Over the next hour-and-a-half, you will climb 600 vertical metres above the canyon floor. At times, you may even need to use your hands to help you up the steeper parts. The trail does zigzag though, which helps take the pain out of it, and it's in shaded forest all the way.

02 Finally, the trail crests a rise and you reach the **Mirador de Calcilarruego**. It's an incredible viewpoint with views up and down the canyon.

THE PYRENEES/53

After you've caught your breath and soaked up the views follow the path eastwards.

You're now on the **Faja de Pelay**, a narrow trail etched into the cliff face. It's impossible to get lost on this part of the trail. If you turn right then you'll walk straight into a cliff. If you turn left then you'll walk straight off a cliff...Despite all this, it's not as scary as it might look in pictures and as long as you stick to the path and there's no ice or snow, it's not dangerous at all (we've done it with 10- and seven-year-old children).

For the next two hours, the path gently descends, with every footfall revealing another startling view. Keep your eyes peeled for golden eagles, griffon vultures and even the mighty **lammergeier** soaring on the thermals rising out of the canyon.

03 Eventually, the trail drops you down to a small bridge at the base of the **Cola de Caballo** (Horse Tail) waterfall at the very head of the **Circo de Soaso**. On its own, the waterfall would be impressive enough but in this setting, it barely generates more than a mere glance. The headwalls of the *circo* (cirque) lead the eyes up to the banded grey rock and chunky glaciers of Monte Perdido (3355m), the third-highest peak in the Pyrenees. Around you are vast pastures fringed with the rainbow-coloured canyon walls and laced through by the liquid-blue headwaters of the Río Arazas. Marmots and izard (chamois) are commonly seen around here.

04 After bathing in the beauty of the setting, spin around 180 degrees and, following the standard canyon floor path, head southwest back down the canyon. After about 45 minutes you'll pass the waterfalls of **Gradas de Soaso** where the glacial turquoise waters scramble over multiple steps and ledges.

05 A further 40 minutes downhill and the trail opens out to a viewpoint over the **Cascadas del Estrecho** and the **Cascadas de Arripas**, two sets of waterfalls a short way apart.

06 The path then enters an old-growth beech forest where mosses hang heavy on the branches and the leaves turn a russet red in autumn. It's one of the largest such ancient beech forests in western Europe and it will now be with you until the end of this walk. The trail twists and turns gently downwards for the next hour until, finally, at the end of this long, but immensely rewarding walk, you emerge back into the car park where your adventure began.

Faja de las Flores

You will likely see photos of people walking this route all over the Ordesa region. Enticing as the pictures make it look, there are some things you should know about the eight-hour (min/max altitude 1320/2380m) Faja de las Flores trail. The route, which runs along the northern wall of the canyon, climbs up the canyon walls at a dauntingly steep angle and then works its way eastwards along a very narrow and highly exposed path that literally hangs in the air hundreds of vertical metres above the canyon floor. Incredible though it is, this is absolutely not for everyone to walk. It can be very dangerous and is really only reserved for experienced mountaineers with a head for heights. Crampons, ropes and ice-axes might be needed. There are sections with fixed ropes. All up, it makes the Faja de Pelay look like a walk in the park.

TAKE A BREAK

When you've started the walk there is nowhere to buy a snack or meal. But full meals, drinks and snacks are available at the **Bar-Restaurante La Pradera de Ordesa** (Pradera de Ordesa; platos combinados €9-11, bocadillos €5-6, set menus €18; 7am-9pm) next to the main car park from Easter to early November.

12

PUERTO DE BARROSA

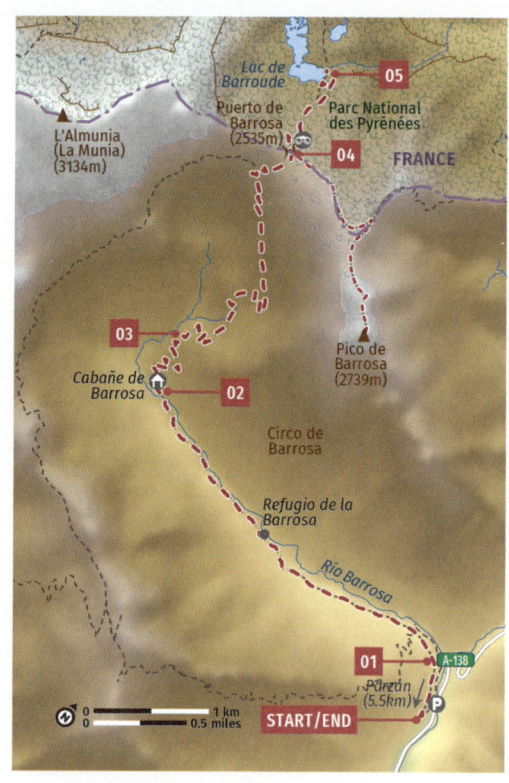

DURATION	DIFFICULTY	DISTANCE	START/END
5½hr return	Hard	15km	Hospital de Parzán

TERRAIN	Mountain trail

This exhilarating walk (min/max altitude 1480/2535m) takes you up the charming, forested Valle de Barrosa (Barrosa Valley) to the Cabane de Barrosa at the foot of the grand, but little known, Circo (Cirque) de Barrosa. This first part of the walk makes an ideal family stroll of 2½ hours (return). For everyone else, the route continues onwards and upwards along an old mule track to the Puerto de Barrosa for views to a lake- and glacier-spotted wilderness and down into France.

This is a well-signed and easy-to-follow route, but if you're going all the way to the Puerto (pass) de Barrosa, the length and significant altitude gain (1054m) make it quite demanding.

GETTING HERE

The walk begins from the Hospital de Parzán. The nearest village is Parzán, 5.5km to the south along the A138. The larger town of Bielsa is a further 3km south along the same road.

STARTING POINT

There is a small roadside parking area (with very limited car spaces) and no other facilities.

01 From the roadside parking area follow the dirt track uphill. The path zigzags to and fro and passes remnants of the area's mining past. After around 20 minutes of climbing through forest the valley suddenly opens up and reveals the **mountains ahead**. The walking gets easier as you amble through pine forest, along the banks of the Río Barrosa.

Pic de Barrosa

Need to push yourself a bit more? From the Puerto de Barrosa it's a 45-minute, 230m climb to the Pic de Barrosa, the rounded ridge just to the southeast. To get there, follow the ridge line east from the pass until you reach another small pass (2674m). At this point leave the faint trail and head southeast over a ridge and then to the summit of the Pic de Barrosa (2739m) for a memorable view over the Circo de Barrosa. Note that this route is not clearly waymarked, though there are some rock cairns. Allow 1¼ hours return from the pass.

02 After an hour, you enter the bottom part of the huge **Circo de Barrosa**, a vast amphitheatre of barren, snow-carpeted rocky peaks culminating in **L'Almunia** (La Munia; 3134m). Head over the grassy valley towards the unstaffed **Cabane (cabin) de Barrosa** (1745m). For families, this is a good place to picnic before returning to the car. For everyone else, the route continues up towards France.

03 The now fairly lightly trodden trail continues up in a generally northerly direction. There are numerous sharp switchbacks through tough grass pastures (keep your eyes peeled for **marmots** around here). The climb becomes increasingly steep, but the path is always obvious and the compensation for your effort is the increasingly good valley and mountain vistas.

04 Finally, some two exhausting hours after leaving the Cabane de Barrosa, during which you will have gained 790m in vertical height, you reach the high, windy pass of the **Puerto de Barrosa** (2535m) and are rewarded with amazing views over a wilderness of rock, scree, ice and, below you down into France, the glacial blue **Lac de Barroude** (2355m; pictured).

05 If you have the energy to burn, you can descend to the lake (allow 1½ hours return), but don't expect to find any nourishment at the refuge there. It burned down several years ago and there are no plans to rebuild it. Otherwise, return by the same route. From the pass to the car should take 2½ hours.

 **TAKE A BREAK**

There are no facilities. Bring a picnic to enjoy snuggled up on the floor of the cirque near the Cabane de Barrosa.

13

CIRC DE COLOMÈRS

DURATION	DIFFICULTY	DISTANCE	START/END
5½hr return	Hard	14.2km	Taxi drop-off point Estanh Major de Colomèrs
TERRAIN	Mountain trail		

Every step you take on this lake-splattered, circular route (min/max altitude 1944/2593m) will reveal something new and beautiful. Lower down there are idyllic flower meadows fringed with mountain vistas; higher up are tundra-like grass plateaus and rocky mountain bowls, plus there's the thrill of a high pass crossing. But, above and beyond all else, there are the lakes. It's said that there are a denser concentration of lakes in this part of the range than anywhere else in the Pyrenees. In fact, there are so many lakes, ponds and pools, all of which are linked by clear gushing rivers, you'll fast lose count of how many you've passed (we're told there are around 40). Each lake is a varied shade of opaque green or shiny jewel blue and the presence of so many liquid treasures helps to make this one of the iconic walks of the Pyrenees.

GETTING HERE

The best base is the small, stone village of Salardú. You'll need your own vehicle to get from Salardú to the walk start point. The car park is 8km south of town at Banhs de Tredos (Plan de Banhs). From the (free) car park hop in one of the minibus taxis (€4 one-way, 15 minutes) that ferry hikers to the trailhead every 15 minutes or so. The first one leaves at 9am and the last one returns at 6.30pm. The taxis only run between mid-June and mid-September, so outside this period, you'd need to walk all the way from the car park, which would add a good 2½ hours to the overall hike time.

STARTING POINT

The walk starts from the taxi drop-off point below the Estanh Major de Colomèrs. There are no facilities here.

01 Follow the well-signed trail uphill towards the **Refugi Colomèrs** (pictured left) until you reach the base of the large dam at the northern end of the Estanh Major de Colomèrs. The refuge is on the western (right) side of the dam. Instead, turn east (left) and follow the clear path marked with the red and white GR11 waymarkers (there's also a signpost for the Refugi d'Amitges).

02 Twenty minutes later, the first of the major lakes springs into view, and what a beauty it is. The **Estanh Clots de Baish** is a curvy bubble of a lake surrounded by flower meadows. The main trail actually bypasses it but you can take a side trail down to the lakeshore and then follow a minor trail along the lake's eastern shore for a few minutes until rejoining the main GR11 trail just short of the second major lake, the appropriately named Estanh Long.

03 Backed by fir trees and meadows, the **Estanh Long de Colomèrs** snakes its way up the valley. About halfway along its length, you will pass a sign pointing west (right) back to the Refugi Colomèrs or straight on (south) to Estanh Obago. We're going to carry on to the Estanh Obago.

04 Pass another smaller lake, **Estanh Redon**, and then start to climb. Just before you reach the top of the rise, take a look back the way you came and you'll be rewarded with a stunning view of the lakes laid out in deep blues below you. **Estanh Obago** is one of the larger lakes and certainly one of the more beautiful.

 Family Treats

Walking families can still get a taste of this corner of the Pyrenees on a short two-hour circular hike. Follow the instructions here to the signpost for the Refugi Colomèrs mentioned in stop 03. Take the trail towards the refuge. You'll meet up with the main route at stop 10. Then follow the instructions for stops 11 and 12.

05 Around halfway along this lake, the trail branches. The main GR11 turns southeast (left) towards the Refugi d'Amitges. Our route is the smaller one continuing straight ahead in a southerly direction. The waymarkers now consist of orangey-red paint splashes. It's easy to miss this junction as it's not signed.

06 The trail starts climbing now. You pass more lakes, trees fade away and the landscape becomes much rockier. The views back down the valley are more arresting with every step. Eventually, you will reach the **Estanh de Podo**. Cold and glacial blue, it sits within a tight bowl of mountain walls and is the final lake before the pass. The next 20 to 25 minutes up to the pass are a hard slog over a giant's chessboard of boulders torn off the surrounding mountain slopes by aeons of icy winters.

07 At 2593m, the **Podo pass** is a wind-scoured and bleak place. The **Gran Tuc de Colomèrs** (2934m) and a series of lesser peaks rise up in a jagged U-shaped cirque around the southern end of the pass. Immediately over the pass is another lake, the **Estanh Gelat**. In Catalan, *gelat* means frozen, which is an appropriate name as the lake remains frozen late into summer.

08 The trail heads northwest and slowly descends. Laid out ahead is a vast upland plateau dotted with an extraordinary number of **lakes**, all of which are the liquidy blue of Scandinavian eyes. The next hour, during which you'll stroll over flat **tundra-like moorland** past many of these lakes, is a sheer delight.

09 Leaving the plateau you pass the sizeable **Garguilhs de Sus** (a lake) in a bowl to your west (left). In a few more minutes the trail crosses a lively stream via a series of stepping stones. A short time after that is a signpost. Go straight on (north) towards the Refugi Colomèrs, which is signed as being just 20 minutes away. In reality, it's further than that.

10 The path continues to the next bit of eye candy, the **Estanh Mort**. Despite the name (Lake of Death), this is perhaps the loveliest lake of them all, and if time allows you'll want to mellow in the flower meadows that surround it.

11 As soon as you leave the shores of the Estanh Mort, you'll reach the edge of a ridge. Below you is the **Estanh Major de Colomèrs** and the refuge. But, oh what a drop! The trail abseils steeply downwards in a series of zigzags. At one point a **short chain** is attached to the rock face to help you safely down (though it's not really needed unless it's icy or very wet). It's all a bit of a rude shock to tired legs. Soon enough though you'll reach the Refugi Colomèrs. Head around the back of it and follow the trail to the building at the western end of the dam wall.

12 Descend to the base of the dam wall and, instead of following the wall back over to the path you took at the start of the day, take the smaller trail heading northeast. It wriggles downwards through **woodlands** and along the riverbank until, five minutes later, it rejoins the original trail by a wooden bridge and the boardwalk you crossed at the start of the walk. Now simply follow the trail back to the waiting taxis.

TAKE A BREAK

The **Refugi Colomèrs** (973 25 30 08, reservations 973 64 16 81; www.refugicolomers.com; Parc Nacional d'Aigüestortes i Estany de Sant Maurici; half-board €49) serves drinks and snacks to non-guests, but it's nicer to take a picnic and eat beside one of the many lakes.

Also Try...

MIGUEL MOYA MORENO/SHUTTERSTOCK ©

BALCÓN DE PINETA & LAGO MARBORÉ

A spectacular, high-altitude and very challenging walk to a natural viewpoint and near eternally frozen lake with views to the glacier that tumbles off the eastern side of Monte Perdido (3355m).

Starting from near the Parador de Bielsa, this very difficult route (in early summer crampons and ice-axes required) climbs relentlessly up (min/max altitude 1300/2595m) the steep-sided walls of the Circo de Pineta, past the impressive Marboré waterfalls and up onto a moonscape plateau of broken rocks and sheer walls. The views back into the Pineta valley are the kind that would normally be reserved for mountaineers. Carrying on upwards, you will reach the Lago Marboré where blocks of ice float year-round and Monte Perdido (pictured above) is reflected in the glassy lake waters. Take note that this hike is not suitable for the inexperienced.

DURATION 8hr return
DIFFICULTY Hard
DISTANCE 18km

FAJA TORMOSA

Not one for the faint of heart, this exhausting walk (min/max altitude 1240/1960m) tiptoes along airy ledges hundreds of metres above the floor of the Pineta valley with spellbinding views all the way and a bevy of streams and crashing waterfalls to cross. It's rightly considered one of the classic walks of the Spanish Pyrenees, but is reserved only for experienced mountain walkers without a fear of heights.

Kicking off from the Refugi de Pineta, the path climbs fast up the western side of the Circo de Pineta and, once it's found the ledge, continues up to the head of the valley before dropping back to ground level again. Be warned that there are a couple of steep sections where fixed chains and ladders have been attached to the cliff face. Do not attempt this walk in wet, icy or snowy conditions.

DURATION 5½hr return
DIFFICULTY Hard
DISTANCE 11.5km

LAGO DE CREGÜEÑA

Hike through glorious woodlands to reach a savage rocky mountain bowl and the high-altitude Lago (lake) de Cregüeña at the foot of the giant Mt Maladeta (3312m).

This is an exhilarating walk to the third-largest lake in the Pyrenees and definitely one of the more spectacular. On the way you'll cover steep, then flat, then very steep, rocky and technical terrain to arrive at the western fingertip of the lake. Although the considerable elevation gain (min/max altitude 1451/2650m) makes this a tough walk, the route is always clear and easy.

DURATION 5½hr return
DIFFICULTY Moderate
DISTANCE 11.5km

REFUGIO DE ARMEÑA

A dreamlike, family-friendly walk through meadows full of butterflies to a quiet elf-green lake and a refuge (unstaffed) with huge views.

This short and easy walk (min/max altitude 1420/1860m) is an ideal way to introduce children to the delights of the mountains. The trail is clear and easy, the scenery varied and the lake and views from the refuge a big reward for little feet. The walk begins from the Parking Armeña, which is 3km down a dirt track from the tiny village of Barbaruens.

DURATION 3½hr return
DIFFICULTY Easy
DISTANCE 10km

PORT DE RATERA D'ESPOT LOOP

This loop takes in several glowing, blue mountain lakes and a viewpoint in the heart of the Parc Nacional d'Aigüestortes i Estany de Sant Maurici (pictured).

Starting from the shores of Estany de Sant Maurici, you quickly leave the crowds behind as you skip through pine forest and on into high pastures where a series of lakes lies splotched across the landscape. The trail takes you past the Refugi d'Amitges and up to the Port de Ratera d'Espot. On the return leg, the trail passes the Mirador de l'Estany viewpoint.

DURATION 5hr return
DIFFICULTY Moderate
DISTANCE 14km

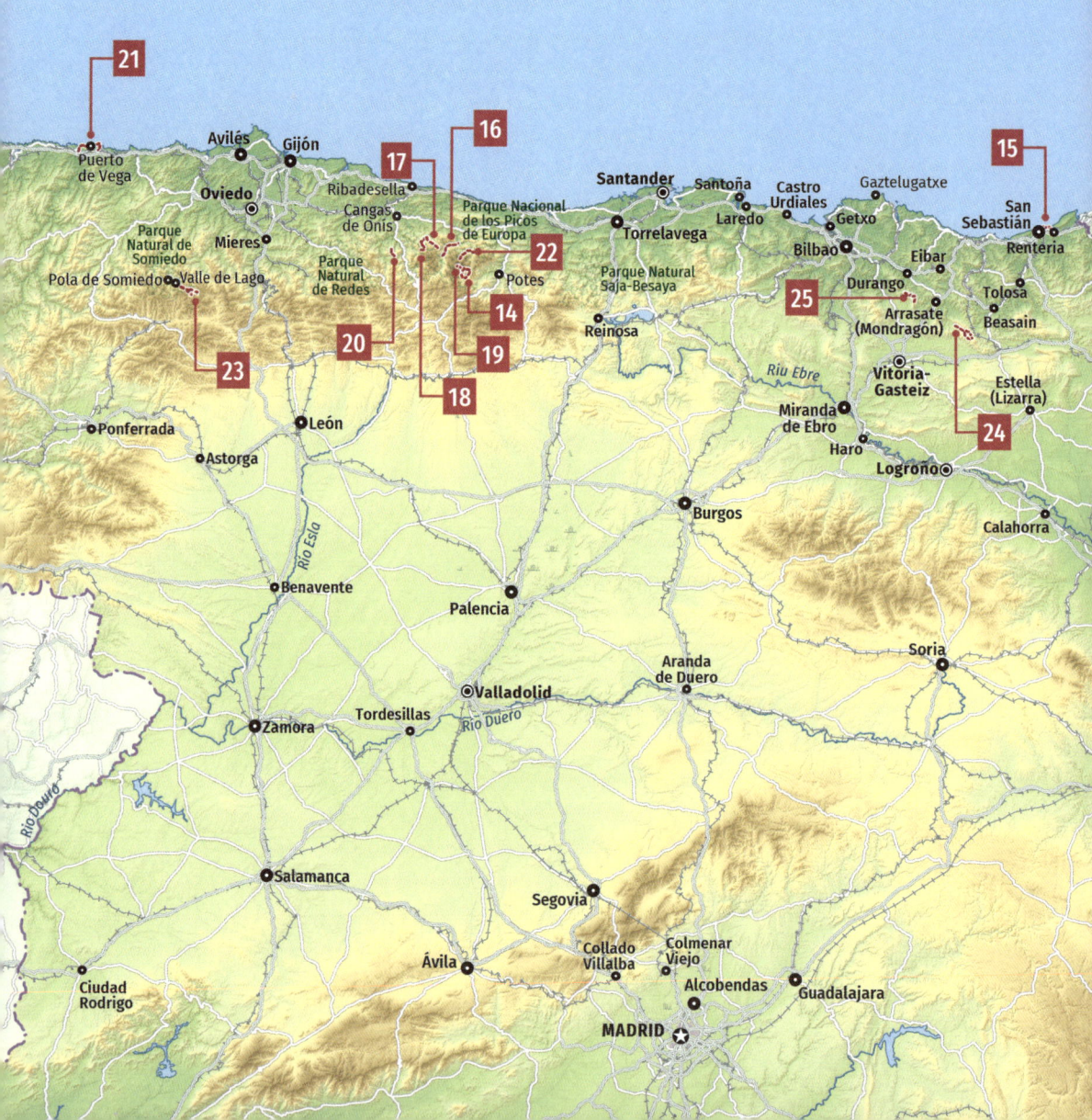

PICOS & NORTHERN SPAIN

14 **Puertos de Áliva** Downhill from Picos de Europa through mountain pastures and dense woodlands. **p68**

15 **San Sebastián to Pasai Donibane** An outing through the coastal forests from the Basque culinary and beach centre. **p70**

16 **Ruta del Cares** Breathtaking walk through a 1000m-deep Picos de Europa gorge. **p72**

17 **Vega de Ario** Ascent from mountain lakes to an upland valley with spectacular vistas. **p74**

18 **Mirador de Ordiales** Climb through a wild limestone landscape to a stunning Picos viewpoint. **p76**

19 **Horcados Rojos** Exhilarating high-mountain walk from the Fuente Dé cable car. **p78**

20 **Picu Pierzu** Panoramic Cordillera Cantábrica ridge walk. **p80**

21 **Costa Naviega** Twenty kilometres of cliffs, beaches and roaring seas. **p82**

22 **Picu Urriellu** Hike up to the awe-inspiring 500m-high rock pillar at the Picos' heart. **p84**

23 **Somiedo Lakes** Five mountain lakes amid the gloriously green Parque Natural de Somiedo. **p86**

24 **Arantzazu, Aizkorri, San Adrián** Everything a good Basque walk should have. **p90**

25 **Anboto** This Basque Country peak is a thrilling hiking challenge. **p92**

PICOS & NORTHERN SPAIN/65

Explore
PICOS & NORTHERN SPAIN

The Cordillera Cantábrica range, stretching 300km east to west, inland from Spain's north coast, contains dozens of 2000m-plus peaks and boundless great walking. It reaches its most spectacular heights in the Picos de Europa – arguably the greatest concentration of mountain drama in the country – and the Parque Natural de Somiedo. To the east, lower but still exciting ranges run across the Basque Country. The coast itself, a scenic sequence of cliffs, coves and beaches, is a walker's delight in its own right.

CANGAS DE ONÍS

A convenient base for the northern Picos de Europa, largely modern Cangas has loads of accommodation and restaurants, plus a few supermarkets and shops specialising in outdoor gear. **La Sifonería** (985 84 90 55; www.lasifoneria.net; Calle de San Pelayo 28; dishes €9-20; noon-4pm & 8pm-midnight Wed-Mon) is a top spot for tucking into good Asturian cooking at good prices. The Picos national park's **Casa Dago information office** (985 84 86 14; Avenida de Covadonga 43; 9am-2pm Mon-Fri, 10am-2pm & 4-8pm Sat & Sun) is here too.

POTES

The small valley town of Potes, with a delightful cobbled old heart, is an enjoyable base for forays into the southern Picos de Europa. There are good restaurants and a few supermarkets. The Picos national park's Sotama visitor centre is 4km north on the N-621.

POLA DE SOMIEDO

The only town in the Parque Natural de Somiedo, plain Pola has a bank, ATM, two small supermarkets, a petrol station, the park information office and several places to eat and sleep. There are further options in some villages, including **Valle de Lago**, 8km up the hill from Pola.

BILBAO

Home to the famed **Museo Guggenheim Bilbao** (94 43 59 08; www.guggenheim-bilbao.eus; Avenida Abandoibarra 2; adult/student & senior/child €15/7.50/free; 10am-8pm, closed Mon Sep-Jun), the Basque Country's largest urban centre is a lively riverside city with all the services you could want. Plaza Nueva, the main square of the old town, is ringed by *pintxo* (tapas) bars, making it a great place to start exploring the inventive Basque food scene.

WHEN TO GO

June to September are the ideal months for walking here; at this time it's generally warm (but not too warm) and with the lowest likelihood of rain, fog or cloud to spoil your day. Choose June or September to avoid the main holiday crowds. Coastal and low-altitude walks

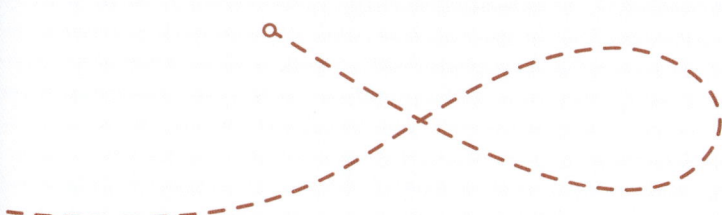

(such as the Ruta del Cares) are practicable year-round as long as the weather is not too vile, but don't plan mountain walking for the winter months – rain and cloud can make route-finding hard, and snow and freezing conditions can be positively dangerous.

Snow can linger into June or July at higher elevations in the Picos: ask locally before setting out. Note that there's very little shade or shelter above the treeline (around 1300m to 1400m) anywhere in the Picos.

TRANSPORT

Bilbao, Santander and Asturias airport (47km northwest of Oviedo) all receive flights from several Spanish cities. Bilbao has the largest range of flights from other European countries; Santander has a few (by Ryanair). These main cities have reasonable to good road, rail and bus connections with the rest of Spain.

Travel to the walk areas is almost always easiest with your own vehicle. For the Picos de Europa, Cangas de Onís has at least seven daily Alsa (www.alsa.com) buses from Oviedo (€7.25, 1½ hours), and summer buses from Cangas will take you to some walks; there is limited summer service between Potes and Fuente Dé (€2.10, 45 minutes).

WHERE TO STAY

Picos de Europa and Somiedo access towns have plentiful accommodation, but the highlight places are often out in the villages or countryside. Such are **Posada del Valle** (www.posadadelvalle.com), a superb country hotel and walking base 11km from Cangas; family-run **Hotel Peña Castil** (www.hotelpenacastil.com) in the Picos village of Sotres; and the larger but cosy **Hotel del Oso** (www.hoteldeloso.es) in Cosgaya outside Potes.

An attractive option in Arantzazu is **Goiko Benta** (http://goikobenta.com), an ancient inn with modernised rooms and a fine restaurant. Bilbao and San Sebastián have vast ranges of places to stay. San Sebastián is on the expensive side.

It's advisable to book at least a few days ahead everywhere in July and August.

Resources

Adrados Ediciones (www.infopicos.com) Outstanding maps of the Picos de Europa, widely available locally.

Parque Nacional de los Picos de Europa (www.miteco.gob.es/es/red-parques-nacionales/nuestros-parques/picos-europa) Official site of the Picos de Europa national park. For walking routes click Guía del Visitante then Itinerarios.

Spanish Trails Los Picos de Europa (www.spanishtrailsco.com) Excellent English-language walking guide by Phil Lawler.

Basque Country (http://tourism.euskadi.eus/en) Official Basque Country tourist information.

WHAT'S ON

Descenso Internacional del Sella (www.descensodelsella.com) A thousand-plus paddlers race down the Río Sella from Arriondas, on the fringe of the Picos de Europa, to Ribadesella on the coast, in this massively attended canoeing event on the first weekend after 2 August.

Aste Nagusia Bilbao and San Sebastián celebrate summer in a big way for eight or nine days in mid-August. Street parties, concerts, parades of giants, Basque rural sports (like chopping wood and lifting heavy stones) and nightly fireworks are part of the fun in both cities.

14

PUERTOS DE ÁLIVA

DURATION	DIFFICULTY	DISTANCE	START/END
4hr one-way	Easy	14km	Teleférico de Fuente Dé upper station/ Fuente Dé

TERRAIN	Unpaved roads, forest paths

Soar 753m up from the green Fuente Dé valley on the Picos de Europa's southern edge, 23km west of Potes, to the Picos' rocky higher reaches by the spine-tingling **Teleférico de Fuente Dé** (📞942 73 66 10; www.cantur.com; adult/child return €18/7, one-way €11/4; ⏰10am-6pm early Feb-Jun & mid-Sep–early Jan, 8am-7pm Jul–mid-Sep, hours may vary; 🅿) cable car. Then walk 1km up to a track junction where you continue ahead following the Áliva-Espinama-Fuente Dé sign. From here on, the always well-marked PRPNPE24 is downhill all the way, across bucolic mountain pastures and through delightful, shaded woodlands, back to Fuente Dé.

With the rock pinnacles of **Peña Olvidada** and **Peña Vieja** (2613m) towering above, the track winds down past the **Chalet Real**, a century-old mountain villa that once hosted King Alfonso XIII, to the **Hotel Refugio de Áliva**, a former mountain refuge that's now a hotel and convenient refreshment stop (open June to mid-October).

Continue 4km down the vehicle track to the **Portillas de Boquejón** (a short defile between rocks), then turn right across a **footbridge** signposted PRPNPE24 Fuente Dé. A stony footpath, with yellow-and-white PR markers, heads downhill to join a larger path after some 400m.

You now have nearly 6km through dense **oak and beech woods**, with level as well as descending stretches, back to Fuente Dé. The huge crags of **Peña de Valdecoro** tower above while your route alternates between footpath and rough vehicle track. Finally you parallel the infant **Río Deva** back to its source, welling out under a rock in front of the **Parador de Fuente Dé** hotel, and continue a little further back to the bottom cable-car station or wherever you left your vehicle.

15
SAN SEBASTIÁN TO PASAI DONIBANE

DURATION	DIFFICULTY	DISTANCE	START/END
3½hr one-way	Easy	11.5km	San Sebastián/ Pasai Donibane
TERRAIN	Footpath (stone-paved or earth), streets		

For a delightful complement to the famed food and beach pleasures of San Sebastián, head up through the lush woodlands of Monte Ulía (234m), with spectacular coastal views, and down to the quaint estuary-side village Pasai Donibane, one of four waterside settlements collectively called Pasaia (Pasajes in Spanish).

GETTING HERE

San Sebastián has flights from Madrid and Barcelona. Biarritz (France), 48km away, has international flights. You can also reach San Sebastián by bus or slow train from other parts of Spain, or by train from France with a transfer in Hendaye.

STARTING POINT

San Sebastián's *ayuntamiento* (city hall), overlooking the wonderful city beach Playa de la Concha.

01 From the *ayuntamiento* take the **waterside walkway** north then west, then round the Monte Urgull headland to **Puente Zurriola** bridge.

02 Cross the bridge and continue straight. Approaching the end of Playa de Zurriola, follow the road round to the right then take the first left, **Zemoria Kalea**. Steps shortcut Zemoria's zigzags, then it merges into a steeper set of steps, which become a trail climbing to a paved road.

03 Turn left along the road. San Sebastián panoramas open out; after 400m fork left onto a path curving upwards through shaded woods. From here, follow signs to Pasaia, and/or

Shortcuts & Detours

At the start, you can shave off 1.8km by walking east from the *ayuntamiento* direct to Puente Zurriola. For another shortcut, skip the trip down to Illurgita.

Most importantly, 10 minutes past the Illurgita turn-off you'll encounter two forks in quick succession. At research time a sign at the second fork announced that the later route section after the Faro de la Plata was closed by *desprendimientos* (landslides). You could still walk to the viewpoint below the lighthouse, then return (30 minutes each way) – or you can immediately return to the first fork and turn left to emerge on a paved road. Go left here, turn right after 100m, and wind your way down into Pasai San Pedro.

JOHN NOBLE / LONELY PLANET ©

the red-and-white paint stripes of the GR121 trail, at all junctions as you wind up and down through the woods to Pasai Donibane. An open, level stretch reveals spectacular **views down to Monpás point** with its ruined 19th-century fort.

04 Cross a paved road 2.5km further on; 600m later, a small unsigned path heads down to the left. Wind your way 10 minutes down to the rocky, usually deserted bay **Illurgita**. It's swimmable on calmer days.

05 The main path continues through woods, passing two short stretches of abandoned aqueduct, to emerge on a paved road below **Faro de la Plata** lighthouse. A **viewpoint** here overlooks the Pasaia estuary: you may witness an outsize ship inching into Pasaia's narrow entrance channel.

06 Head south on the paved road. After 650m, take the signposted path left down into the woods. Turn left at a picnic area to find the zigzag footpath descending steeply past **Senokozulua lighthouse** to the estuary-side walkway. In 10 more minutes, you'll reach the little passenger **ferry** (€0.80 one-way) from Pasai San Pedro (this west side of the estuary) to Pasai Donibane (the east side).

07 Happily, several of the waterside buildings in **Pasai Donibane** (pictured) are bar-restaurants. When suitably refreshed, return to Pasai San Pedro and walk 500m west to the bus stop for buses to San Sebastián (€1.85, 10 minutes) every 15 minutes.

TAKE A BREAK

Pasai Donibane's waterside **Ziaboga Bistrot** (943 51 03 95; www.ziaboga bistrot.com; Donibane Kalea 91; 9am-8pm Wed-Mon) does an excellent range of seafood, meat, salads and cheeses in all sizes from *pintxos* (€1.80 to €4.50) to main-course platters (€14 to €22).

16

RUTA DEL CARES

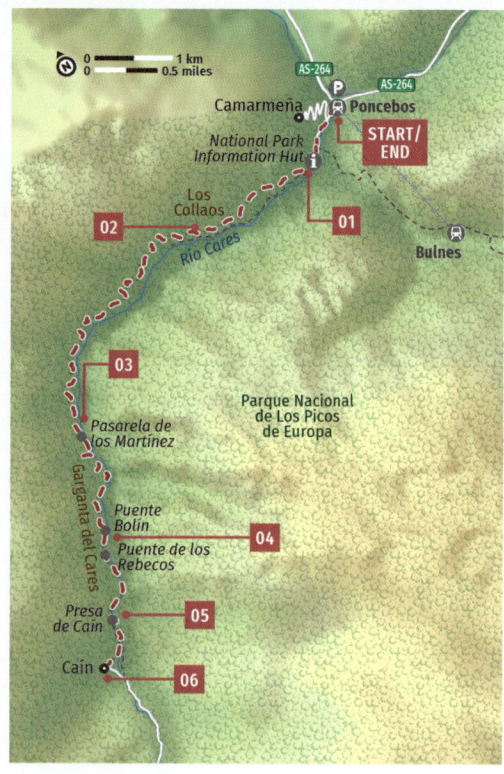

DURATION	DIFFICULTY	DISTANCE	START/END
6½hr return	Moderate	23km	Poncebos

TERRAIN	Earth/gravel/stony footpath, easy gradients

The 1000m-deep canyon separating the Picos de Europa's western and central massifs is probably the most popular mountain walk in Spain – with good reason: the breathtaking scenery never lets up for one moment as you wend your way along the gorge with pinnacle peaks piercing the sky above and the beguilingly blue Río Cares tumbling far below.

There are steep, sometimes perpendicular, drops from the path almost the whole way, but the path is always 1m to 2m wide and there's no need to walk along its edge.

GETTING HERE

Poncebos (the hamlet at the walk's northern end, 6km south of Arenas de Cabrales) is overall a more accessible start/end point than Caín (the village at the southern end). On a quiet day, drivers can park several hundred metres past Poncebos towards the gorge; on the busiest days you might have to park 2km back towards Arenas. From about mid-July to early September, Alsa (www.alsa.com) operates several daily buses from Arenas to Poncebos (€3) and back. Some people choose to do the walk in one direction only, arranging transport from the far end, but the return walk is within the capacity of any reasonably fit walker and is logistically far easier!

STARTING POINT

The bridge over the Cares at Poncebos.

01 Walk southwest up the road towards the gorge, passing two hotels. Jagged rock pinnacles will already be towering high above you. After 800m, at a seasonally open **national park**

The Cares Canal

Here and there along the Ruta del Cares, you'll notice a fast-flowing canal just above or just below the path. The footpath owes its existence to this canal, which channels some of the Cares' water 11km from the dam at Caín to the village of Camarmeña, from where the water shoots 200m downhill inside pipes to power the hydroelectric station at Poncebos. The canal, with 71 hand-drilled tunnels, was constructed between 1915 and 1921; the path was added between 1945 and 1950 to facilitate canal maintenance. Both are considerable engineering achievements; they cost the lives of 11 and two workers respectively.

information hut, turn right up the path signed 'PRPNPE3 Senda del Cares'.

02 This well-made path climbs gradually westwards. Nearly 2km (40 minutes) from the info hut, you reach its highest point, **Los Collaos**. From here, you can just enjoy the awe-inspiring scenery as you wend your way along the gorge. You get glimpses up side-valleys and pass over side-streams, under rock overhangs and through a few tunnels.

03 Between 1km and 4km after Los Collaos, the path's overall direction bends southwards and the gorge narrows. At the **Pasarela de los Martínez**, a 23m-long boardwalk – named after a celebrated local mountaineering family – straddles a break in the path caused by the collapse of an entire section of cliff in 2012.

04 Two kilometres before Caín, the **Puente Bolín** transfers you to the east side of the gorge. The **Puente de los Rebecos** (pictured) returns you to the west side 500m later.

05 The river rises closer to the path and a 150m stretch of damp tunnels brings you to a third bridge and the little **Presa de Caín** dam.

06 The final stretch is alongside the river and across one more bridge to little **Caín**. Rest assured: the gorge is no less marvellous on the way back!

TAKE A BREAK

There are several places to replenish your energies in Caín. **Hostal La Ruta** (987 742 702; www.facebook.com/HostalLaRuta; Travesía del Cares 15; Mar-Oct; P), one of the first you come to, is a good bet, serving *bocadillos* (long-bread sandwiches, €5) and *platos combinados* (meat/sausage/eggs/fish with chips and salad/veg, €7 to €9) in a dining room and on an ample outside terrace.

17

VEGA DE ARIO

DURATION	DIFFICULTY	DISTANCE	START/END
6½hr return	Moderate	16km	Lagos de Covadonga
TERRAIN	Earth/grassy/stony mountain paths		

From the Lagos de Covadonga, you ascend over pastures alive with the tinkle of livestock bells and bare limestone expanses to a spectacular view of the Picos de Europa's central massif across the Cares gorge. Gradients are mostly gentle but you rise 600m en route.

GETTING HERE

The walk starts near the Lagos de Covadonga, two beautiful mountain lakes 22km southeast of Cangas de Onís (and 10km past Covadonga village). During main tourist periods (usually a week or more over Easter, daily from June to September, and some other weekends), private vehicles cannot drive up past Covadonga village between 8.30am and 9pm, but a shuttle bus operates from Cangas de Onís bus station to the Lagos and back (day ticket adult/child €9/3.50,

45 minutes each way). At other times of year, you can drive to the Lagos any time, but there's no bus. A taxi from Cangas costs €30 each way.

STARTING POINT

The Buferrera car park at the Lagos de Covadonga, where the shuttle bus stops. Drivers can save 1km of walking by driving up to the car park near Lago de la Ercina (if it's not full). There's also usually a minibus service (€1) between the two car parks.

01 Walk up the path from the Buferrera car park to the Centro de Visitantes Pedro Pidal and on to picturesque **Lago de la Ercina**. Your path, the PRPNPE4, heads across the grass to the left of the lake. When you leave the lake, any crowds immediately evaporate. The clear path, with occasional yellow-and-white PR markers along its route, passes beneath the right side of a rock outcrop and round a couple of shepherds' cabins.

Picos Wildlife

A few wolves survive in the Picos and the odd bear might wander through, but you have a far better chance of spotting chamois (*rebeco* in Spanish), a goat-antelope with short curved horns. About 6000 chamois skip with amazing agility around the rocks and slopes in higher parts of the Picos.

Huge raptors and vultures soar in the skies. Commonest is the griffon vulture, but you may also see the majestic golden eagle and, in summer, the Egyptian vulture. If very lucky you might spot a lammergeier (*quebrantahuesos* in Spanish). This enormous vulture with up to 3m wingspan is being reintroduced after falling extinct here in the 1950s.

JOHN NOBLE/LONELY PLANET ©

02 At the top of a steeper rocky section about 1.25km from the lake, you get your first sight of jagged peaks in the distance, then descend into a grassy bowl, the **Vega Las Bobias**, with several red-tile-roofed shepherds' cabins and livestock shelters, and beech woods over to the right.

03 Past the cabins is a large flattish-topped rock with a spring on its left side. Take the path heading up the rocky slope ahead. After 700m cross a stream flowing out of a soggy depression called **Llaguiellu** and follow the Vega de Ario signpost up a steepish slope.

04 You climb fairly steadily for 2.5km, with the heather and gorse thinning out and limestone increasingly dominant. A short upwards zigzag finally brings you to the flattish limestone area **El Jitu**, with superb vistas of the jagged pinnacles of the Picos' central massif to the southeast. The tallest summit, with the flattish top, is Torrecerredo (2648m), the highest peak in the entire Cordillera Cantábrica.

05 Follow the cairns across El Jitu to a round stone engraved with arrows pointing to major peaks, then take the signposted trail to the **Refugio Vega de Ario**, the end-point of the PRPNPE4. Have a wander round the *vega* (grassy basin) where the *refugio* is situated, then head back to Lago La Ercina. Take care not to stray downhill to the right as you round the hillside after Llaguiellu.

TAKE A BREAK

The **Refugio Vega de Ario** (Refugio Marqués de Villaviciosa; ☎984 092 000, 656 843095; www.refugio vegadeario.es; ⏱late May–mid-Oct) is a friendly spot for a drink and snack at the top of your walk. Try some of its homemade bread and local Gamoneu cheese.

18

MIRADOR DE ORDIALES

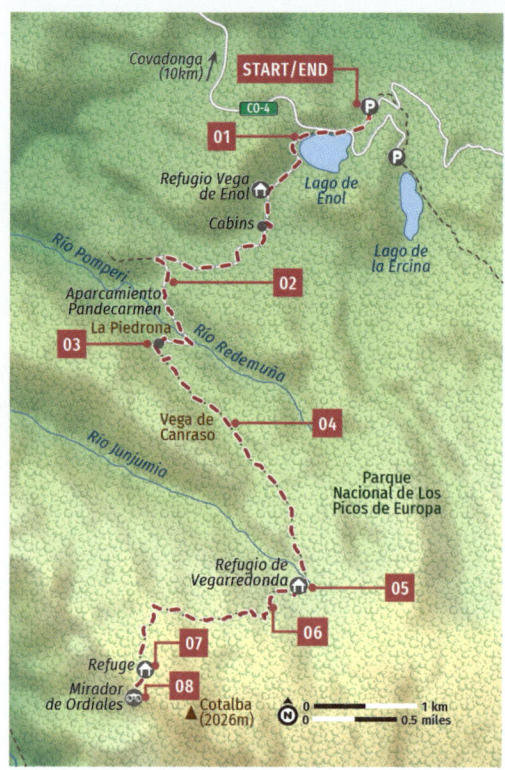

DURATION	DIFFICULTY	DISTANCE	START/END
7hr return	Moderate	23km	Lagos de Covadonga
TERRAIN	Earth/grassy/stony mountain paths, dirt road		

Walk a good, clear path (the PRPNPE5) up from mountain lakes and gentle pastures at around 1050m altitude to a stunning Picos de Europa viewpoint at about 1700m, via wild terrain of limestone crags and rocks.

GETTING HERE

The walk starts near the Lagos de Covadonga, two lakes 12km up a mountain road from Covadonga, which is 10km southeast of Cangas de Onís. During the main tourist periods (usually a week or more over Easter, daily from June to September, and some weekends in other months), private vehicles cannot drive up past Covadonga between 8.30am and 9pm, but a shuttle bus operates between Cangas de Onís bus station and the Lagos (day ticket adult/child €9/3.50, 45 minutes one-way). A taxi from Cangas to the Lagos costs €30 one-way.

STARTING POINT

The Buferrera car park at the Lagos de Covadonga, where the shuttle bus stops. Drivers can save about 3.5km of walking in each direction by driving (track conditions permitting) as far as the small Aparcamiento Pandecarmen parking area.

01 From Buferrera car park, walk up the road and along the north side of **Lago de Enol**, then branch left onto a path signposted PRPNPE5, which winds round the lake to join a dirt road.

02 Crossing gentle pastureland, pass the Refugio Vega de Enol and several red-tile-roofed shepherds' cabins, reaching the **Aparcamiento Pandecarmen** 2.5km from the lake.

03 The track becomes rougher as it enters woodland and starts to climb. It dwindles to a footpath shortly before the large rock **La Piedrona**.

 Pedro Pidal

You'll notice inscriptions in the natural rock parapet of the Mirador de Ordiales, with an artificial platform in front. This is the tomb of Pedro Pidal (1870–1941), Marqués de Villaviciosa, an Asturian politician, hunter, sportsman – and the driving force behind the creation in 1918 of Spain's first national parks, Picos de Europa and Ordesa.

Pidal also, with Gregorio Pérez, a shepherd from Caín, made the first ascent of Picu Urriellu (Naranjo de Bulnes), in 1904. He loved the Picos so much that he chose to be buried right here on the lip of the Ordiales precipice, in what he called 'the enchanted kingdom of the chamois and the eagles'.

04 Climb steadily along the clear path, with varying steepness, passing along the brilliantly green **Vega de Canraso** valley with jagged pinnacle peaks up ahead. Grey limestone starts to replace green grass as the predominant colour.

05 Nearly 3km from La Piedrona, the **Refugio de Vegarredonda** (pictured) appears in a broad limestone basin.

06 Past the refuge follow the path signed 'Mirador de Ordiales', **climbing steeply** through a world of limestone rock for about 30 minutes, with yellow-and-white PR markers now more frequent. Then there's a more level westwards stretch across rocky expanses for 1km or so, before a leftward bend heralds the final upward push.

07 A grassy slope leads up to a small, unstaffed **refuge** (providing shelter if needed), then the path swings right past a large **sinkhole** and on up towards the rocky skyline.

08 Just before a V-shaped gap in the skyline (which can be particularly windy), head up to the right where the rock forms a natural wall. This is the **Mirador de Ordiales**. Peer over the edge with extreme care to look 1000 almost perpendicular metres down to the Angón valley far below.

To return to the walk's starting point, go back the way you came.

 TAKE A BREAK

In decent weather, it's hard to beat a picnic up in the Vega de Ordiales, the grassy area with the unstaffed refuge below the mirador. Lower down, the **Refugio de Vegarredonda** (985 922 952, 626 343366; www.refugiovegarredonda.com; Mar-Nov) serves snacks, meals and drinks.

19

HORCADOS ROJOS

DURATION	DIFFICULTY	DISTANCE	START/END
4hr return	Moderate	11km	Teleférico de Fuente Dé lower station
TERRAIN	Unpaved roads, stony mountain paths		

An exhilarating high-mountain walk that starts with a ride on the spectacular Fuente Dé cable car then takes you higher into a universe of rock, culminating in a view to Picu Urriellu in the heart of the Picos de Europa. Total walking ascent and descent: 600m.

GETTING HERE

From Fuente Dé (23km west along the Deva valley from the town of Potes), the **Teleférico de Fuente Dé** (📞 942 73 66 10; www.cantur.com; adult/child return €18/7, one-way €11/4; ⏰ 10am-6pm early Feb-Jun & mid-Sep-early Jan, 8am-7pm Jul-mid-Sep, hours may vary; 🅿) whisks you high up the southern wall of the Picos' central massif – an ascent of 753m in less than four minutes. It's a scenic ride, if you dare open your eyes. Cable cars depart continually throughout the day, weather permitting. Book online at least 24 hours ahead to avoid queues. A taxi from Potes to Fuente Dé costs about €25.

STARTING POINT

Teleférico de Fuente Dé upper station.

01 From the upper cable car station (altitude 1823m) walk up the track through the rocky landscape. At the **Horcadina de Covarrobres** junction after 1km, go left following the PRPNPE23 Horcados Rojos sign.

02 The stony track heads northwest beneath the towering crags and cliffs of Peña Olvidada. Below are two small, clear mountain lakes, the Pozos de Lloroza. At **La Vueltona**, a sharp left-hand bend in the track, take the path to the right signposted Refugio Cabaña Verónica.

The Long Way Down

For a longer, more varied and complete outing – and avoiding a downwards ride on the *teleférico* – don't turn right to the *teleférico* station when you get back to the Horcadina de Covarrobres, but continue straight on to join the Puertos de Áliva route (p68).

This takes you down to Fuente Dé via mountain pastures and dense woodlands – a total distance on the day of 23km (about eight hours' walking), with 750m of ascent and 1520m descent.

JOHN NOBLE / LONELY PLANET ©

03 You start climbing immediately, with the cliffs of Peña Vieja (2613m) rising to your right. There is now nothing but rock all around you. At a **fork** after a steep zigzag section, go left.

04 In a kilometre you reach another fork, with **Cabaña Verónica** signposted left. Go right, following yellow-and-white markers.

05 After half a kilometre uphill, you reach the **Collado de Horcados Rojos** pass (2340m). Below you is the Jou de los Boches basin; ahead, sticking up like a giant thumb, is Picu Uriellu (Naranjo de Bulnes; 2519m). All around are other high peaks of the central Picos. Paths starting east from the Collado head up Torre de Horcados Rojos (2503m) and down to the Jou de los Boches (and from there to the foot of Picu Uriellu), but these are steep, airy routes only recommended for experienced walkers (and not recommended at all with snow).

06 Head half a kilometre back down, and from the path junction walk up to the tiny **Refugio Cabaña Verónica** (pictured) to enjoy its spectacular location and views and learn about its unique history. Then return to the main path and back to the *teleférico*.

TAKE A BREAK

If the **Refugio Cabaña Verónica** (☎663 516456; www.facebook.com/Refugio.Cabana.Veronica; breakfast/lunch/dinner €7/15/15; ⊙approx Apr-Nov) looks like a warship gun turret, well, it was. The turret was obtained in 1961 by the Federación Española de Montaña from the US aircraft carrier *Palau*, which was being broken up near Bilbao. Today, it can lodge four to six people (by reservation) and serves drinks when the warden is home.

PICOS & NORTHERN SPAIN/79

20

PICU PIERZU

DURATION	DIFFICULTY	DISTANCE	START/END
4-4½hr return	Moderate	10km	Collado Llomena

TERRAIN	Dirt track, earth/stony/grassy paths

There's a lot more to the Cordillera Cantábrica than the Picos de Europa. The mountains and valleys of the Parque Natural de Ponga, the Picos' western neighbour, are a perfect place to start exploring. Picu Pierzu (1552m) is not Ponga's highest peak but it's exceptionally scenic, with a dramatic ridge-top approach. Note that the ridge is almost devoid of shade or shelter, so you're exposed to whatever weather the day brings.

GETTING HERE

You need a vehicle. From Puente Vidosa, 21km south of Cangas de Onís by the N625, drive 7.5km west up the PO2 through Viegu (Viego) village to Collado Llomena (altitude 993m), which has a convenient parking area.

STARTING POINT

Collado Llomena at Km 5.1 on the PO2.

01 From Collado Llomena head north along an unpaved road into the woods. After 300m you get your **first glimpse** of Pierzu ahead (the further peak is the summit). The track, ascending imperceptibly, alternates between woodlands and more open areas. The western massif of the Picos de Europa, about 12km away, peeps over the eastern horizon, while the dark bulk of Tiatordos (1950m) and, to its left, Maciédome (1903m) loom to your southwest. The views of all these will get better and better as the walk goes on.

02 After 2.2km turn right off the track, up a **small path** with a 'Pico Pierzu PRAS211' sign. Now the work starts. The path winds steeply uphill for some 400m, with yellow-and-white paint markers helping to show the way,

ℹ Mountain Encounter

They came out of nowhere, bounding down the Asturian mountainside with a noise somewhere between a howl and a bark. OH MY GOD. I didn't even have time to panic before they reached me – wagging their tails. They weren't wolves after all, but *mastines* (mastiffs), guarding a herd of cattle. The biggest dogs I'd ever seen – but undoubtedly friendly. They wore viciously spiked collars, a defence *against* wolves, which like to grab their prey by the throat. *Mastines* are commonly used to guard livestock in the Asturian hills. They can be aggressive if they think you're a threat to their animals, so give them a nice wide berth.

JOHN NOBLE / LONELY PLANET ©

then strikes north, gradually ascending the ridge. Superb panoramas open out in all directions.

03 The grassy Valle de Aranga, with two small lakes (the smaller one may be dry in summer), appears down to the left. At the **Majada de Cerboes**, a small group of shepherds' huts, the path swings to the right across the grass in front of the largest of these. Small cairns show the way over a short rocky section, then you cross a steepish slope before veering north again, climbing, on the east side of the ridge.

04 Cross the side of a small **grassy bowl**. At the top of the rise from that, you're on the west side of the ridge again, with a steep grassy hillside sweeping down to your left.

05 As you crest another rise 300m later, the summit, with its concrete pillar, is now agreeably close. Small cairns become the most useful route markers. Cross a small saddle and in another 600m you're at the **summit**. Bare serrated ridges stretch away to the northwest; Tiatordos and other high, rocky summits of the Cordel de Ponga fill the western horizon; Cangas de Onís can be glimpsed 13km to the north; and the pinnacles of the Picos de Europa rise above everything to the east. Soak up the panoramas, then head back down the way you came.

 TAKE A BREAK

After your walk, stop into cosy **La Corralada** (☎985 843 073; www.facebook.com/Bar-Restaurante-La-Corralada-1500849460126589; mains €8-11, lunch menu €12; ⏱9am-midnight), by the roadside in Viegu, for well-priced, home-style Asturian dishes including *fabada*, a bean stew with meat, sausage and black pudding, or sausage/ham/bacon with eggs and chips for €8.

PICOS & NORTHERN SPAIN/81

21

COSTA NAVIEGA

DURATION	DIFFICULTY	DISTANCE	START/END
6hr one-way	Moderate	20km	NV2 Km 9.85/Navia

TERRAIN	Footpaths, dirt tracks, streets

Twenty kilometres of cliffs, beaches, rocky coves and roaring seas – all the drama of Spain's north coast is packed into the Senda Costa Naviega (PRAS293) along Asturias' western coast. It's well marked with yellow-and-white PR markers.

GETTING HERE
A taxi from Navia is €11 to the walk's starting point. An alternative is to take an **Alsa** (www.alsa.com; several daily) bus or **FEVE** (www.renfe.com/es/es/cercanias/cercanias-feve; two daily) train from Navia, Luarca, Oviedo or elsewhere to Villapedre village, then walk 1km east along the quite busy N-634.

STARTING POINT
Km 9.85 on the minor NV-2, 400m north off the N-634 at Km 515.5, 9km east of Navia.

01 Go east along the dirt track from the information board at NV-2 Km 9.85, forking left after 100m. The path U-turns after another 100m. Ignore a sharp right turn 100m later and head on through mixed **woodlands**. The little Río Barayo eventually accompanies you. Ignore signs to Playa de Barayo, unless you want an early beach detour.

02 Reaching a car park 2.4km from the walk's start, turn right. After 700m, the path turns left to run along the **clifftops** for nearly 4km, with the sea crashing on jagged rocks below and open fields on your left – classic Asturias coast. At times, the path comes within a metre of the cliff edge, but it's plenty wide enough.

03 Wind your way down into the small town of Puerto de Vega and round its colourful little **fishing harbour**.

Navia

Less pretty-pretty than some other small towns along the western end of the Asturias coast, Navia still makes an agreeable base for this walk. It has an oldish heart around its market square, the **Plaza de Abastos**, and a range of hotels, including **Palacio Arias** (www.palacioarias.es), a century-old *palacete de indianos* (mansion built by a returned emigrant to the Americas). **La Magaya** (www.sidrerialamagaya.com; Calle Regueral 12), on the main street, is a bright, modern take on a traditional Asturian *sidrería* (cider bar) with a good restaurant section.

Best for

COASTAL VIEWS

ISA FERNANDEZ FERNANDEZ/SHUTTERSTOCK

04 Coming up to the street opposite Restaurante Jorge, turn left then first right. Take the middle street (Calle Jovellanos) at a three-way fork after 50m. At its end, turn left, then immediately right along Calle La Atalaya, and follow this to the panoramically sited **Capilla de la Atalaya** chapel.

05 Head west along the footpath here for another scenic clifftop stretch, 3km to the long sweep of beautiful **Playa de Frejulfe** (pictured). After 300m across its sands, take the path up into the tall eucalyptus woods, turning left at the Km 12 marker.

06 After 2km, the path climbs up behind the cliff-backed **Playa Fabal**; 700m further on, don't miss a sharp right downhill turn. Where an asphalt road comes in from the left 400m later, continue ahead on a footpath.

07 Wind along near the cliffs and go left at a track junction after 1.3km. At an **unsigned fork** 150m later, go right.

08 In 600m, you reach a paved road. Head along this, and the mouth of the Río Navia comes into view. Turn down to the **Monumento al Emigrante** and the car park below. Head south through a woodland area till you reach a paved road among sports installations. Continue south and, in 1km, you're in the middle of Navia.

 ## TAKE A BREAK

Puerto de Vega has several seafood-focused eateries, but if you'd rather go further before stopping, head for **Chiringuito La Mar de Fondo** (📞644 074950; dishes €7-20; ⏱noon-midnight or later, approx Jun-early Sep; 🅿), which serves seafood and salads on a deck overlooking Playa de Frejulfe. It's advisable to call ahead for a table.

22

PICU URRIELLU

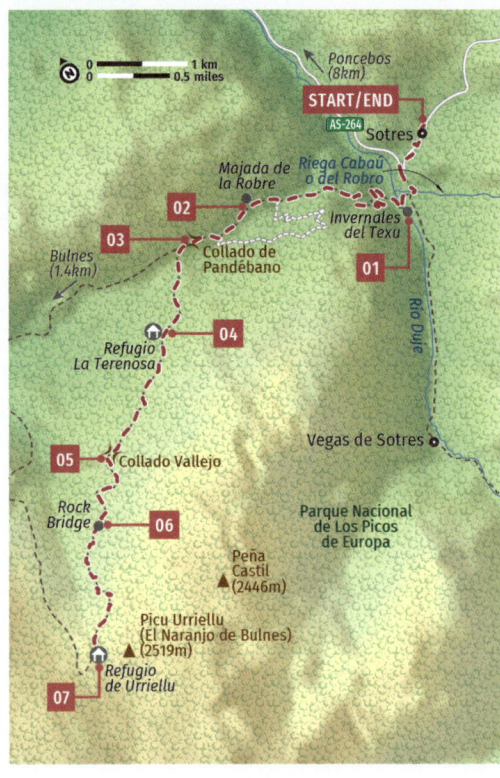

DURATION	DIFFICULTY	DISTANCE	START/END
7hr return	Hard	21km	Sotres

TERRAIN	Grassy/stony mountain paths, unpaved road

The magnificent rock pillar Picu Urriellu (Naranjo de Bulnes; pictured) towers like a gigantic thumb 500 very vertical metres from its base in the heart of the Picos de Europa to its 2519m-high summit. Urriellu is the greatest emblem of the Picos and draws climbers from far and wide to its breathtaking limestone walls. Just getting to the bottom of it is a thrill for any hiker. The easiest approach is via the Collado de Pandébano, a grassy saddle most easily reached from the Picos' highest village, Sotres. The route (PRPNPE21) is clear and hard to lose.

GETTING HERE

Sotres sits at an altitude of 1045m, 11km up a twisting mountain road, the AS-264, from Poncebos, which is 6km south of Arenas de Cabrales. The only ways to reach Sotres are to drive, walk or take a taxi (around €20 from Arenas de Cabrales).

STARTING POINT

The start point is Sotres. Drivers can cut a useful 4km off the distance in each direction by driving, with care, via the unpaved road through the Invernales del Texu as far as a cattle grid below the Collado de Pandébano.

01 Walk down the paved AS-264 from Sotres, and on a right-hand hairpin after 800m, take the unpaved road heading straight ahead (south). After 350m turn right down a footpath, which brings you down to another unpaved road among the **Invernales del Texu**, a collection of tile-roofed winter livestock shelters.

Urriellu or Naranjo?

Urriellu, the age-old local name for the mountain, is thought to derive from *ur,* a pre-Roman term denoting a high place. The origin of the name Naranjo de Bulnes is a mystery. It first appeared on an 1855 map of Asturias by German geologist Guillermo (Wilhelm) Schulz. Bulnes is the nearest village to the peak; *naranjo* is Spanish for orange-coloured – a possible reference to the rock's hue at sunset.

The daunting peak was first scaled in 1904 by Pedro Pidal, Marqués de Villaviciosa, and a local guide from Caín, Gregorio Pérez 'El Cainejo'. Since then its walls have become a magnet for daring climbers, and over 70 different routes have been opened to the summit.

Best for

WILDLIFE

ANTON PETRUS/SHUTTERSTOCK ©

02 Follow the road zig-zagging up through woodlands then climb gradually to another set of cabins, the **Majada de la Robre**, and on to a cattle grid, around which drivers park. A hundred metres further, a PRPNPE21 sign points you up the grassy slope to the right.

03 In a few minutes, you're up on the pastures of the **Collado de Pandébano** (1200m), and Picu Urriellu is peering over the shoulder of the hill to the southwest, with Neverón de Urriellu (2549m) and Picu L'Albu (2442m) to its right.

04 Follow the PRPNPE21 signpost and in 1km you'll pass **Refugio La Terenosa**. The path becomes stonier and steeper. Thick woodlands slope down to the right towards tiny Bulnes village, far below.

05 The landscape changes dramatically at **Collado Vallejo**, 1.5km from La Terenosa. As you come round a bend, the hillside suddenly plunges down to the right. A few steps later, a magnificent view of the towering Urriellu, with the path snaking round the hillside towards it, unfolds before you.

06 One kilometre later you cross a **natural rock bridge** over a gully and the climb becomes markedly steeper.

07 The path zigzags up through rocky terrain, with the pillar of Urriellu drawing you ever closer. Finally you reach the **Refugio de Urriellu** (1953m) at the foot of the mighty monolith. When you're ready, return the way you came.

Stop a while in the Vega de Urriellu, the rocky basin below Picu Urriellu. The **Refugio de Urriellu** (☏ 638 278041, 650 780381, www.refugiodeurriellu.com; Vega de Urriellu; breakfast €5, lunch or dinner €15; ⓗ mid-Mar–mid-Dec) serves *bocadillos*, drinks and plates of cheese, cured meats or sausage. There's a potable spring here too.

23

SOMIEDO LAKES

DURATION	DIFFICULTY	DISTANCE	START/END
8½hr return	Hard	26.5km	Valle de Lago
TERRAIN	Unpaved roads, earth/rocky/grassy paths		

Emerald-green valleys, jagged-pinnacled mountains, upland pastures alive with the tinkle of cow bells, hillsides clothed in dense deciduous forests – this is the Parque Natural de Somiedo (www.parquenaturalsomiedo.es) in southwest Asturias, one of the most outstandingly beautiful parts of the Cordillera Cantábrica.

This walk takes in five mountain lakes, high pastures and some wonderful mountain and valley scenery. We rate it hard because of its length: there are shorter options (p87) if you don't fancy the full 26.5km.

GETTING HERE

Valle de Lago village is 8km up a twisting mountain road from Pola de Somiedo (the only town in the area). An Alsa (www.alsa.com) bus departs Oviedo bus station for Pola de Somiedo (€9, two hours) at 5pm Monday to Friday and 10am Saturday and Sunday, returning from Pola at 6.45am Monday to Friday and at 4.30pm or 5.30pm Saturday and Sunday. There's no public transport between Pola and Valle de Lago: a taxi will cost about €20.

STARTING POINT

Casa Cobrana restaurant in Valle de Lago.

Place-naming in the first part of the walk is not too imaginative. We're following the Río del Valle (River of the Valley) from the village of Valle de Lago (Lake Valley) up the Valle del Lago (Valley of the Lake) to the Lago del Valle (Lake of the Valley). There are two possible routes: the Camino del Sol (Sun) and the Camino de la Sombra (Shade). They coincide for just 400m or so about halfway to the lake. We take the prettier and more interesting Sombra route.

01 Facing the entrance of Casa Cobrana, take the lane along the right side of the building. After 300m, just before the **church**, turn left along a concrete road signed PRAS16. Fork left off this after 100m onto an unpaved track with a yellow-and-white X 'wrong way' marker (it's not the wrong way for us), and follow this as it heads southeast, paralleling the south bank of the little Río del Valle and sometimes narrowing to a footpath.

02 Keep your eyes open for vultures circling around the jagged, multi-pinnacled crags above the valley. After 2km you pass a **teito** (broom-thatch cabin characteristic of the Somiedo area) on the left. Ignore a track forking up to the right 100m later. In another 500m, you cross the river and come out on a wide unpaved road. Go right, then after 400m veer right along a footpath into trees, emerging after 150m at a fork of tracks. Take the lower, right-hand track (not the even lower footpath): this crosses back over the river and starts climbing.

03 Where the track makes a sharp right turn about 1.2km past the river, fork left onto a footpath. This rises across grasslands to reach the retaining wall of the **Lago del Valle** (pictured pp88-9) in a further 1.2km. You have, perhaps surprisingly, risen 330m in altitude reaching this point (1560m) from Valle de Lago village. The lake, Asturias' largest at 240,000 sq metres, occupies a classic glacial cirque with steep mountains on all sides except the valley you have just walked up.

 Shorter Options

If you feel like heading back from the Lago del Valle to Valle de Lago by the shortest route, take the path heading northwest from the lake. This quickly becomes a good unpaved road – the Camino del Sol – and returns you to the village in 6km.

A way to cover much the same ground as our whole walk in less distance is the PRAS15 trail, running from the Alto de la Farrapona to Valle de Lago village via the Lagos de Saliencia, Lago del Valle and Camino del Sol in about 14km, predominantly downhill. It is, however, a one-way route so you need transport. A taxi from Valle de Lago to the Alto de la Farrapona costs about €45.

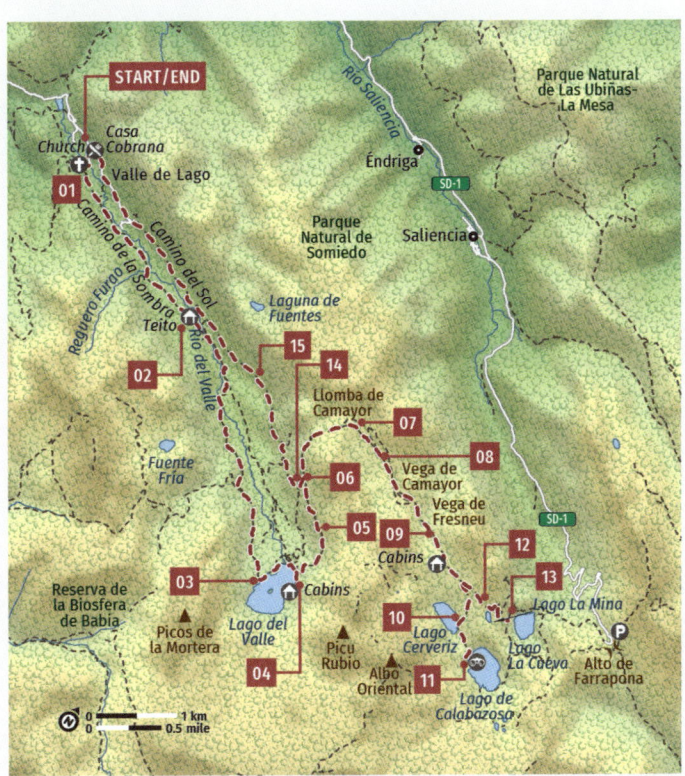

04 Head left round to the far (east) side of the lake where two **cabins** (one a *teito*, the other with a slate roof) stand on a grassy rise above the shore. This is a perfect spot to take a break and enjoy the beautiful vistas over the lake, the valley and the mountains framing everything.

05 To continue, take the path heading uphill from the northeast corner of the lake. It has a 'Lagos de Saliencia PRAS15' sign, though this may be pointing in the wrong direction (thanks to winds). The path quickly bends left, passes between two rocks and then bends right, climbing. At a fork of paths within 100m, go left. The **narrow but clear path** (pictured p86) works its way up and across the hillside, beneath crags on the right, with a decent number of PR markers to confirm its course.

06 Lovely views of the Lago del Valle, the spiky peaks framing the valley, and the mixture of fields and woodlands below, open up as you climb. Two kilometres from the lake the path crosses a sloping **stone field**.

07 Half a kilometre later the path veers right (northeast) and continues climbing. In another 400m you reach its highest point, the **Llomba de Camayor** (1750m); continue ahead following the sign to Alto La Farrapona.

08 The path soon bends right to pass along the delightful springy turf of the broad, grassy **Vega de Camayor**

JOHN NOBLE / LONELY PLANET ©

valley, about 1.2km long, beneath imposing cliffs on the right.

09 Over the rise at the end of the Vega de Camayor, another valley, the **Vega de Fresneu**, stretches ahead. As you mount the end of this after 1km, two cabins appear to the right and your path bears left.

10 **Lago Cerveriz**, the first of the four Lagos de Saliencia, appears down to the right and a track leads down to its eastern end – a picturesque spot with the cliffs of Albo Oriental (2109m) reflected in the waters and, quite likely, a herd of tan-coloured cattle grazing the pastures. In contrast to the Lago del Valle, which flows out as the Río del Valle, the Saliencia lakes all sit in the bottom of mountain bowls and have no above-ground outlets. They occupy limestone sinkholes or depressions that were filled in by impermeable deposits allowing lakes to form.

11 From Lago Cerveriz walk east across a grassy basin then a rocky dip to a viewpoint overlooking the biggest of the Saliencia lakes, **Lago Calabazosa**. You can only actually see about two-thirds of the lake from here: for a fuller view, take the steep, rocky path down in front of the viewpoint and walk along the lake shore to the right for about 100m.

Bear Spotting

The Cordillera Cantábrica is the main stronghold of Spain's biggest animal, the brown bear (*oso pardo*). With the help of conservation efforts, bear numbers in the Cordillera have passed 300, from as low as 70 in the 1990s.

Two companies, **Wild Watching Spain** (www.wildwatchingspain.com; per day adult/child €90/50) and **Somiedo Experience** (www.somiedoexperience.com; half/full day per person €40/70), offer bear-watching outings from Pola de Somiedo. Observation is normally from a distance through telescopes or binoculars. The best times for sightings are May (if it's warm), June, late August and September.

12 Return to Lago Cerveriz and back up to the main track. Turn right and in 500m **Lago La Mina** appears down to your right. The smallest of the Saliencia lakes, it is in fact often dry in summer and autumn.

13 The track then zigzags to a point with a great view over the fourth lake, **Lago La Cueva**, at the bottom of a deep bowl with steep slopes of green grass and grey rock all round – except at the northern corner where two cabins, one of them a *teito*, overlook it from a grassy slope. There is no need to walk down to Lago La Cueva unless you really want to. (The track in fact continues 2km to meet the paved SD1 road at the Alto de la Farrapona, at the head of Somiedo's Saliencia valley.)

14 Turn round and retrace your steps until you're descending back into the Valle del Lago. On the descent ignore a 'Valle del Lago' sign pointing straight down the hillside (this is a possible shortcut but the first part is steep, rough and trackless). Continue across the stone field you crossed on the way up but at a **fork**, where the part of the stone field above the path comes to an end, continue on down (not left towards the Lago del Valle).

15 In 200m the path veers to the right, going round a small building and changing direction from southeast to northwest. It develops into a gently **descending dirt track**, which, in 3km, brings you out on the Camino del Sol. Continue along this for a further 3km back to Valle de Lago village.

TAKE A BREAK

The Lago del Valle is an idyllic picnic spot, especially the grassy rise with the two cabins on its eastern shore. There's a good, drinkable spring behind the cabins too.

24

ARANTZAZU, AIZKORRI, SAN ADRIÁN

DURATION	DIFFICULTY	DISTANCE	START/END
6–7hr return	Hard	23km	Arantzazu

TERRAIN	Unpaved roads, footpaths, some rocky with steepish sections

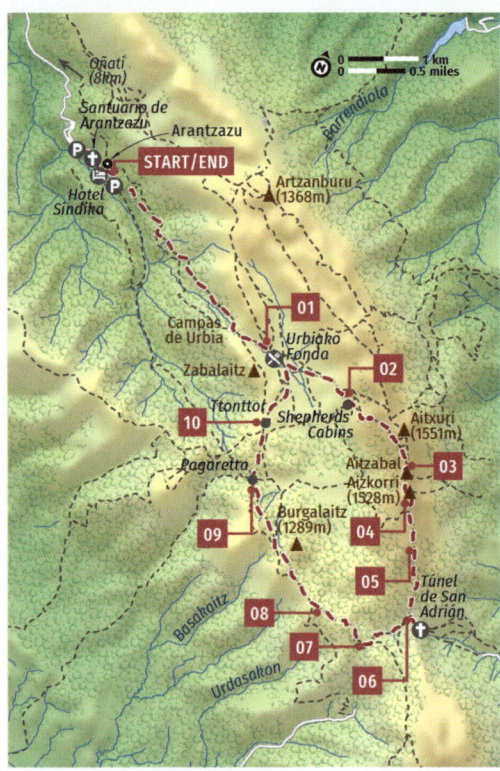

This route has everything a good Basque Country walk should have: steep-sided peaks, dense beech woods, pastures alive with livestock bells, and a dose of cultural-historical interest. There's some 1200m of ascent and descent.

GETTING HERE
Arantzazu is 10km south of Oñati, which is served by Pesa buses (www.pesa.net) from Bilbao (€7.25, 60 minutes, three daily) and elsewhere. Buses link Oñati and Arantzazu on Sundays, but otherwise you'll need a taxi (around €10) or your own wheels.

STARTING POINT
The Santuario de Arantzazu.

01 Walk east along the road from the monastery. At a parking area 500m after Hotel Sindika, take the left-hand track signed Urbia and Aizkorri. This gradually climbs 3km through **beautiful woodlands** to a broad grassy valley, the **Campas de Urbia**, where the **Urbiako Fonda** makes a good refreshments stop.

02 Some 100m past the Urbiako Fonda, veer left across the pasture for 300m to meet a dirt road. Go left and after 1km enter a group of **shepherds' cabins** to find the path up towards Aizkorri.

03 After about 40 minutes' ascent on the clear path, you reach a **grassy pass** where views along the ridge's steeper east face open up.

04 Pass across the west flank of Aitzabal (1508m; pictured) before climbing to the superbly panoramic summit of **Aizkorri** (1528m). A chapel and a walkers' refuge sit just below the peak.

Among Thorns, You?

The origins of the **Santuario de Arantzazu** (☎943 78 09 51; www.arantzazu.org; Barrio de Arantzazu; ⏱9am-8pm) go back to shepherd Rodrigo de Baltzategi's reported discovery of a statuette of the Virgin among thorn bushes in 1468. The miraculous spot quickly became a pilgrimage site, a chapel was built and a monastic community was established. Baltzategi is said to have exclaimed *'Arantzan zu?'* ('Among thorns, you?') on finding the statue, hence the monastery's name – and that of the many women called Arantza/Arantxa/Arancha. The large complex owes its current austere but highly original look to a 1950s rebuilding by Basque architects.

JOHN NOBLE/LONELY PLANET ©

Best for

BRINGING THE PAST TO LIFE

05 Descend south-southeast along the crest and fork right after 100m. In another 150m, turn left and descend a rocky path into a **beech wood**.

06 About 50 minutes down from the Aizkorri summit, you emerge in a grassy clearing, with a partly stone-paved path running across its far side. This is part of the Camino Vasco del Interior, a branch of the Camino de Santiago. Walk 250m left, down to the **Túnel de San Adrián**, a remarkable natural tunnel with a chapel inside.

07 From the tunnel head back up the Camino Vasco, which climbs gradually through woodlands. About 1km past the grassy clearing, turn right down a **path signposted to Urbia and Arantzazu**. Keep a sharp lookout for red-and-white GR markers through the maze of woodland paths from here, the first at an easily missed right-hand turn after just 80m, also marked by a small cairn.

08 In 20 minutes, you reach a **clearing** with views over to the Aizkorri range, then emerge on an unpaved road. Go right, then veer off to the right after 100m. Some 800m later, rejoin the unpaved road very briefly before veering left.

09 A kilometre through woodlands brings you to a clearing around the prehistoric **Pagarreta monolith**.

10 Take the path signposted Urbia. This joins an unpaved road leading past a farmhouse called **Ttonttor** selling prize-winning sheep's cheese. Continue down the road to Urbiako Fonda, and Arantzazu.

 TAKE A BREAK

Atmospheric, stone-walled **Urbiako Fonda** (platos combinados €8-14; ⏱approx 8am-9pm daily May-Oct, Sat & Sun Dec-Apr) in the Campas de Urbia is the perfect pit stop either on the way out or the way home.

25

ANBOTO

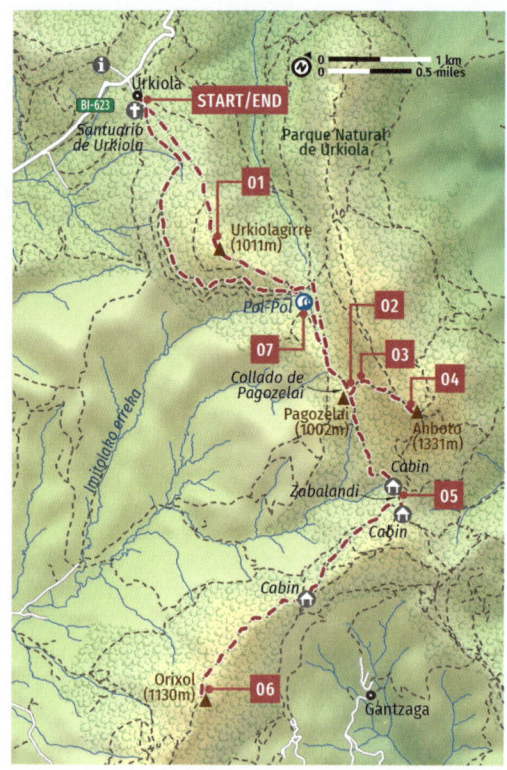

DURATION	DIFFICULTY	DISTANCE	START/END
7-7½hr return	Hard	25km	Urkiola
TERRAIN	Unpaved roads, footpaths, some rocky and steep		

Anboto, the high point of a knife-edged limestone ridge, is arguably the Basque Country's most thrilling hiking challenge. We rate it hard because of the downright scary final section to the top, which requires hands as well as feet (and guts!). But don't panic: there's no shame in skipping the final ascent. The itinerary also visits another panoramic peak, Orixol (also spelled Oriol or Orisol). Total ascent and descent: 1400m.

GETTING HERE

Álava Bus (http://araba.eus/alavabus) runs at least six daily Durango-Vitoria (and vice versa) buses, stopping at Urkiola (€1.90, 20 minutes from Durango). **Bizkaibus** (http://web.bizkaia.eus/es/web/bizkaibus) runs frequent Bilbao-Durango buses, though weekend connections in Durango are poor.

STARTING POINT

Santuario de Urkiola church in tiny Urkiola on the Durango-Vitoria road.

01 Immediately past the highest level of the car park above the church, take the path to the left, crossing a stile after 60m. Head up across pasture and through pines to **Urkiolagirre** (1011m), where the Anboto range stretches out ahead.

02 Descend 1km ahead and cross a stile to an unpaved road. Go left, climbing gradually, then fork left (signed Zabalandi) after 1km. In 300m, at the **Collado de Pagozelai** (Beech Tree Pass), a signpost points left to Anboto, with the bare-rock mountain looming behind it.

03 Follow the Anboto sign, then veer right after 100m. A tangle of paths heads steeply up through the **woods** for about 25 minutes. From

 ## Trail Options

If you don't fancy the ascent of Anboto, you can save 1½ hours' effort by continuing straight on towards Zabalandi from the Collado de Pagozelai. Secondly, you could turn round at Zabalandi and save about 2½ hours' walking to Orixol and back.

For the intrepid, it's possible to make an airy and daring descent direct from Anboto to Zabalandi. From the summit the path continues along the crest a short way then veers right, initiating a steep descent on the limestone slope. But be warned: the first part of this runs close to a terrifyingly sheer drop.

ANDRES CERVINO ALVAREZ/SHUTTERSTOCK ©

the very topmost tree take the path straight uphill. In five minutes, you're at the **foot of the final ascent** to Anboto's summit. At the sight of this steep rocky slope with perilous drop-offs, many people understandably decide to go no further.

04 If you go for the summit, take it slow and steady, use your hands and don't look down. The first rocky slope reaches a false summit, from which you have a slightly less steep stretch of about 75m (with perilous drop-offs) to the **summit of Anboto** (1331m; pictured).

05 Return to the Collado de Pagozelai and turn left. The path joins an unpaved road (with a good fresh-water **fountain** just up to the left after about 600m) leading to **Zabalandi**, a five-way junction.

06 Take the path signed Oriol into beech woods. After about 400m, fork left (uphill); 450m later, in a rockier, more open section, take the lower, right-hand fork. Occasional red-and-white markers assist. At a small pasture with a cabin, take the path along the back of the cabin. This winds 2km up through wonderful mossy beech woods to the rocky top of **Orixol** (1130m), with superb valley views.

07 Return to Zabalandi, Pagozelai and the junction 300m later. Take the track signed Asuntza, but after 150m veer left down a grassy path, which reaches the iron-tasting three-spout fountain **Pol-Pol**. Ascend to the unpaved road, turn left and walk 3.5km back to Urkiola.

TAKE A BREAK

On the main road below the Urkiola church, **Restaurante Bizkarra** (946 81 20 26; BI623, Urkiola; platos combinados €9-17; 9.30am-7.30pm) does hearty *platos combinados,* salads and *bocadillos.*

PICOS & NORTHERN SPAIN/**93**

Also Try...

JOHN NOBLE/LONELY PLANET ©

LA PERAL TO VILLAR DE VILDAS

A superb medium-length walk (the PRAS14, well marked) through some of the best Somiedo scenery.

From La Peral village (altitude 1350m) ascend the Trabanco valley, with high peaks rising to the south. Your highest point (1720m) comes at a fork of tracks 1.2km past Fuente Las Machadas: take neither track but head left of the left-hand one, passing a water trough. The path descends, via the Collado de Enfistiella pass, to Braña Viella (Braña de los Cuartos), a collection of cabins formerly used by cattle and their herders. From here, descend the bright green Pigüeña valley to La Pornacal, the best preserved of Somiedo's *brañas,* with 33 thatched cabins, and on to Villar de Vildas village (altitude 850m). The ends of this route are a €50 taxi ride apart. If you want to finish where you started, we suggest walking from Villar de Vildas to Braña Viella and back.

DURATION 3½hr one-way
DIFFICULTY Moderate
DISTANCE 13km

RIBADESELLA TO LA ESPASA

Follow a beach-strewn stretch of the Camino del Norte pilgrimage route from the lively small Asturias town of Ribadesella. The way is marked with Camino de Santiago scallop-shell symbols and yellow arrows.

At the far end of Ribadesella's Playa Santa Marina, go left along the street, then take the second of two roads to the right at the first intersection. Country lanes lead through San Pedro village and down through Vega village to Playa de Vega (pictured above), a 1.5km surf beach with a few bars (good for a halt). Continue to Berbes village, after which you have 1km along the N632 (beware traffic) before heading down to Playa Arenal de Morís. Then it's across fields and along 2km of beaches and low cliffs to Playa La Espasa, with another handful of restaurant-bars. Try a squid *bocadillo* at Chiringuito La Espasa!

DURATION 3½hr one-way
DIFFICULTY Easy
DISTANCE 15km

JM ARBONES/SHUTTERSTOCK ©

VEGA DE LIORDES

A great Picos de Europa walk, taking you to a spectacular high-level green valley between lines of high, rugged peaks. There are sections of steep ascent and descent.

The well-marked route (PRPNPE25) works upwards through woodlands from Fuente Dé (1100m), then climbs grassy hillsides and a steep, rocky gully, the Canal de Pedabejo. From the pass at the top (2040m), the Vega de Liordes valley unfolds before you. Descend into the *vega*, then return to Fuente Dé by a long, long zigzag down the steep Canal del Embudo gully.

DURATION 5½hr return
DIFFICULTY Hard
DISTANCE 11km

GAZTELUGATXE

This is a place with a touch of magic. It's a rocky, chapel-topped islet with natural rock arches, linked to the cliff-lined Basque coast by a causeway and a zigzag path climbing 231 steps – a setting dramatic enough to have starred as Dragonstone in *Game of Thrones*.

From Easter to September you need to reserve a time slot online (www.tiketa.eus/gaztelugatxe) to ensure access. Gaztelugatxe (pictured above) is 35km northeast of Bilbao. There's a steepish 200m descent to the causeway from the parking areas.

DURATION 1hr return
DIFFICULTY Easy
DISTANCE 3km

RUTA MACIZO DE ÁNDARA

Introduction to the mountain and valley scenery of the Picos de Europa's eastern massif.

The well-marked trail (PRPNPE28) starts and ends at Jitu de Escarandi, 3.5km east of Sotres on the road towards Tresviso. It takes in dense beech woods, mountain pastures, the towering cliffs of Macondiu (1999m) and relics of abandoned mine workings. Total ascent and descent: about 600m. Some versions of the route include an extension to Bejes village and back. This adds an extra 12km and 530m of descent and ascent.

DURATION 4½hr return
DIFFICULTY Moderate
DISTANCE 16km

GALICIA

26 **Illas Cíes** Sail out from the Rías Baixas to walk wildly beautiful national park islands. **p100**

27 **Parada de Sil Circuit** An inland gem in the plunging Sil canyon. **p102**

28 **Castro Caldelas Magical Forests** A rural dream of woodland streams, vineyards and ancient churches. **p104**

29 **O Vicedo to Porto de Espasante** Cliffs, beaches, enormous panoramas and Spain's most famous bench. **p106**

30 **Muxía to Lires** A spectacular day along one of Spain's most dramatic coasts. **p108**

31 **Lires to Cabo Fisterra** Unforgettable coastal hike to the lighthouse at the 'end of the earth'. **p110**

Explore
GALICIA

Galicia, the unique region occupying Spain's northwest corner, is the destination of Spain's most famous long walk, the Camino de Santiago, but is also laced with a huge variety of great shorter hikes along its dramatic coast of cliffs, capes, beaches and snaking *rías* (inlets), and inland among its deep-green valleys, rolling hills, stone-built villages and age-old vineyards. Everywhere you go you'll find signs of Galicia's distinct identity: the sound of bagpipes, superb seafood from the 1200km coastline, wayside *cruceiros* (carved stone crosses) and *hórreos* (traditional stone grain stores on stilts), the Galician language *galego*, the *castro* fort-villages of Galicians' Celtic ancestors...

SANTIAGO DE COMPOSTELA

Galicia's capital is the final stop on the epic Camino de Santiago pilgrimage trail, a place where long-gone centuries live on in arcaded streets and magnificent stone architecture. Yet Santiago has a strong Galician character too, with the skirl of bagpipes wafting across plazas, and countless restaurants and bars specialising in fine Galician seafood and wines.

FISTERRA

Galicia's coastline is arguably at its most spectacular along the Costa da Morte (Coast of Death, so-called for its many shipwrecks), northwest of Santiago. The town of Fisterra (Finisterre in Castilian Spanish) holds an almost magnetic attraction for travellers. It's a colourful fishing port with plenty of services and a scenic headland, once thought to be the end of the world, that's still the destination of great walks.

OURENSE

The plunging valleys of the Ríos Sil and Miño in the southeast, together known as the Ribeira Sacra (Sacred Riverbank) because of their many medieval monasteries, are perhaps the most beautiful of Galicia's inland regions and are endowed with many lovely, well-marked walking trails. The nearest urban hub is Ourense, with an appealingly labyrinthine historic quarter, a lively tapas scene and delightful riverside thermal baths perfect for soothing weary limbs.

VIGO

The main gateway to the Illas Cíes, Vigo is a busy modern port city, but also with a historic centre, the Casco Vello, and plenty of green parks. There's a buzzing after-dark scene in the many tapas bars, restaurants and clubs.

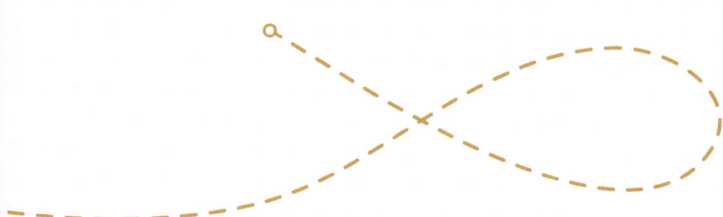

Resources

www.turismo.gal Official Galicia tourism information; multiple languages.

www.iatlanticas.es Parque Nacional de las Islas Atlánticas de Galicia, including the Illas Cíes.

http://turismo.ribeirasacra.org Select English then click 'Plan' and 'Download Maps & Guides' for Ribeira Sacra walking routes.

www.caminodosfaros.com The Camiño dos Faros.

☀ WHEN TO GO

Galicia is one of Spain's wettest regions (that's why it's so green). July and August are the driest months, with June and September not too far behind, so these are the optimum months for walking, and likely to be warm but not too warm. On any walk, try to pick a day of decent weather. There's not too much fun in battling rain, wind or fog, whether on the wild coast or in the inland forests.

 TRANSPORT

Santiago de Compostela has Galicia's main airport, with flights from 12 European cities (some seasonal) as well as domestic services. Buses fan out around Galicia from the city's bus station and there is fast train service between Santiago and Vigo, Ourense and A Coruña. Trains from Madrid to Galicia's main cities mostly take five to seven hours.

Vigo, the main jumping-off point for the Illas Cíes walk, also has a domestic airport. For other walk areas, a vehicle makes things a lot easier. For the Costa da Morte, a few daily buses run from Santiago de Compostela to Muxía and Fisterra. Public transport options for the north coast are limited to a few daily buses from A Coruña, Ferrol, Lugo or Santiago, and the FEVE narrow-gauge railway running east from Ferrol towards Oviedo in Asturias. The Ribeira Sacra has some limited bus services from Ourense.

🛎 WHERE TO STAY

On the Costa da Morte, Muxía, Lires and Fisterra are equipped with numerous hostels (geared primarily to Camino de Santiago walkers) and a number of mostly small hotels. Outstanding options include **Casa Fontequeiroso** (www.casafontequeiroso.com) at Queiroso near Lires, a very welcoming little country hotel with superb home-style meals, and the larger, top-end **Parador Costa da Morte** (www.parador.es), just outside Muxía.

The Ribeira Sacra offers a few very appealing bases such as **A Casa da Eira** (www.acasadaeira.com), a cosy, cleverly renovated granite-and-timber farmhouse 10km from Parada de Sil, and the **Parador de Santo Estevo** (www.parador.es), the area's grandest monastery now turned into an indulgent hotel.

Hotels along the north coast are mostly modest but if you have a vehicle, **Hotel Herbeira** (www.hotelherbeira.com) at Cedeira is a perfect mix of design, comfort and practicality.

Vigo has accommodation for all budgets: **Hotel América** (www.hotelamerica-vigo.com) is an excellent midrange choice.

👍 WHAT'S ON

Festival Ortigueira (www.festivaldeortigueira.com; ⏱mid-Jul) Galicians celebrate their Celtic roots with this four-day international Celtic music festival at Ortigueira in the Rías Altas.

Fiestas del Apóstol Santiago (Feast of St James; ⏱25 Jul) Two weeks of festivities in Santiago de Compostela for the Día de Santiago peak with a spectacular lasers-and-fireworks display on the night of 24 July.

26
ILLAS CÍES

DURATION	DIFFICULTY	DISTANCE	START/END
4–4½hr	Easy	14.5km	Ferry dock, Praia de Rodas
TERRAIN	Good earth and paved footpaths		

Sail out from Galicia's southern coast to the these wildly beautiful islands at the mouth of the Ría de Vigo, part of the Parque Nacional de las Islas Atlánticas de Galicia, and spend a day walking well-signed paths to clifftop viewpoints, lighthouses and pristine sandy beaches. Bring drinking water, and a swimsuit if you can tolerate water temperatures that rarely reach 20°C. The islands are vehicle-free and their nature pristine, but up to 3000 visitors are allowed at one time and this limit is often reached in July and August. Several trails here are wheelchair-accessible and the national park can provide wheelchairs and other facilities for travellers with disabilities: see p17 for more information.

GETTING HERE

Sailing to the islands is part of the fun. Ferries normally operate daily from Vigo and Cangas during Easter week and from June to mid-September, and on variable other weekends and holidays. Between them, **Naviera Mar de Ons** (www.mardeons.es) and **Nabia Naviera** (www.piratasdenabia.com) sail up to 14 times a day from Vigo and 12 times from Cangas. There are also summer sailings from Baiona.

The crossing takes about 45 minutes from any of the ports; return tickets are €16 to €19 (free to €8 for children). Book as far ahead as possible, online or by phone (with a credit card) or at the departure ports. From mid-June to mid-September you need a free national park authorisation, available at http://autorizacionillasatlanticas.xunta.gal or ferry companies' websites, before buying boat tickets.

ⓘ Relics of a Hidden Past

Traces of a Bronze Age settlement, the **Castro das Hortas**, have been found on the hillside between the Faro de Cíes and Faro da Porta. The remains of the medieval monastery of Santo Estevo lie beneath the visitor centre, which occupies a former artillery store built over the monastery ruins in 1810. A long history of raids by Vikings, North Africans and English (including Francis Drake) eventually led to the Cíes' abandonment in the 18th century, but two fish-salting plants were founded here in the 19th century. Restaurante Rodas by the ferry dock occupies one of their sites.

Best for  **WILDLIFE**

STARTING POINT
The ferry jetty at the northern end of Praia de Rodas.

01 Walk 200m inland to the national park information kiosk and turn left. The path crosses a **causeway** from the northern to the middle island and passes the campground and **visitor centre**.

02 Next, climb lighthouse-topped Monte Faro in the southwest of the island, detouring to the **Pedra da Campá**, a rock framing a nice sea view, and a **birdwatching hide** overlooks large cliffside nesting colonies (February to August) of shag and yellow-legged gulls.

03 From the **Faro de Cíes** lighthouse, there are superb views over the rocky south island (not accessible by public ferries) and along the ocean-battered, west coasts of the middle and north islands.

04 Descend from Monte Faro to the short but sandy **Praia de Nosa Señora** – usually less populated than the islands' other main beaches.

05 Return to the north island and walk to the **Alto do Príncipe**, another superb clifftop viewpoint.

06 Head on through the woods to the **Faro do Peito** lighthouse and another **birdwatching hide**. To the north look for the Illa de Ons.

07 Head back south to delightful **Praia das Figueiras**, half a kilometre of powdery sand backed by tall pines and eucalyptus, before returning to the jetty for your boat back to the mainland.

☕ TAKE A BREAK

There are restaurants at the ferry dock and campground, but **Restaurante Serafín** (☏679 349065; mains €9-18; ⊙1.30-4pm & 9-11pm approx Jun-mid-Sep), south of the campground, is more secluded and serves dishes on a pleasant shaded terrace.

27

PARADA DE SIL CIRCUIT

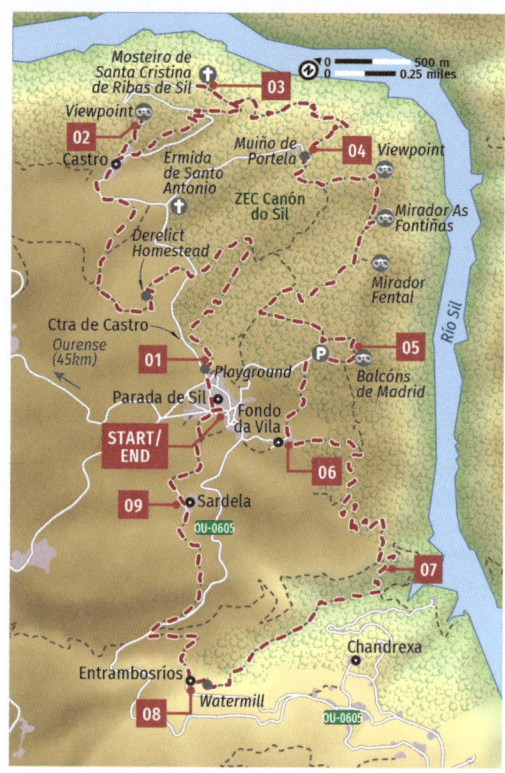

DURATION	DIFFICULTY	DISTANCE	START/END
6¼hr	Moderate	19km	Parada de Sil
TERRAIN	Country paths, cart tracks, paved roads		

Everything you could hope for in a Ribeira Sacra walk: viewpoints over the plunging Sil canyon, mossy-walled paths through chestnut and oak woods, steep-sloped vineyards, lost-in-the-woods hamlets, a gem of a Romanesque monastery. The walk (PRG98, well indicated with signs and yellow-and-white markers) combines two loops from Parada de Sil village, so you can just do one if you like, though both are well worth the effort! Be ready for over 800m of ascent and descent.

GETTING HERE

Parada de Sil is a 46km drive east of Ourense. Gavilanes buses (http://empresagavilanes.com) leave Ourense bus station for Parada de Sil (€4.50, 1¼ hours) at 2pm and 6.30pm, Monday to Friday only. The single bus back leaves Parada de Sil at 6.45am Monday to Friday.

STARTING POINT

Praza do Barquillero in the middle of Parada de Sil.

01 Head southwest up the main road (OU-0605) and take the first road off to the right. Just past the town hall turn right past a **playground**. The path winds its way for about 5.5km, mostly through woodlands, down to the Santa Cristina monastery, occasionally crossing or briefly rejoining the road.

02 In Castro hamlet, it's well worth making a short detour at a 'Castro de Cividá' signpost to the remains of a **Bronze Age fortified settlement** (probably Celtic) and a superb canyon **viewpoint**. Return to the road and, at the end of the hamlet, fork left onto a footpath indicated by yellow-and-white markers.

Monasteries of the Ribeira Sacra

Early Christian hermits and monks were drawn to the remote Sil and Miño valleys as far back as the 6th century. Of the surviving monasteries, most enchanting is the tiny, rock-carved **Mosteiro de San Pedro de Rocas** (www.centrointerpretacionribeirasacra.com) dating from 573, 11km south of Luintra with an informative Ribeira Sacra interpretation centre adjacent. Grandest is the **Mosteiro de Santo Estevo**, 6km east of Luintra, with three magnificent cloisters and a Romanesque-Gothic church. It's now a *parador* (luxurious state-owned hotel). The main monumental parts and the cafe and restaurant are open to all.

Best for

BRINGING THE PAST TO LIFE

03 Little **Mosteiro de Santa Cristina de Ribas de Sil** (www.paradadesil.es; €1; church 11am-2pm & 4-6pm mid-Jun–Oct, hours vary at other times, exterior 24hr), secluded among chestnut woods with a 12th-century Romanesque church, is one of the loveliest Ribeira Sacra monasteries.

04 From Santa Cristina, the route leads down, down, then up, up through woods to an old watermill, the **Muíño de Portela**.

05 You ascend to a more level stretch giving access to several canyon viewpoints. Particularly worth detouring to are the **Mirador As Fontiñas** and the **Balcóns de Madrid**, 300m to 400m above the river. If you want to return to Parada de Sil at this point, just head 800m along the paved road from the Balcóns de Madrid parking area.

06 Otherwise, turn left on a footpath into the woods after 100m. This brings you to **Fondo da Vila** hamlet, then you descend about 2.5km by a series of paths, tracks and steps almost down to the level of the Río Sil.

07 You'll pass through beautiful woodlands with ferns and hanging moss, and some of the renowned steep Ribeira Sacra **vineyards**.

08 At the foot of the descent, follow a woodland stream southwards past another old watermill to the lost-in-time hamlet of **Entrambosríos**.

09 Then climb through woods to **Sardela**. Just after Sardela, the route veers left onto another woodland path, which leads 700m back to Parada de Sil.

 TAKE A BREAK

Casa Mercedes (Praza do Barquillero 2, Parada de Sil; raciones & grills €3.50-12; 9am-midnight) does fine pre- or post-walk food – burgers, egg dishes, salads, potatoes, chicken.

GALICIA/103

28
CASTRO CALDELAS MAGICAL FORESTS

DURATION	DIFFICULTY	DISTANCE	START/END
6½hr	Moderate	21.5km	Castro Caldelas

TERRAIN	Country paths and tracks

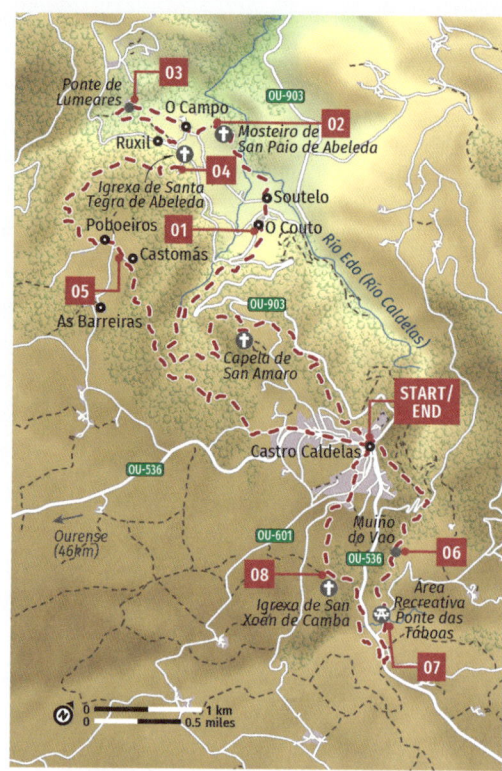

A walk of gentle but outstanding Ribeira Sacra beauty, the well-marked PRG213 (Sendeiro Os Bosques Máxicos) takes you to glorious chestnut and oak woods, tiny hamlets, exquisite woodland streams and ancient churches, monasteries, vineyards and watermills. It combines two loops (*bucles*) from the castle-topped village of Castro Caldelas, the 16km Bucle Longo and the 5.5km Bucle Curto – both good walks in their own right. There's 700m of descent and ascent.

GETTING HERE
Castro Caldelas is a 49km drive east of Ourense. Buses leave Ourense for Castro Caldelas (€6, 50 minutes) at 11am Saturday and Sunday, 2.45pm Monday to Friday and 6.30pm daily. Return services go through Castro morning and afternoon.

STARTING POINT
Praza do Prado, Castro Caldelas' central plaza.

01 Starting with the Bucle Longo, head northwest down Rúa dos Pilos and in 70m a signpost sends you down a path to the left. The route winds down through wonderful dense chestnut and oak woods for 5km then, around **O Couto** and **Soutelo** hamlets, between vineyards.

02 From Soutelo, descend to the Río Edo (or Río Caldelas) then climb briefly to the large **Mosteiro de San Paio de Abeleda**. It was once an important monastery, but was abandoned in the 19th century and, now, is sadly locked up. You can peer into the church through a crack beside its door jamb.

03 From O Campo hamlet, walk between stone walls to the **Ponte de Lumeares** over the little Río do Porto.

104/GALICIA

Heroic Viticulture

Growing grapes in the impossibly steep Sil and Miño gorges began in Roman times. The activity still defies mechanisation and the challenges have earned it the label *viticultura heróica* (heroic viticulture). The Ribeira Sacra DO (Denomin-ation of Origin) is today prod-ucing ever-improving vintages, principally reds from the native *mencía* grape. Three interesting smaller wineries where you can visit (and taste) are **Adega Algueira** (www.adegaalgueira.com) at Doade, 16km north of Castro Caldelas, and **Ponte da Boga** (www.pontedaboga.es) and **Adega Vella** (www.adegavella.com) on the OU-903 a few kilometres nearer Castro. They're normally open daily but it's advisable to call ahead.

Best for
OFF THE BEATEN PATH

JOHN NOBLE / LONELY PLANET ©

04 Continue up the river, then climb to Ruxil hamlet and turn right up into woods opposite the **Igrexa de Santa Tegra de Abeleda**. Turn sharpish right opposite a water-storage structure after 400m.

05 The track levels off through **Poboeiros** and **Castomás** hamlets, then traverses more woods before re-entering Castro Caldelas by the OU-536.

06 To start the Bucle Curto head down the OU-903 (signposted Teixeira and Mon-forte) from Praza do Prado, and turn right at the PRG213 sign after 90m. Head downhill through woods for nearly 1km to a paved road. Go left across a bridge, then immediately right for a dreamlike 1.5km passage up beside the Río Edo as it ripples along beneath trees, between ferns and over tiny waterfalls, passing a grass-covered stone bridge and the mossy remains of the **Muíño do Vao** watermill.

07 From the **Área Recreativa Ponte das Táboas** picnic area, the route leads to an underpass beneath the quite busy OU-536. Head northwest for 1km then veer up to the left just before reaching the OU-536 again.

08 You emerge from the woods at the **Igrexa de San Xoán de Camba**, a large church in the middle of nowhere. It was once part of a monastery: a few ruined structures remain on its south side. Finally, head 2km through woods, beside fields and along roads back to Castro Caldelas.

TAKE A BREAK

Café Bar Rubio (Praza do Prado 2, Castro Caldelas; dishes €5-11; 8am-11pm) is the best bet for refreshments, with egg dishes, burgers and toasted sandwiches.

GALICIA/105

29
O VICEDO TO PORTO DE ESPASANTE

DURATION	DIFFICULTY	DISTANCE	START/END
5½hr one-way	Moderate	20km	O Vicedo/ Porto de Espasante
TERRAIN	Country lanes (paved and unpaved), footpaths		

Galicia's northern coast is blessed not just with stunning cliffs, capes, beaches and *rías* (inlets) but also with an excellent, very well signed, 154km walking trail, the **Camino Natural de la Ruta del Cantábrico** (Camiño Natural da Ruta do Cantábrico in Galician; www.mapa.gob.es/es/desarrollo-rural/temas). Our walk, between a pair of small fishing and beach towns, follows most of the route's seventh and last stage.

GETTING HERE
Espasante (1.5km south of Porto de Espasante) and Vicedo (at O Vicedo) stations are on the FEVE railway (www.renfe.com/es/es/cercanias/cercanias-feve) between Ferrol (Galicia) and Oviedo (Asturias). You can leave a vehicle at Espasante, take the 9.43am train to Vicedo (€1.65, 18 minutes), then walk back. Trains also stop at Loiba (2km south of Picón) and O Barqueiro. Arriva (http://arriva.gal) buses serve both Porto de Espasante and O Vicedo.

STARTING POINT
Praia do Fomento, O Vicedo.

01 Walk to the southwest end of Praia do Fomento's grassy foreshore area and up to a street, where you turn left then first right. Camino Natural signs direct you along a seafront walkway and then along roads and paths that bring you down alongside **Praia de Arealonga** beach.

02 Passing through pines, you reach three parallel **bridges** over the **Río Sor**, carrying a road, a railway and your footpath.

03 Across the river, pass **O Barqueiro train station**, with postcard-perfect views of the

The Best Bank of the World

Stories abound about how the famed bench on the Loiba clifftops got the English name by which it's best known (which plays on two meanings of the Spanish *banco*: bench and bank). One version says it was coined by Scottish musicians from the annual Celtic music festival at nearby Ortigueira in 2010. There's certainly no question about the magnificence of the bench's outlook, along the savagely jagged coast all the way from Cabo Ortegal (Spain's northwestern corner) to the Punta da Estaca de Bares (Spain's northernmost point). Today it's so popular that you may have to queue up to sit on it.

JOHN NOBLE/LONELY PLANET ©

fishing village (pictured). Follow Camino Natural indicators up to the AC-862 road, down to O Barqueiro's cemetery, then along a country lane for nearly 1km.

04 Cross a bridge over the railway and climb to another paved road. Go left 900m to the parking area for **Praia do Esteiro**. Go left along a boardwalk across wetlands and a small river, then turn right to reach a headland overlooking the bay.

05 Now take a footpath climbing left to begin the highlight section along the Acantilados de Loiba (Cliffs of Loiba). Reaching **Picón** hamlet, follow the road to the right, passing above Praia do Picón.

06 Fork right 200m after the Chiringuito De Furnas to reach the celebrated Banco de Loiba, better known as **'The Best Bank of the World'**.

07 You now head 4.5km through woods and open countryside to meet a paved road on the edge of Mazorgán hamlet. Turn right, then left where the paving ends after 150m. You cross fields, pass a couple of clifftops and through woods, then descend to **Praia de Bimbieiro**.

08 A boardwalk leads from Praia de Bimbieiro towards 1km-long **Praia de Santo António**. An inconvenient rock outcrop blocks the middle of Santo António, so the Camino Natural heads inland, uphill, for 700m, then 1.2km along a paved road to the middle of **Porto de Espasante**.

 **TAKE A BREAK**

Halfway along the walk, rustic **Chiringuito De Furnas** (Picón; items €4-12; 11am-9pm Apr-Oct) will replenish your energies with *bocadillos* (long-bread sandwiches) or *huevos rotos* (broken fried eggs) with ham.

30
MUXÍA TO LIRES

DURATION	DIFFICULTY	DISTANCE	START/END
8½hr one-way	Hard	28km	Muxía/Lires

TERRAIN	Earth and grassy paths, paved and unpaved roads

A long but truly memorable Costa da Morte day as sandy beaches, panoramic hilltops, rocky coves and cliffs succeed one after another. You could continue with the Lires to Cabo Fisterra walk for a magnificent two-day trip (p110). The walk mostly follows the **Camiño dos Faros** (www.caminodosfaros.com), whose waymarkers of small green arrows or paint blobs can be easily missed, but most of it is shown in Google Maps' Street View.

GETTING HERE

Hefe SL (www.grupoferrin.com) runs two daily buses from Santiago de Compostela to Muxía (€8, 1½ hours). Taxis from Lires to Muxía or Fisterra cost €15 to €20. You could shorten the walk by arranging a pick-up at Cabo Touriñán or Nemiña beach, or staying at Casa Fontequeiroso (p98).

STARTING POINT

Muxía's legend-infused Santuario da Virxe da Barca.

01 Walk up to the cracked-rock monument A Ferida (remembering the 2002 *Prestige* oil spill), then follow Camino de Santiago yellow arrows along the west side of town and out along the DP-5201. Green arrows on a roadside barrier send you down to **Praia de Lourido**.

02 Walk along the beach, then follow some unusually good Camiño dos Faros signs above the rocky shore. Great panoramas reward the 20-minute climb up **Monte Cachelmo** (174m).

03 A green arrow points down a westwards descent. Meeting an unpaved road, go 350m left to the DP-5201. Walk 450m to the right, then turn right down a gravel road to **Coído de Cuño** bay. Here head south to cross the Regato de Cuño stream, then immediately start climbing to the left.

The Most Westerly Point

Cabo Touriñán (9° 18' W) is the western extremity of mainland Spain. But opinions are divided about which of its rocky protrusions merits the actual 'western-most point' title. Some favour Punta de Sualba, 300m north-northwest of the light-house, while others opt for Illa Herboso, 500m south-southwest of the lighthouse, which does extend further west but is joined to the mainland at very low tides only.

JOHN NOBLE / LONELY PLANET ©

04 The green arrows are particularly elusive through these woods: ignore broad tracks up to the left 750m and 1km after the stream, and go straight at a track crossroads 250m later. A steepish 20-minute path up **Monte Pedrouzo** (272m) rewards with fabulous panoramic views.

05 The path heads down towards the sea before turning southwards as a cart track: 600m along this, turn right following green arrows to descend to **Praia de Moreira**.

06 Paths, tracks and roads, with reasonable green-arrow waymarkers, take you across to and along the 2km promontory of **Cabo Touriñán**. From the **lighthouse** (pictured), return down the cape's west side to rejoin the paved road.

07 Fork right up an unpaved road after 250m, then turn right down a small path opposite a gate 500m later. Reaching a paved road after 1km, head south, then after 1km fork right down an unpaved road. Wiggle through **Talón** hamlet and across fields to glorious **Praia de Nemiña**.

08 Walk 500m along the beach then up to the road and turn right. One kilometre after you enter pine woods, green arrows indicate a right turn down a footpath, which becomes a cart track in 400m. In another 500m there's a right fork onto a lesser track with easily missed green markers. The final 1km into Lires is straightforward, crossing a **bridge over the Río Castro** en route.

 **TAKE A BREAK**

Restaurante A Marina (Avenida A Marina 30, Muxía; raciones & mains €6-17; ⏰8am-11pm; 📶), facing Muxía's harbour, opens at 8am with hearty hikers' breakfasts.

GALICIA/109

31

LIRES TO CABO FISTERRA

DURATION	DIFFICULTY	DISTANCE	START/END
6½hr one-way	Hard	22.5km	Lires/Cabo Fisterra
TERRAIN	Dirt tracks, grass/earth paths, paved roads		

Long, wild beaches, high cliffs and jagged rocks line the spectacular route to the lighthouse at the 'end of the earth', the Faro de Fisterra on Cabo Fisterra. The name Fisterra (Finisterre in Castilian Spanish) comes from the Latin *finis terrae* (end of earth).

Much of this walk follows the **Camiño dos Faros** (www.caminodosfaros.com), whose waymarkers of small green arrows or paint blobs are sometimes easily missed. But its website is very helpful and most of the route is shown in Google Maps' Street View. There's some 630m of ascent and descent.

GETTING HERE
There's no bus service to Lires. A taxi costs €15 to €20 from Muxía or Fisterra. A taxi from Cabo Fisterra into Fisterra town (3.5km) costs €5. Monbus (www.monbus.es) runs at least four daily buses from Fisterra to Santiago de Compostela (€9.85, 2¼ to 3¼ hours) and can get you to Muxía with a transfer at Cée (Monday to Friday only).

STARTING POINT
The road junction in front of As Eiras hotel, effectively the centre of Lires.

01 Wind your way down through Lires, cross the bridge over the Ría de Lires and follow the road along to the right. It ends at a small **parking area** above the mouth of the *ría*. Take the track up ahead signed 'To Fisterra along the coast'.

02 As you ascend, stop to look back and take in the views along the **Praia de Nemiña**. The track passes above cliff-foot beaches. At a fork after 500m, take the lower, right-hand track, which narrows to a path. At another fork 100m later, go straight ahead. The path bends right, down towards Area Grande beach, then turns left uphill, away from the beach. Head through a **gap in a wall**.

03 The path broadens into a rough vehicle track, levelling off across heath-like country above the cliffs. Where it bends left a half-kilometre after the gap in the wall, turn right down a lesser track then immediately left onto a path across grassland. After about 170m, you go through another **gap in a wall**, this time with cliffs dropping away on the far side. Take care! Turn left and follow the path beside the wall. It bends right and runs along a fairly open hilltop. At a path junction about 800m after the gap in the wall, turn 90 degrees right.

04 You now wind down quite steeply towards the cliffs but at a path junction after 200m, go left across the thornbush-covered hillside, passing a **signboard for Punta do Narís** (a headland below). The path bends left, leading into woods. At a track crossroads 200m into the woods, go right, towards the sea.

05 Emerging from the woods, turn left down a grassy path. The full wild glory of **Praia do Rostro** now stretches ahead of you: a broad 2km stretch of sand with the Atlantic surf pouring endlessly in from the west (unfortunately, it's not safe for swimming). Follow the path down to the beach and walk along it.

06 Just before the end of the beach, go left around the back of a rocky outcrop. Continue 150m up to a parking area and take a sandy path to the right, up to the panoramic headland **Punta do Rostro**.

Camino Walks

The **Camiño dos Faros** (Lighthouses Way) is a 200km trail along the Costa da Morte ending at Cabo Fisterra, originally established by a group of local friends in 2012.

This is not a seaside stroll, but more like mountain hiking by the coast, with ups, downs, cliffs and some rough terrain. It's quite distinct from the Camino de Muxía-Finisterre, which is one of the many **Camino de Santiago** pilgrim routes, though the two routes occasionally coincide. While the rugged Faros trail covers 51km between Muxía and Cabo Fisterra, the Santiago route is 31km, mostly through gentle countryside.

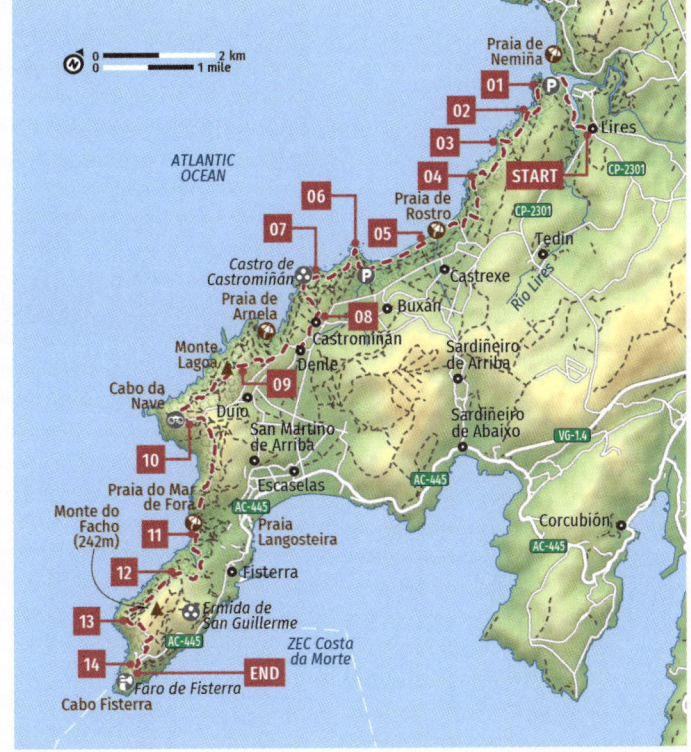

07 Take the track going left from the top of the Punta, go right at a fork after 350m, and follow the path across the green hillside. Where the path bends left 800m from the fork, take a small path to the right, climbing the top of the small elevation here. This is the site of the strategically located Iron Age hill fort **Castro de Castromiñán**. As you walk up, you can discern the lines of two defensive ramparts stretching off to your right.

08 Return to the main track. Here the Camiño dos Faros immediately turns right along a small path indicated by a few green markers, but this is the start of nearly 1km across steep hillsides falling away in cliffs at the bottom, which anyone without a head for heights will probably hate. So, we continue ahead on the main track and go left where it forks after 100m. The track winds across the hilltop, passes through pine woods and emerges on a paved road in **Castromiñán** hamlet.

09 Head to the right (south) along the road and turn up the first paved road to the right, after 600m (now in the hamlet of Denle). The **Camiño dos Faros** joins this road from the right after 300m, then turns off right again after another 350m, down a green track signposted Praia de Arnela. That leads to another section across steep hillsides above cliffs, so to avoid that, continue 15m along the road then fork right along a grassy track. In 200m go right at a track crossroads. You bend left and climb through **pine woods** for nearly 1km.

10 Emerging from the woods the track splits: take the right-hand grassy track heading towards the antennae on top of Cabo da Nave a kilometre ahead. You descend for some 200m then veer left and soon start climbing towards the antennae. Pass through the antennae to come out on a paved road where a superb **ocean panorama** opens out over infinite expanses of the Atlantic, 230m below you, with Cabo Fisterra and the top of Fisterra town to the left.

11 Walk 450m left down the road to where three tracks turn off right into the woods. Take the left-hand one and immediately fork right off it. You head through pine woods, then along the edge of pine woods. About 800m from the road there's a fork of two tracks that meet again after 450m. The right-hand path runs along open hillside above the ocean cliffs – more scenic but ever so slightly vertiginous. At a fork 200m after the two paths rejoin, now descending, go to the right around the trees, then left after 30m. You now descend quite steeply to **Praia do Mar de Fora** (pictured p110), another wild, sandy beach with ocean breakers roaring in (unsafe for swimming).

San Guillerme

Cabo Fisterra, where the sun sinks below the horizon later than almost anywhere else in Europe, has been a place of spiritual significance since long before it became a goal for Camino de Santiago pilgrims continuing beyond Santiago de Compostela.

As you descend towards the Fisterra lighthouse, you'll pass a 'San Guillerme' sign pointing along a track to the left. This leads to the mysterious Ermida de San Guillerme, a ruined medieval chapel and rock shelter that some believe may originally have been the location of a legendary *ara solis* (altar of the sun), site of pre-Roman sun-worship and fertility rituals.

12 Walk along the beach then zigzag up the boardwalk, which becomes a stone-paved path. Fork right after greenhouses on your right, and turn right on reaching a paved road at the top of Fisterra town. The road quickly narrows to a cobbled footpath, the **Camiño da Insua**, running uphill between stone walls. You emerge from the woods onto a rough vehicle track that immediately forks: take the level, straight-on option. You're now walking along the west side of Cabo Fisterra, 100m above the ocean, which stretches away to the horizon.

13 Take the lower, right-hand track at another fork after 600m; then the upper, left-hand option 350m later; then go left, uphill, 200m after that. As you now **climb steeply**, the Fisterra lighthouse comes into view, perched at the end of the cape.

14 Turn right on reaching a paved road and now just 1.4km remains down the road to the lighthouse. Pass the former lighthouse-keeper's residence (now a hotel), and head down to the rocks just past the **Faro de Fisterra** (Fisterra Lighthouse), the end point not just of the Camiño dos Faros but also, for many, of the Camino de Santiago. A sculpted bronze boot on one of the rocks is a fitting symbol of the journey that all have made to reach here.

 TAKE A BREAK

Breakfast well before leaving Lires – the bright cafe at **LiresCa** (661 464345; www.liresca.com; Lires 31; Apr-Oct;) is a good option – and carry food and water for the whole walk. At Cabo Fisterra you can relax with drinks and food at the cafe-bar in the hotel **O Semáforo de Fisterra** (it serves snacks all day) or the adjacent **Bar O Refuxio** (items €4-15; 11am-8pm). Fisterra town, a colourful fishing port, has plenty of good eating options.

GALICIA/113

Also Try...

ILLA DE ONS

An island of the Parque Nacional de las Islas Atlánticas de Galicia, 5.6km-long Ons is less famous than the Illas Cíes, but it's wild and unspoiled and you can combine its walking trails for a great day out.

From the tiny village where boats arrive, head up to the Faro de Ons lighthouse, then continue to the island's north end and back to the village by the Ruta Norte, via the best beach, Praia de Melide. Then take the Ruta Sur round the southern half via the Fedorente viewpoint and the Buraco do Inferno, a collapsed sea cave. Naviera Mar de Ons (www.mardeons.com) and other companies sail to Ons from Sanxenxo, Portonovo and Bueu on the Ría de Pontevedra several times daily from about late June to mid-September, and on other variable dates (30 to 60 minutes each way; return fares adult/child €14/7).

DURATION 4hr return
DIFFICULTY Easy
DISTANCE 12km

RUTA CAÑÓN DO RÍO MAO

This superb Ribeira Sacra walk (PRG177) traverses dense woodlands, vineyards, remote hamlets, some fascinating historical relics and a pair of canals for hydroelectric schemes.

The route, well signalled with yellow-and-white markers, starts at the Albergue A Fábrica da Luz (a small hydro-plant converted to a hostel and activities hub), 11km east of Parada de Sil. You descend the Mao canyon (initially on an 850m boardwalk) to Barxacova village, then climb 1.5km past vineyards to San Lourenzo village (pictured above) and continue upwards to A Miranda and Forcas villages. Then, return to San Lourenzo via the medieval bridge of Conceliñas, the new canal, the old canal (dry) and the medieval necropolis of San Vítor. From San Lourenzo, descend direct to the Fábrica da Luz. For shorter outings, the route divides easily into separate loops of 5km and 11.5km.

DURATION 6½hr return
DIFFICULTY Moderate
DISTANCE 16.5km

RUTA COSTA DA MORTE

The rugged coastline west and north of the small fishing town Camariñas is one of the most scenic and interesting stretches of the Costa da Morte.

Path PRG158, named the Ruta Costa da Morte, takes you to the Faro de Vilán lighthouse, the sandy beaches of Pedrosa, Balea and Reira, and the Cemiterio dos Ingleses, the lonely burial ground from a tragic 1890 shipwreck that took the lives of 172 British naval cadets. You return across the low inland hills. Get a map-leaflet from Camariñas' tourist office or www.turismocamarinas.net.

DURATION 6½hr return
DIFFICULTY Moderate
DISTANCE 24km

CABO ORTEGAL

At this mother of Spanish capes, where the Bay of Biscay meets the Atlantic Ocean, great stone shafts drop sheer into the ocean from such a height that the waves crashing on the rocks below seem pitifully benign.

Start from the Miradoiro Gabeira viewpoint, a few hundred metres along the Ortegal road from the workaday port of Cariño. The Senda de San Xiao path leads 1.6km to the San Xiao do Trebo chapel, with grand views en route. Walk 250m up to rejoin the road for the last 1.5km to the cape. Retrace your steps to return.

DURATION 2hr return
DIFFICULTY Easy
DISTANCE 6.7km

MONTE DE SANTA TREGA

Santa Trega hill rises above the town of A Guarda at Galicia's southwest tip. Work your way to its 341m summit for stupendous panoramas up the Río Miño, across to Portugal and out over the Atlantic.

Get a map of the hill's PRG122 path network at www.turismo aguarda.es/en/monte-santa-trega. The Atallo Vello route feeds into the Volta do Promonte, which loops round the hilltop to join the motor road for the final 600m to the top. Detour briefly along the Camiño da Citania to visit the Castro de Santa Trega (pictured above).

DURATION 3hr return
DIFFICULTY Moderate
DISTANCE 7.5km

CENTRAL SPAIN

32 **Laguna Grande de Gredos** A gem of a mountain lake ringed by towering peaks. **p120**

33 **San Lorenzo de El Escorial to Machota Baja** Escape into the hills around the famous Escorial monastery. **p122**

34 **Peñalara** The Guadarrama's highest peak and a rocky ridge leading to mountain lakes. **p124**

35 **Siete Picos** Scenic ridge walk with return along a beautiful forest trail. **p126**

36 **La Mira** Hike up to a high Gredos pass and panoramic peak. **p130**

37 **El Morezón** Dramatic high peak with unrivalled views of the Gredos cirque. **p134**

38 **Ruta de Carlos V** Follow an emperor's route over the mountains of northern Extremadura. **p136**

Explore CENTRAL SPAIN

From the middle of Spain to the Portuguese border stretch the high, handsome ranges of the Sistema Central, with superb walking along rivers and ridges to 2000m-plus peaks and mountain lakes – beloved of *madrileños* but little known to outsiders. The Madrid plains are fringed by the Sierra de Guadarrama. Further west is the region's crown jewel, the Sierra de Gredos, over 100km long.

MADRID

Many Sierra de Guadarrama walks can be done as day trips from Spain's capital, using private or public transport. Madrid is a city not just of world-famous art museums and a fabulous food scene but of boundless Spanish energy, with great live music and nightlife that goes till the next day, should you not be getting up in the morning for a hike.

SAN LORENZO DE EL ESCORIAL

San Lorenzo is an enjoyable place to stay a night or two, with pleasant parks and gardens around the grand Real Monasterio. See www.sanlorenzoturismo.es for walk ideas. We like **Petit Verdot** (www.petitverdotvinos.com; Calle Floridablanca 30) for its creative salads, wraps, wines and alternative atmosphere.

HOYOS DEL ESPINO

Modest but pretty Hoyos del Espino, about 2½ hours' drive west of Madrid, is the best village launching pad for the Sierra de Gredos' spectacular central section. It possesses a small but well-stocked supermarket (next to its tourist office), two bakeries, a greengrocer, a healthy smattering of places to stay, eat and drink, and the **Casa del Parque Pinos Cimeros** (920 34 90 46; cp.gredos.hoyos@patrimonionatural.org; Carretera de la Plataforma; hours & days variable, closed Jan & Feb), an information office of the Parque Regional Sierra de Gredos.

JARANDILLA DE LA VERA

Jarandilla is dominated by the imposing 15th-century Castillo de los Condes de Oropesa, now the **Parador de Jarandilla** hotel, whose cafe, classy restaurant and fine Renaissance courtyard are open to all. Down in the town, **El Patio de la Posada** (Calle Francisco Pizarro 1-3) does good meals in a lovely stone-walled garden-patio.

 ## WHEN TO GO

The climate is pretty continental here. July and August are blisteringly hot on the plains, so people escape to the hills, where it's still hot but more bearably so. Winter brings snow to the higher elevations. The best months to walk are

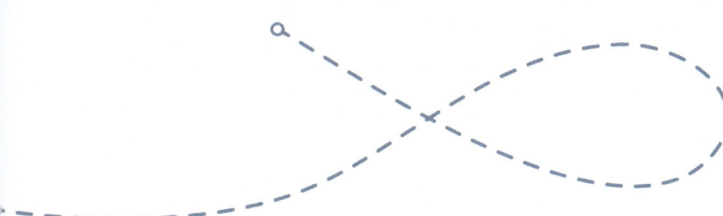

June and September, though snow may linger on some Gredos passes and gullies till early July. There's little shade on any Gredos mountain walks.

TRANSPORT

Madrid is the hub of Spain's transport system, with a busy international airport and trains and buses fanning out all round the country. The Sierra de Guadarrama is well served by bus (and to some extent by train) from the city. Public transport to the Sierra de Gredos and Ruta de Carlos V is more limited: your own vehicle makes things much easier.

WHERE TO STAY

Madrid offers every variety of accommodation from backpacker hostels upwards. If you should want to stay in the Sierra de Guadarrama, friendly **El Refugio de Cotos** (www.refugiodecotos.com) in Cotos railway station, offers dorm beds with half-board for €35, and there are a few small hotels in Puerto de Navacerrada. San Lorenzo de El Escorial has a range of hotels, many of them near its monumental monastery. **Hotel Florida** (www.hflorida.com) is a reliable midrange choice.

Little Hoyos del Espino, a Gredos jumping-off point, has a good amount of accommodation, from campgrounds to the boutiquey **El Milano Real** (www.elmilanoreal.com). In Barajas, 4km east, **Hostal Refugio de Gredos** (www.refugiodegredos.com) is a welcoming small hotel with rooms for €50 to €70 including breakfast. A few kilometres further east is the **Parador de Gredos** (920 34 80 48; www.parador.es; AV941 Km 10, Navarredonda de Gredos; s/d incl breakfast from €96/112; P 🛜), the very first of the luxury *parador* chain to be opened (in 1928, by King Alfonso XIII). It has a good deal of atmosphere, and very comfortably updated rooms.

Easily the best option in Tornavacas is the welcoming, good-value **Antigua Posada** (www.facebook.com/antiguaposadatornavacas; Calle Real de Abajo 32) in an 18th-century stone-and-wood building. Jarandilla de la Vera, at the other end of the Ruta de Carlos V, offers a much wider choice, including the splendid **Parador de Jarandilla** (927 56 01 17; www.parador.es; Avenida de García Prieto 1; d €90–210; P ❄ 🛜 🏊) in the castle where King Carlos I stayed.

WHAT'S ON

Fiestas de San Isidro Labrador (🕓 around 15 May) Madrid's big week of processions, parties, bullfights and concerts throughout the city, around.

Fiestas Patronales, Hoyos del Espino (🕓 8 Sep) Village fiesta with music, married-versus-unmarried football games (masculine and feminine), and religious events honouring Nuestra Señora del Espino (Our Lady of the Hawthorn Bush).

Resources

Parque Nacional de la Sierra de Guadarrama (www.parquenacionalsierraguadarrama.es) Official park site, in Spanish and English.

Spanish Trails: The Mountains of Madrid (Phil Lawler & Tim Price; www.spanishtrailsco.com) English-language walking guide to the Sierra de Guadarrama.

Sierra de Gredos Mapa + Guía (Editorial Alpina; www.editorialalpina.com) Map (1:25,000) and booklet with route descriptions in English and Spanish.

Andando Gredos (http://andandogredos.com) Gredos walking routes, in Spanish only, with maps, photos and elevation profiles.

Hoyos del Espino (http://hoyosdelespino.net) Interesting Spanish-language site on the village and the Gredos.

32
LAGUNA GRANDE DE GREDOS

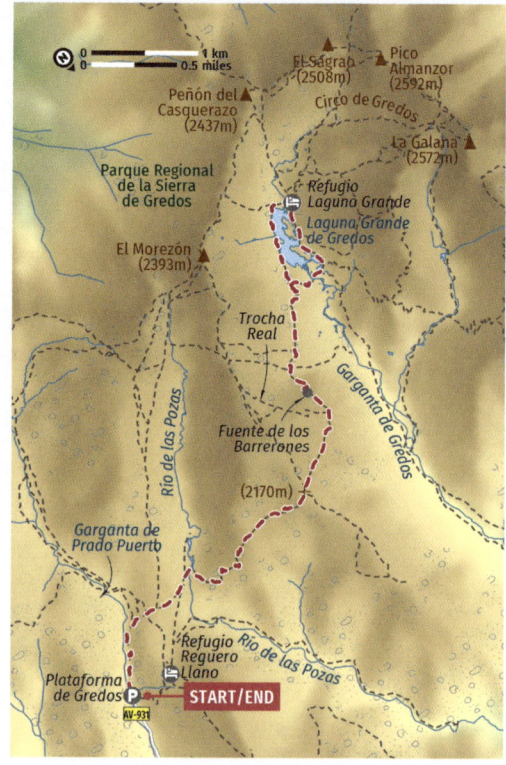

DURATION	DIFFICULTY	DISTANCE	START/END
5½hr return	Easy	14km	Plataforma de Gredos

TERRAIN	Footpath, mostly stone paved

Few sights in Spain's mountains surpass the beauty of the crystal-clear Laguna Grande de Gredos ringed by the high, jagged peaks of the Circo de Gredos. Until about 17,000 years ago, during the last glacial period, this 630m-long lake was the bottom of a 300m-thick glacier that filled most of the cirque. The path to it (PRAV17) is clear and unmissable, though much of it is paved with uneven stones, which don't make for particularly comfortable walking.

The walk starts at the **Plataforma de Gredos** (altitude 1760m), a parking area at the end of the AV931 road, which runs 12km south from Hoyos del Espino village. Walk up the path heading south from the Plataforma – a steepish uphill 800m before the path bends right across open grassland and becomes more level. At a concrete bridge over the **Río de las Pozas**, you start to climb steadily again.

After 1.8km, at the walk's **highest point** (2170m), the peaks of the Gredos cirque start to come into view. The path runs roughly level between broom bushes for 600m, then starts descending. At a left-hand bend comes your first view of **Laguna Grande** (pictured), with the majestic mountain ring behind it – Pico Almanzor (2592m) in the southwest is Gredos' highest peak.

It's downhill nearly all the way to the lake (1940m), passing the **Fuente de los Barrerones** (with good drinkable water) en route. Head along the lake's eastern shore and round to the **Refugio Laguna Grande**, where you can get food and drink, then return along the western shore to rejoin the main path near the lake's northeast corner and head back to the Plataforma.

33

SAN LORENZO DE EL ESCORIAL TO MACHOTA BAJA

DURATION	DIFFICULTY	DISTANCE	START/END
4½hr return	Moderate	12.5km	San Lorenzo de El Escorial
TERRAIN	Hill paths, unpaved roads		

Escape the crowds on a walk up Machota Baja (1404m) from San Lorenzo de El Escorial in the foothills of the Sierra de Guadarrama, 47km northwest of Madrid. The walk, with an ascent of 450m, is a perfect complement to San Lorenzo's cultural/historical attractions, centred on its monumental palace-monastery built by Felipe II in the 16th century.

GETTING HERE
Buses 661 and 664 run several times hourly to San Lorenzo (€4.20, one hour) from platform 30 at Madrid's Intercambiador de Moncloa.

STARTING POINT
Real Monasterio de San Lorenzo (pictured).

01 From the monastery's west side, go south through the arches. Head straight, then bend right, on Paseo Carlos III, and at the end of the stone wall turn left between **stone columns** into the Bosque de La Herrería, an extensive woodland, park-like in its lower areas, that extends into the Machotas foothills.

02 The track passes along an avenue of plane trees, crosses the M505 road and continues, now paved, into the woodlands ahead. On the first right-hand bend take a path to the left; where this meets the road again, follow the path left into the trees. You'll notice red-and-white paint markers. Follow these uphill to the **Silla de Felipe II** (Felipe II's Seat), a rock where, according to tradition, Felipe II sat to observe the progress of work on his monastery. Recent research suggests it was more likely a sacrificial altar of the area's pre-Roman inhabitants, the Vetones.

Real Monasterio de San Lorenzo

After Felipe II's victory over the French in the Battle of Saint-Quentin on St Lawrence's Day, 10 August 1557, he commissioned a **monastery-palace** (📞 902 044454; www.patrimonio nacional.es; adult/child, senior & student €12/6, EU & Latin American citizens & residents free Wed & last 3hr Sun; ⏱10am-8pm Tue-Sun, to 6pm Oct-Mar) in the saint's name above the hamlet of El Escorial. The austerely grand complex was overseen by the great Spanish Renaissance architect, Juan de Herrera.

Felipe died here in 1598. It's an extraordinary place filled with art treasures by the likes of El Greco and Titian. Almost all Spain's monarchs since Carlos I (Felipe II's father) are interred here.

JOHN NOBLE/LONELY PLANET ©

03 Pass the nearby cafe and take the path and steps south up to the Casa del Sordo (Deaf Man's House), an old forest ranger's house. Follow the path round to the right here, and turn left on meeting an unpaved road in 300m. After 100m, at the gate of the property Los Ermitanos, bear right along a footpath that starts to climb through **boulder-strewn woodlands**.

04 After 500m turn left through an iron gate and along the side of a stone wall. The path, still with red-and-white markers, levels and the woodland thins out. Go through a **revolving gate** in a wall where a sign announces that you're entering the property La Machota.

05 Another 600m uphill and you reach the **Collado de Entrecabezas** pass (1275m). Machota Baja is up to your left.

06 Follow a south-eastwards path up through boulders onto a ridge. Go left at a fork and round a subsidiary peak. Reaching a second, boulder-piled 'hump', make your way left across some slightly sloping slabs for about 20m till the path reappears. Between the second and a third, also boulder-piled, hump, fork left up past a solitary evergreen oak. The **summit rock** is just beyond: climb up from the back (east) side. There are fab views from the top, with the monastery and Siete Picos to the north, and the towers of Madrid to the east. If you need water on the way back, there's a good drinkable **fountain** 300m downhill to the left from the Collado de Entrecabezas.

 **TAKE A BREAK**

Buy supplies in town for a food stop at the Collado de Entrecabezas or Machota Baja's summit.

34
PEÑALARA

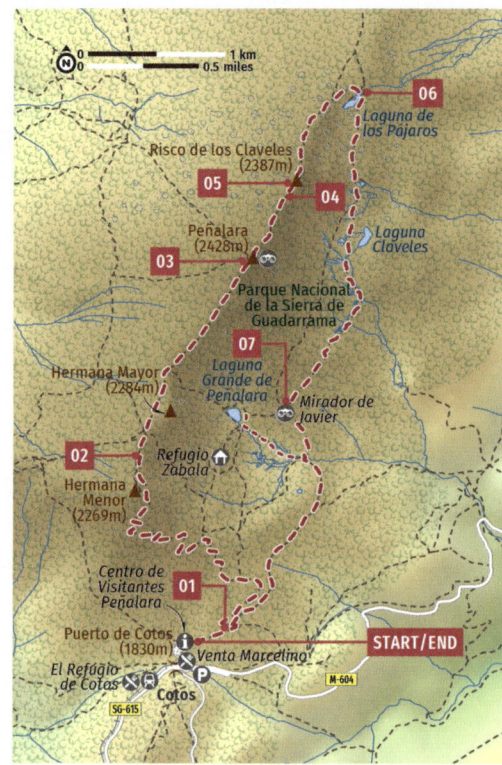

DURATION	DIFFICULTY	DISTANCE	START/END
4½hr return	Moderate	12km	Centro de Visitantes Peñalara
TERRAIN	Earth and stony footpaths, rocky ridge		

Climb the highest peak in the Sierra de Guadarrama (2428m) for superb long-distance views, a rocky ridge-top trail and a return via picturesque mountain lakes.

GETTING HERE

Puerto de Cotos is a pass at 1830m on the SG615 road, roughly an hour's drive north of central Madrid. Bus 691 departs Madrid's Intercambiador de Moncloa for Puerto de Cotos (€5.10, 1¼ hours) at 8.30am and 9.30am, Monday to Friday (every 15 or 30 minutes 8am to 9.30am Saturday and Sunday). Last buses down leave at 6.35pm, Monday to Friday (6.25pm Saturday and Sunday). You can also get here by train. *Cercanías* (suburban trains; www.renfe.com) from Madrid's Chamartín station, every two hours from 8.15am to 4.15pm, will get you to Cotos station (€8.70, two hours), 400m from the walk starting point, with a change at Cercedilla onto a narrow-gauge mountain line, which climbs 719m in just 18km. Downward trains depart Cotos every two hours, 10.43am to 6.43pm.

STARTING POINT

The national park's Centro de Visitantes Peñalara at the Puerto de Cotos.

01 Take the track east into the **pine forest** from the visitor centre. It heads steadily upwards and starts zigzagging more steeply uphill after emerging onto a less densely forested hillside. Follow Pico Peñalara and/or RV2 signs at all forks.

02 Eventually, you reach the relatively level **Loma de Dos Hermanas (Two Sisters) ridge**. Pass a low-stone-wall shelter on your right, and at a fork 250m later take the rockier right-hand option. Blue-topped wooden posts marked RV2 now help to show the way.

💬 Guadarramismo

Easily accessible from Madrid, the Sierra de Guadarrama played a key role in developing Spaniards' appreciation of nature and mountains from the late 19th century. Leading parts were taken by the Institución Libre de Enseñanza (Free Teaching Institution), which promoted the health, educational and artistic benefits of the sierra, and the Real Sociedad Española de Alpinismo Peñalara, an early mountaineers' group (still going strong). This wave of enthusiasm for the sierra even engendered a new word: *guadarramismo*. But it wasn't till 2013 that the Parque Nacional Sierra de Guadarrama came into existence, protecting 340 sq km of the sierra's higher reaches.

JOHN NOBLE/LONELY PLANET ©

03 The final approach to the **summit of Peñalara** is another bit of ascent, but the views are more than worth the effort – Cuerda Larga to the south, Siete Picos to the southwest, Segovia down on the plains to the northwest.

04 From the peak you could return the way you came up, but the best is yet to come if you continue north along the ridge. A moderately clear path passes right of the first crag then descends to a more level section where you have to pick your way through a **jumble of rocks**. The ridge is high and steep-sided, but nowhere are you walking along the edge of a precipice.

05 Go down round the left side of the forbidding-looking crag **Risco de los Claveles**; the path is pretty clear here and a couple of tiny cairns help.

06 A few minutes of steepish descent are followed by a clear and easy walk down to the **Laguna de los Pájaros** (Lake of the Birds; pictured) – a nice halt though its shore is off-limits for conservation reasons.

07 Pick up a clear path (RV8) heading south from the lake's east side and it's a straightforward 1½-hour walk, nearly all gently downhill and passing several small lakes, back to the Centro de Visitantes. To reach the largest lake, the Laguna Grande de Peñalara, you'll have to detour half a kilometre (each way) after descending from the **Mirador de Javier** viewpoint.

 **TAKE A BREAK**

El Refugio de Cotos (📞602 221006; www.refugiodecotos.com; mains €8-9; ⏰8am-7pm; 📶) at Cotos station and **Venta Marcelino** (www.ventamarcelino.com; bocadillos €6; ⏰daily) at Puerto de Cotos are both fine places for drinks and small or big eats after your walk, with ample open-air terraces. The *refugio* opens at 8am for breakfast, too.

35

SIETE PICOS

DURATION	DIFFICULTY	DISTANCE	START/END
3½-4hr return	Moderate	10km	Puerto de Navacerrada
TERRAIN	Earth and stony footpaths		

A defining feature of the skyline from far and wide, the Siete Picos (Seven Peaks) are strung along a high ridge of the Sierra de Guadarrama about 45km northwest of central Madrid. These castle-like excrescences and other weirdly eroded granite formations, along with fabulous long-distance panoramas, make for a great ridge walk from the small settlement of Puerto de Navacerrada. Then, you return along the Camino Schmid, a lovely path through pine forests. Parts of the ridge are a maze of paths, so a good digital map is helpful for finding your way here.

GETTING HERE

You can do this in a day trip from Madrid using public or private transport, though there are a few accommodation options if you want to stay in the hills. Puerto de Navacerrada is a small settlement and ski station at the pass of the same name (altitude 1880m) on the M601 road from Collado Villalba to Segovia – roughly an hour's drive northwest of central Madrid.

Bus 691 departs Madrid's Intercambiador de Moncloa for Puerto de Navacerrada (€5.10, 1¼ hours) at 8.30am, 9.30am, 2.55pm and 4.55pm Monday to Friday, every 15 minutes 8am to 9.45am Saturday, and every 30 minutes 8am to 9.30am Sunday. It heads back down at about 11.10am, 4.40pm and 6.40pm Monday to Friday, and hourly from 3.30pm to 6.30pm Saturday and Sunday. Buses stop on the main road right outside the car park where the walk starts.

You can also go by *cercanías* (suburban trains; www.renfe.com), though it's a half-kilometre steepish uphill walk from Puerto de Navacerrada station to the start of the walk. Departures from Madrid's Chamartín station every two hours from 8.15am to 4.15pm will get you to Puerto de Navacerrada (€8.70) in 1¾ hours via a change at Cercedilla onto a narrow-gauge mountain line.

STARTING POINT

The car park beside Arias restaurant at Puerto de Navacerrada.

01 From the main road walk to the far end of the car park beside Arias restaurant, then continue ahead to a metal **gate**. Turn right here up a steep, stony track.

02 Reaching the fence of a ski run, your path bends left alongside it for 50m. It then bends left again before veering right to make a steep, stony ascent to meet the fence again higher up. Turn left and go round the left side of a small **telecommunications tower**, bending right to join a broad path coming from the top of the ski lifts.

03 Now head southwest, forking right after 130m, then forking left 100m later. Cross a rocky elevation with a statue of the Virgen de las Nieves (Virgin of the Snows) and continue to another rocky elevation, the **Alto del Telégrafo** (1978m).

04 Continue along the broad ridge to an open, boulder-strewn area known as the **Pradera de Siete Picos**. On clear days you can see the towers of Madrid far to the southeast, Peñalara to the northeast and Segovia down on the plains to the north. Beside a boulder pile on the right look for a carved stone pillar, one of several set in these hills to mark a land purchase by King Carlos III in the 18th century.

 Tors

The crags of the Siete Picos are known in geology, in Spanish as well as English, as tors.

The word refers to hard rocks, such as the granite here, which stand out because they have resisted the forces of erosion better than what's around them – but have cracked, without falling or shifting. In some cases this yields improbable piles of rock slabs, which you'd think would find it easier to topple down than stay in place.

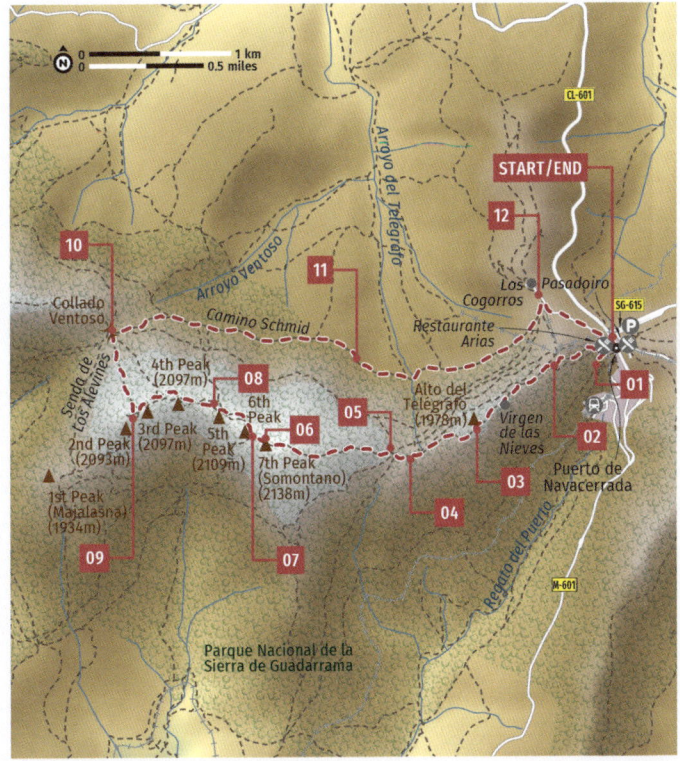

CENTRAL SPAIN/127

05 At a **five-way junction** of paths just past the boulder pile, go straight on, then after 30m fork left up a cairn-marked path.

06 Climb through trees, then out of them, to reach, 1km from the five-way junction, what turns out to be a false summit. But from here your first of the seven peaks, and the highest of all (2138m), is just 100m in front of you. This is in fact the **seventh peak** (also called Somontano) as they are conventionally counted from west to east, and this is the easternmost. Climbing it is a scramble, best done from the northeast. Coming down is more unnerving than going up. If you don't fancy it, there is no obligation.

07 The **sixth peak**, less than 200m further along the ridge, is an easier proposition (still with a minor scramble). From here you're going to head along the north side of the ridge as far as the second peak. There are numerous forks and minor paths, and this is where that digital map comes in handy. Don't forget to enjoy the exceptional panoramas and the weird rock formations as you go!

08 From the northeast base of the sixth peak, follow the path round the peak's north side for some 60m, then take a small, steep-looking path down to the right. It's easier than it looks, and in two minutes you come down to a smoother, wider track. Go left. In 150m, with the rock jumble of the fifth peak (2109m) up to your left, take a left fork to pass a particularly **precariously balanced large rock** on your right within 100m.

09 You pass the fourth peak (2097m) in another 250m, and the third peak (also 2097m) 300m after that. The **second peak**, just ahead, is split in two – the left-hand part (2093m) is marginally higher than the right-hand part.

10 Turn right downhill just before the second peak. Segovia is dead ahead in the far distance. Your path immediately becomes obvious as you descend into the pines. In 15 to 20 minutes you come down to a broad, level clearing with paths heading off in several directions. This is the **Collado Ventoso** (Windy Pass). Either side of the clearing you'll notice two more of Carlos III's carved stone pillars.

11 Turn right (east) at Collado Ventoso. You are now on the **Camino Schmid** (pictured p126), a broad, beautifully constructed path, marked with a few yellow paint circles on trees, that leads you 4km through the pine forest – the first half in gentle descent, the second half in gentle ascent – back to Puerto de Navacerrada. It was laid out in the 1920s by Eduardo Schmid, a member of the Real Sociedad Española de Alpinismo Peñalara (Peñalara Royal Spanish Mountaineering Society) to connect the society's hostel in the Valle de la Fuenfría (to the west) with another at Puerto de Navacerrada.

12 The Camino Schmid emerges on a paved road where you'll see **Los Cogorros**, a Spanish air force residence, along to the left. Turn right and walk 600m back to the middle of Puerto de Navacerrada.

The First Peak

'What happened to the first of the seven peaks?', you might ask as you turn off the ridge at the second peak.

The first peak is a lower southwestern outlier, Pico de Majalasna (1934m), not part of the ridge-top chain. If you're keen to visit it, take the mostly level Senda de los Alevines path south-southwest from Collado Ventoso for just over 1km (then come back).

TAKE A BREAK

There are a few roadside cafe-restaurants at Puerto de Navacerrada where you can get some breakfast before starting out and lunch or a *bocadillo* (long-bread sandwich) or snack on return. **Pasadoiro** (www.pasadoiro.com; M601, Puerto de Navacerrada; bocadillos €6-8;) opens at 8am and has an open-air terrace.

36

LA MIRA

DURATION	DIFFICULTY	DISTANCE	START/END
6hr return	Hard	18.5km	AV931 Km 6

TERRAIN	Dirt roads, earth or stony footpaths, some steep and ill-defined

An outstanding Sierra de Gredos walk with great variety, showcasing both the gentler and more rugged faces of the range. You walk up a river valley to the Puerto del Peón, a centuries-old drovers' pass across the Gredos, then along the ridge to the wonderfully panoramic peak La Mira (2343m), and back down by the little-walked, initially steep Los Conventos valley. Total ascent and descent: 840m.

GETTING HERE

The walk starts at Km 6 of the AV-931 road, which runs south from Hoyos del Espino village. Public transport is limited. **Cevesa** (www.cevesa.es) runs buses from Madrid's Estación Sur to Hoyos del Espino (€13, 3¼ hours) at 8.30am Saturday and 10am Sunday (only), starting back from Hoyos at 4.30pm Saturday and Sunday. **Muñoz Travel** (http://munoztravel.es) runs a bus from Ávila to Hoyos del Espino (€5.85, 1½ hours) at 5pm Monday to Friday, returning at 7.35am the same days. All these buses terminate/start at Barco de Ávila, one hour west of Hoyos. A taxi from Hoyos to Km 6 costs €10 or less.

STARTING POINT

The small parking area (with an information board for the route as far as the Puerto del Peón) at Km 6 on the AV-931.

01 Go through the gate across the road from the parking area and follow the dirt road across open, heath-like country. You can soon discern the Puerto del Peón, a noticeable dip in the line of hills ahead to the southeast. As far as the pass, you will be following the PRAV18 walking route and it's well marked. You fork left immediately after a **gate** after 1km, and go right at another fork 500m later, near a red-tile-roofed cabin. (A white X on a post on the straight-ahead track at this last fork tells you that's the wrong way.)

02 In another kilometre, you cross a small stream, the **Arroyo del Charco** (pictured), and the track becomes a footpath. From here on, plenty of cairns confirm the route. Continue gradually up the valley with the Garganta de la Covacha stream down to your right. Los Conventos valley opens up between the hills over on your right: it's a good idea to check water levels in the Garganta de la Covacha here to make sure you'll be able to cross it on your descent later. (If it's too high, plan on returning from La Mira by retracing your steps via the Puerto del Peón.)

03 Two kilometres from the Arroyo del Charco the path starts to steepen; you cross the Garganta de la Covacha (here much smaller than it is lower down) and start zigzagging up on the far side. In half an hour the path flattens out and you reach the **Puerto del Peón** (2028m). The much steeper, more rugged character of the Gredos' southern side is immediately apparent. Over to the right are the sharp crags of Los Galayos and beyond them the hump of La Mira. You can already make out the little turret on La Mira's summit, whose nature will become apparent later.

04 The PRAV18 continues on down the southern slope, but don't follow it – instead take the **clear, stony path**, with some cairns, westwards along the ridge. It dips down to the right of the ridge then climbs up again, to avoid the crags of La Tarayuela, and as you approach the top of this climb La Mira reappears, less than 2km away to the southwest.

Trashumancia

Since time immemorial herders from high, cold Castilla y León have moved their livestock south to lower, warmer Extremadura for winter and brought them back north for summer. The Puerto del Peón was historically one route for this *trashumancia* (transhumance) – a phenomenon that reached epic proportions in late medieval Spain when vast flocks of sheep migrated up and down a 125,000km network of officially protected drove roads. Today, animals are mostly moved by truck, but a few herders maintain old traditions with twice-yearly journeys of 200km to 400km lasting two or three weeks.

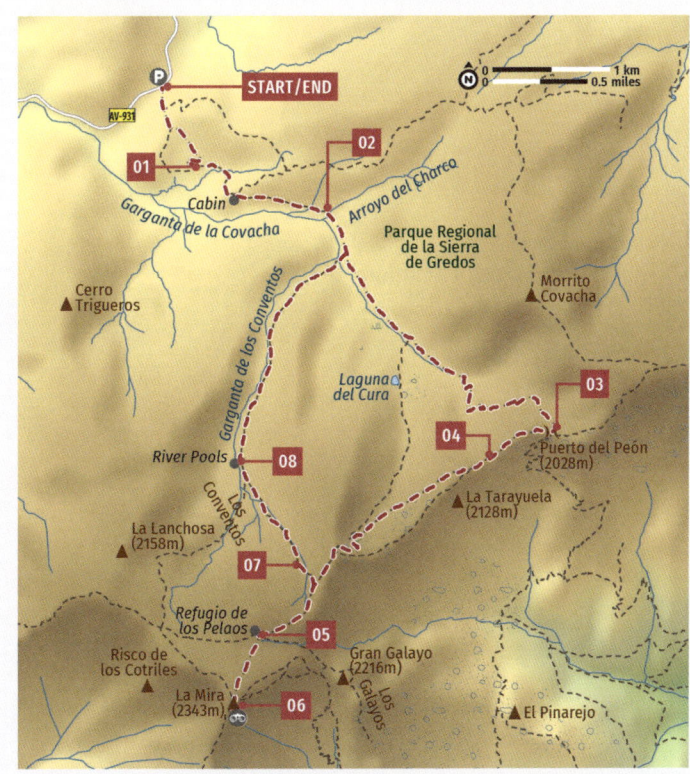

CENTRAL SPAIN/131

05 Follow the stony path to the ruins of the **Refugio de los Pelaos**, a mountaineers' hut built in 1916, with a spring just to its south. Then head south up a gentle slope to the top of La Mira.

06 The path is indistinct but the direction obvious. The views from the **summit** are wonderful. A multi-peaked rocky ridge stretches south, with the plains of the Tiétar valley far below; immediately east are the needle-sharp pinnacles of Los Galayos, a magnet for rock climbers in the Gredos; in the western distance are the jagged peaks of the Gredos cirque, including Almanzor (2592m), the range's highest summit.

As well as enjoying the views, you have an opportunity to contemplate the progress of messaging technology over the past couple of centuries, for the turret-like stone structure on the summit is the remains of an optical telegraph station. Optical telegraph was a mid-19th-century system by which messages were transmitted by visual signals along chains of stations located within sight of each other. It was rendered obsolete almost as soon as it was invented by the appearance of the electric telegraph. You could WhatsApp someone from here to emphasise the technological progress point.

07 Start back the way you came up, but as you head northeast from the Refugio de los Pelaos along the broad ridge, look for occasional cairns that seem to be veering off to the left. These become a discernible sequence and 1km from the Refugio these **cairns** turn left determinedly downhill into the Los Conventos valley. (Note: this route is not recommended in wet weather because the rocks could be dangerously slippery. In this case, or if you already decided that crossing the Garganta de la Covacha at the bottom of the valley is a no-go, just return via the Puerto del Peón; this will add 20 or 30 minutes to the walk time.)

08 Going down into the Conventos valley, there is initially no real path: just keep your eyes peeled for the cairns. Some are very small – occasionally just one or two stones on top of a rock – but they are brilliantly positioned: from each one you can see the next one (or several). An intermittent path even-tually starts to appear and it becomes more discernible after you cross the stream and pass a series of tempting **river pools** on the Garganta de los Conventos to your left. Head on down the valley for another 2km, find a good place to cross the Garganta de la Covacha at the bottom, climb back up to the PRAV18 and turn left to return to the starting point.

The Gredos Ibex

On any mountain walk in the Sierra de Gredos you stand a high chance of seeing ibex (*cabra montés* in Spanish), a large wild goat whose males boast splendid, long, curving horns. The ibex subspecies found in central Spain is *Capra pyrenaica victoriae* and its main population, estimated between 8000 and 10,000, is in the Sierra de Gredos.

Ibex in the Gredos escaped extinction by hunting in the early 20th century only because local councils and landowners gave exclusive ibex-hunting rights to King Alfonso XIII in 1905. The king brought a few hunting parties here during the following decades, but no one else was allowed to hunt them, so ibex numbers bounced back.

TAKE A BREAK

Bring supplies for a picnic (or picnics) at the top of La Mira or the Puerto del Peón or by the Los Conventos pools.

37

EL MOREZÓN

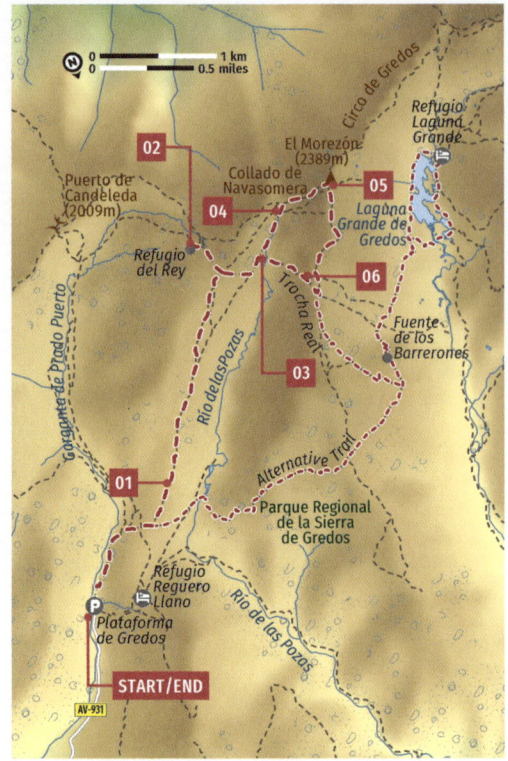

DURATION	DIFFICULTY	DISTANCE	START/END
4½hr return	Hard	12km	Plataforma de Gredos
TERRAIN	Stony footpaths, some clear and paved, others faint and rough		

Climb to a dramatic, high, rocky peak (2389m) with stunning views of the magnificent glacial cirque at the heart of the Sierra de Gredos.

GETTING HERE
The walk starts at the Plataforma de Gredos (altitude 1760m), a parking area at the end of the AV-931 road, which runs 12km south from Hoyos del Espino village, about 2½ hours' drive west from Madrid. There is a €3 charge per car or motorbike to go past Km 7 of the AV931 between 8am and 8pm June to September (8am to 6pm Saturday and Sunday in other months). A taxi from Hoyos to the Plataforma costs €10.

STARTING POINT
Plataforma de Gredos.

01 Head up the initially steepish, stone-paved path south from the Plataforma. As it becomes more level after about 1km, with the Refugio Reguero Llano visible to your right, take the **cairned path** up the gentle grassy slope to the left (south-southwest). Climbing steadily, go left at a fork after 1.5km. Ignore a path to the left 800m later, continuing uphill with the cairns, but turn left at a more major path about 70m after that.

02 This leads in 400m to the tumbledown remains of the **Refugio del Rey** (King's Refuge), built in 1914 to accommodate Alfonso XIII on ibex-shooting trips. It still has regal views – east along the Gredos ridge to La Mira and beyond, south down to the plains of the Tiétar valley.

03 Head back northwest along the path you came on, and follow it bending left into a valley with a **grassy area with a few pools**. Continue

Return via Laguna Grande

Having seen the Laguna Grande from above, it may be hard to resist the urge to get down to it. Do NOT be tempted by any of the gullies heading down from the Morezón ridge. They're all potentially perilous. Instead, follow our main route down as far as the Trocha Real, then turn left, not right. The path immediately swings right to run north along the ridge for 500m, then gradually descends left to meet the main Laguna Grande de Gredos route (p120). Turn left, walk down to the lake and then back to the Plataforma. Your total distance on the day will be 18.5km (some seven hours' walking), with a total ascent and descent of about 860m.

JOHN NOBLE/LONELY PLANET ©

ahead across this and follow cairns up beside a small stream, the upper reaches of the Río de las Pozas.

04 Reaching a plateau, the **Collado de Navasomera**, continue ahead then, just where it begins to slope down slightly, bear right to follow cairns up towards the rocky ridge. The route steepens but cairns and the intermittent path lead you on up through the rocks.

05 Near the top of the ridge the path turns left and in 150m you're at the summit of **El Morezón** (2389m), a jumble of big rocks with precipices plunging away on its west side. The whole of the Gredos cirque is spread out before you (pictured). In the far southwest corner rises Almanzor (2592m), the Gredos' highest peak. In the bottom of the cirque, 450m below your feet, stretches the **Laguna Grande de Gredos**.

06 Having sated your senses on the spectacle, head north along the rocky ridge. A few cairns help guide you. About 600m north of the summit, the cairns turn right, downhill. After a few zigzags they swing north again, and after a half-kilometre descent you meet a very clear path going from right to left. This is part of the **Trocha Real**, a path built, like the Refugio del Rey, in 1914 for Alfonso XIII's shooting trips. To return to the Plataforma de Gredos, turn right and in about 700m you'll reach the grassy area with pools that you crossed on your way up. Follow the path to the left here and in 500m turn left to retrace your steps all the way down to the Plataforma.

 **TAKE A BREAK**

Buy supplies for a peak picnic in Hoyos del Espino.

38

RUTA DE CARLOS V

DURATION	DIFFICULTY	DISTANCE	START/END
9hr one-way	Hard	27km	Tornavacas/ Jarandilla de la Vera
TERRAIN	Unpaved roads, forest and mountain paths		

Walk the historic, highly scenic route (PRCC1) over the mountains of northern Extremadura by which King Carlos I of Spain – also Holy Roman Emperor Charles (Carlos) V, hence the route's name – was carried in 1556 en route to retirement at the monastery of Yuste. The route, across the Sierra de Tormantos, a southwestern outlier of the Sierra de Gredos, involves 900m of ascent and 1150m of descent. It's mostly well marked with yellow-and-white PR markers and signs.

GETTING HERE

Both ends of the route are about three hours' drive west of Madrid. Both have bus services. **Cevesa** (www.cevesa.es) runs two daily buses to Tornavacas from Madrid's Estación Sur (€15, three hours) and two or three daily from Plasencia (€3.20, 45 minutes). Only the 9am from Plasencia gets you to Tornavacas in time to do the walk the same day – and that only when sunset is sufficiently late. The bus stop in Tornavacas is in front of Mesón Los Arcos on the N-110, 100m up the road from the walk starting point. **Samar** (http://samar.es) operates a daily bus departing at 11am from Madrid's Estación Príncipe Pío to Jarandilla (€18, four hours). **Alsa** (www.alsa.com) runs between Jarandilla (Avenida Soledad Vega Ortiz, a few steps from Santander bank) and Plasencia. To bus it from Jarandilla to Tornavacas, you need to change in Plasencia. The 7.10am bus from Jarandilla reaches Plasencia (€6) at 8.30am, enabling you to catch the 9am bus to Tornavacas. A taxi from Jarandilla to Tornavacas costs around €60.

STARTING POINT

N-110 Km 358.8 (opposite La Covacha restaurant on the main road through Tornavacas).

01 A sign at the starting point states that Carlos began his journey here on 11 November 1556. Walk 150m down the road and turn sharp left downhill, then sharp right after 200m, then left after another 200m. This brings you, in 200m more, to a **bridge** over the infant Río Jerte.

02 Turn right then fork right onto a footpath after 175m. The path parallels the river, passing some of the Jerte valley's thousands of cherry orchards (a sea of white blossom for 10 days in late March or April). In 1km continue ahead when you come up onto a paved road. This crosses the **Puente de San Martín** bridge over a stream, becomes concrete then dirt, and reaches a junction of tracks with a large 'Reserva Natural Garganta de los Infiernos' sign. Here take the second of two tracks turning to the right.

03 The track bends left and starts climbing; 200m from the last junction turn right into oak woods along a stone-paved track with yellow-and-white PR markers. At a fork after 400m go left uphill; at a five-way junction 900m later go straight ahead; and meeting a slightly bigger track 600m later go ahead slightly downhill, indicated by a PR post. You cross a cattle grid, see the town of Jerte down to the right, then fork left onto a footpath with 'Ruta Carlos V' signs. Climb through oak and chestnut woods to the **Collado de las Losas** (960m), where you cross a broad track and take the track downhill, opposite.

04 Fork left, indicated by a PR post, after 500m, then fork right onto a footpath, signposted Puente Nuevo, 250m later. Descend through oaks and bracken along a stone-paved

Why Carlos Crossed the Mountain

Worn out after four decades confronting uprisings, wars, Protestantism and the challenges of Spain's new American empire, in 1555–56 the gout-stricken King Carlos abdicated both the Spanish throne and the Holy Roman Emperorship.

Deciding to spend his final years at Yuste monastery in remote northern Extremadura, he sailed from the Low Countries to Laredo (Cantabria) in autumn 1556, and continued overland. Reaching Tornavacas in the Jerte valley, and wishing to take the shortest possible route to his next stop, he asked to be carried directly over the Sierra de Tormantos to Jarandilla de la Vera.

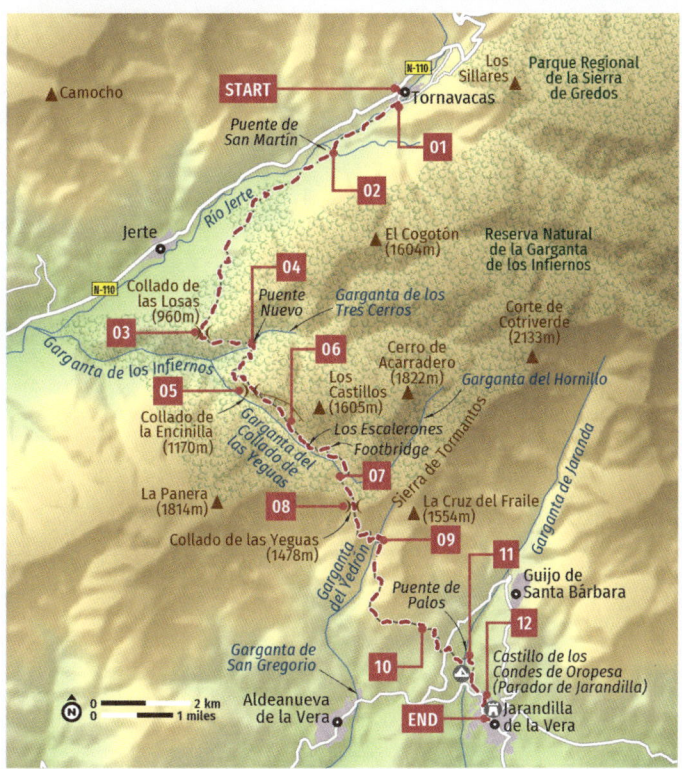

path to the elegant arch of the **Puente Nuevo** (pictured), spanning the Garganta de los Tres Cerros river. Some say this is where Carlos uttered *'No pasaré otro puerto sino el de la muerte'* ('I will not cross another pass except that of death'). The Collado de las Yeguas, later in the route, seems a more likely place for that statement, as it is a *puerto* (mountain pass) and not a bridge – but, either way, the Puente Nuevo is a very pretty spot.

05 Across the bridge, the stone-paved path turns right. At a fork after 150m, go left uphill, signposted 'Jarandilla 18'. You now start the route's stiffest climb, an ascent of 280m to the Collado de la Encinilla, taking you back into woods where route-finding requires care. Just be thankful you're not carrying the Holy Roman Emperor in a sedan chair. After 1km, fork left up a minor path signposted 'Jarandilla 17.5'. About 100m further, at a couple of small cairns, go left up what seems a very minor path. The path becomes a bit more distinct as it weaves its way upwards. Occasional stone-paved sections, cairns and red-and-white GR and yellow-and-white PR markers help confirm your route. At the **Collado de la Encinilla** (1170m), plunging views into the valley of the Garganta del Collado de las Yeguas open up on your right.

06 It's a scenic 1.5km to the **Fuente Peñalozana**, which has good drinkable water. In another 700m you reach a clearing with an 'Escalerones' sign, referring to the step-like rocks along its edge, with a precipitous drop on their far side. The path zigzags up to the left from the clearing and continues gradually climbing. At a plateau-like area with a little roofless stone shelter, bear left to reach a wooden footbridge over a stream in 300m.

07 Pass across moorland to a 'Jarandilla 12.5' sign pointing you down to the right, to a **footbridge over the Garganta del Hornillo** stream. You now enter a vast area that was devastated by fire in 2020. The devastation spread over the ridge ahead of you and far down the southern slopes towards Aldeanueva de la Vera.

08 From the bridge you climb to the **Collado de las Yeguas** pass (1478m), the route's highest point, where views of La Vera (the fertile lowland zone on the south side of the western Gredos) open out, and a signpost tells you, discouragingly, that there's still 11.5km to go to Jarandilla. (We reckon it's less.)

09 Zigzagging down from the pass, go left at a fork after 150m. Your path bends left around a ridge and zigzags on down to a **footbridge over the Garganta del Yedrón** stream. Continue along the clear path down the Yedrón valley, then bending left away from it.

Tornavacas

Tornavacas is a modest little town where things don't seem to have changed a huge amount along the narrow streets of the old centre, with their half-timbered houses and wooden balconies, since King Carlos passed through in 1556. The house where he slept is at Calle Real de Abajo 23; there's an inscription engraved on the lintel above its ancient wooden door, opposite the Antigua Posada inn.

10 The route now becomes more complicated as it approaches Jarandilla, but PR markers and signposts guide you through. At a junction of paths just after a building on the right, nearly 2km from the Yedrón bridge, go left (east). One kilometre later, finally out of the fire-damaged area, turn right onto a smaller path at a junction marked by a Ruta de Carlos V sign and PR markers on stones. This brings you to a flattish, open area where **Jarandilla and its castle** finally come into view.

11 You head down into woods. Meeting another path running from left to right, go right; about 125m later, PR markers tell you to fork right down a small path. In another 150m, at a multiple track junction, take the downhill track with PR posts. Reaching a paved road, go left, then after 100m turn right down a concrete road with PR markers. At a dirt road after 600m, go left then in 150m turn right down a path with a PR marker and a sign 'SLCC56 Ruta de los Puentes, Jarandilla 25 minutos'. Cross the **Puente de Palos** over the Garganta de Jaranda stream and turn right. Pass a campground on your right to come out on a paved road. Go ahead down the hill, turn left at a junction after 100m and you'll meet the main road (EX-203). Turn left into Jarandilla.

12 It's 1km to the **Castillo de los Condes de Oropesa**, where King Carlos arrived after his mountain crossing – and stayed for three months, waiting for his private wing at Yuste monastery, 11km away, to be completed. The multi-turreted castle is now a *parador* (luxurious state-owned hotel) and its handsome Renaissance courtyard and adjoining cafe are open to all.

TAKE A BREAK

Tornavacas has a few shops where you can get basic supplies for the walk: look along Calle Real de Abajo. The riverside rocks at the Puente Nuevo and the panoramic Collado de las Yeguas are good picnic spots. On arrival in Jarandilla you should have at least a drink at the *parador*!

Also Try...

JOSERPIZARRO/SHUTTERSTOCK ©

RUTA DEL EMPERADOR

The perfect follow-up to the Ruta de Carlos V (p136), the Route of the Emperor heads from Jarandilla de la Vera, where King Carlos I stayed after crossing the Sierra de Tormantos in 1556, to the Monasterio de Yuste (pictured), where he retired to live his final years.

You cross mostly level countryside and through Aldeanueva de la Vera and Cuacos de Yuste villages, well directed by Ruta del Emperador signs – except in Cuacos, where it's a good plan to have a wander round the atmospheric old centre, then find your way up to the monastery road. The **monastery** (902 044254; www.patrimonionacional.es; adult/concession €7/4, guide €4, EU & Latin American citizens & residents free Wed & last 3hr Sun; 10am-8pm Tue-Sun Apr-Sep, to 6pm Oct-Mar P) itself, founded in 1409, is a fascinating visit. You can return to Jarandilla on the 4.30pm Samar bus (€1.20, 10 minutes) from Cuacos.

DURATION 3hr one-way
DIFFICULTY Easy
DISTANCE 10.5km

HOYA MOROS

West of the Sierra de Gredos rises the Sierra de Béjar, with peaks over 2400m. One of the best walks is to Hoya Moros, a glacial cirque filled with enormous blocks of granite, popular with boulderers.

A 10km drive up from picturesque Candelario takes you to El Travieso parking area (1850m). Take the path heading uphill 10m before its far end. The clear path, with great long-distance views, rises to 2230m. After about 2.5km there's one short, steepish, rocky bit where you'll want to use your hands a little. Crossing the route's highest part, with a number of tall cairns, head towards the Dos Hermanitos, similarly shaped twin peaks up ahead. Then follow a string of pools downhill to Hoya Moros (2050m). The lawn-like areas along the little river at the foot of the basin are a delightful picnic spot. Return the way you came.

DURATION 4½hr return
DIFFICULTY Moderate
DISTANCE 10km

CUERDA LARGA

The exhilarating but long walk along the ridge that forms Madrid's northern skyline.

The route (PRM11) starts from Puerto de Navacerrada (1880m; 1¼ hours from Madrid by bus 691) with a stiff climb to Bola del Mundo (2262m), then you head east along the panoramic ridge in a series of ups and downs, finally descending to the Puerto de la Morcuera (1777m; you could organise a taxi pick-up here if you wish) and Miraflores de la Sierra (1140m; one hour to Madrid by bus 725). Total ascent/descent is about 1100/1800m. For a track, search 'PR-M 11 Miraflores de la Sierra, Cuerda Larga'.

DURATION 7hr one-way
DIFFICULTY Hard
DISTANCE 26km

GARGANTA DE NAVAMEDIANA

The PRAV38 path follows the tumbling Garganta de Navamediana stream up from tiny Navamediana village on the northwest edge of the Gredos.

Woodlands give way to moorland and then rocky wastes surrounded by high mountains at Las Hoyuelas basin, where the walk ends. The 700m elevation gain is steady, but gradients are not severe. The path is clear almost as far as the Chozo Quemaculos hut after 6km, but then you have to rely on cairns and occasional PR posts. Return the way you came.

DURATION 6hr return
DIFFICULTY Moderate
DISTANCE 15km

RUTA GARGANTA DE LOS INFIERNOS

This circular route on the southeast flank of Extremadura's Valle del Jerte explores mountain streams and the forests of the Garganta de los Infiernos (Hell's Gorge) and its tributaries, though it's more beautiful than scary.

The walk starts at the Centro de Interpretación de la Reserva Natural Garganta de los Infiernos, 3km southwest of Jerte town, and takes in a series of picturesque rock pools (pictured), and the lovely Puente Nuevo bridge over the Garganta de los Tres Cerros (coinciding with the Ruta de Carlos V, p136).

DURATION 6hr return
DIFFICULTY Moderate
DISTANCE 16km

ANDALUCÍA

39 **Castaño del Robledo & Alájar Loop** Idyllic inter-village walk through densely wooded, rolling hills of Andalucía's far west. **p146**

40 **Río Borosa** Simply one of the most beautiful walks in the country. **p148**

41 **Sierra de Cazorla** Forests, peaks, waterfalls and infinite panoramas in Andalucía's northeast. **p150**

42 **Cómpeta to El Acebuchal** Follow a historic mule train route through wild mountain country to lunch in a reborn village. **p152**

43 **Las Negras to Agua Amarga** Coastal drama amid the surreal landscapes of volcanic, desert-like Cabo de Gata. **p154**

44 **La Tahá** Wander paths between Moorish-origin villages and negotiate dramatic ravine-side switchback trails. **p156**

45 **Mulhacén** Summit the highest peak on the Spanish mainland! **p158**

46 **Acequias del Poqueira** Hike up a beautiful valley and return by a high-level path with spectacular vistas of Sierra Nevada peaks. **p162**

Explore
ANDALUCÍA

Spain's southernmost region is a diverse natural wonderland where more than 30% of the territory is environmentally protected. The many mountain ranges provide much of the best walking – notably the Sierra Nevada south of Granada, and the Alpujarras valleys along its southern flank. The sierras around Cazorla in the northeast, and the Sierras Tejeda and Almijara, between Málaga and Granada, are other abrupt, dramatic ranges. Gentler, greener hills in the western Sierra de Aracena also provide particularly lovely walking. Don't forget the coast: the eastern Cabo de Gata peninsula has a surreal beauty unique in the country.

GRANADA

Granada was the fabled capital of the Nasrid emirate, the final flowering (1249–1492) of Moorish power and culture on the Iberian Peninsula, showcased by the lavishly lovely Alhambra palace-fortress. But this is also a contemporary Spanish city of overflowing tapas bars, intimate flamenco clubs and counterculture street art – with outstanding natural areas within easy reach.

CAZORLA

The little white town of Cazorla is the main gateway to the mountain, valley and forest drama of the Parque Natural Sierras de Cazorla, Segura y Las Villas, Spain's largest protected area at 2098 sq km. It's a charming base with two imposing castles (three if you include the one at neighbouring La Iruela) and a core of winding old streets.

CAPILEIRA

Capileira's labyrinthine streets of flat-roofed, white-painted houses slope down towards the Barranco del Poqueira (Poqueira Gorge), amid woodlands and cultivation terraces more than 1400m above sea level. A perfect Alpujarras village, it's the starting point of many fine mountain and valley walks – very popular with visitors, but somehow that doesn't spoil its charm.

WHEN TO GO

The walking is best from April to June and in September and October, when the weather is warm but not too warm, summer crowds (and prices) are absent, and the vegetation is at its most colourful (spring blooms, autumn leaves). July and August are *too* hot for walking in most areas. The exception is the high Sierra Nevada (including Mulhacén), where it's actually best from July to mid-September.

A sunny winter day can be great anywhere, but in the mountains much snow on the trail can make the going difficult, possibly dangerous.

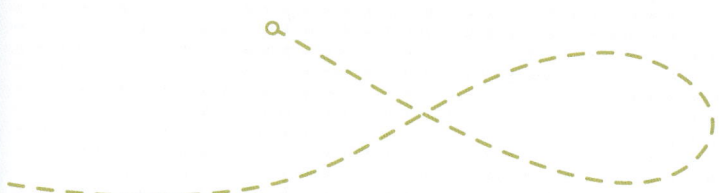

TRANSPORT

Málaga airport is Andalucía's main international entry point. There are also airports at Granada, Almería, Seville, Jerez de la Frontera and Gibraltar. A good road network makes it easy to drive to walk areas; bus services exist for most walks in this chapter, but rarely run more than a couple of times a day.

WHERE TO STAY

Capileira is an ideal village base in the high Alpujarras. Options range from the relatively swish **Hotel Real de Poqueira** (www.hotelespoqueira.es) to the good-value, welcoming **Hotel Rural Alfajía de Antonio** (www.hotelruralalpujarra.com). In Ferreirola, go for rustic-chic **Casa Ana** (www.casa-ana.com) or long-established **Sierra y Mar** (www.sierraymar.com).

Cazorla town is a convenient walkers' base with appealing lodgings such as pretty **Casa Rural Plaza de Santa María** (www.plazadesantamaria.com) and unfussy but immaculate **Hotel Guadalquivir** (www.hguadalquivir.com). The top-end **Parador de Cazorla** (www.parador.es) is 25km from town.

The main accommodation centre in Cabo de Gata is the small town of San José. Beachside villages tend to have few hotels and many holiday apartments. Bright **Hotel Senderos** (www.hotelsenderos.com) and romantic **MiKasa** (www.mikasasuites.com) are top options in Agua Amarga. In Las Negras you can choose between budget **Hostal Arrecife** (950 38 81 40), three-star **Hotel Cala Chica** (www.calachica.com) and four-star **Hotel Spa Cala Grande** (www.calagrande.es).

Over in Cómpeta there's a good range of choices from foreign-owned B&Bs to the pleasant **Hotel Balcón de Cómpeta** (www.hotel-competa.com), but most appealing and original is **Finca El Cerrillo** (www.hotelfinca.com), on a hillside 4km out of town in a revamped former olive mill.

The Sierra de Aracena has a few lodgings well tuned into walkers' needs, with owners who are experts on the area's trails. Castaño del Robledo has a big plus in British-owned **Posada del Castaño** (www.posadadelcastano.com). At Alájar, go for eco-friendly, Spanish- and-English-owned **Posada de San Marcos** (www.sanmarcosalajar.com) or the Dutch-owned cottages **Molino Río Alájar** (www.molinorioalajar.com).

Resources

Ventana del Visitante (www.juntadeandalucia.es/medioambiente/servtc5/ventana/entrar.do) Official Andalucía protected areas site; includes all this chapter's walk areas.

Discovery Walking Guides (www.dwgwalking.co.uk) English-language walking guides and maps for Las Alpujarras, La Axarquía and the Sierra de Aracena.

Spanish Trails: The Sierra Almijara and Tejeda (www.spanishtrailsco.com) English-language walking guide for the hills around Cómpeta and Nerja by Phil Lawler.

Walking Holiday in Cómpeta (www.walkspain.co.uk) English-language digital guide to walks in the Cómpeta area, with downloadable GPS tracks.

WHAT'S ON

Bluescazorla (www.bluescazorla.com; Jul) Remote Cazorla demonstrates a surprisingly cosmopolitan vibe with this three-day blues fest.

Romería de la Virgen de las Nieves (5 Aug) Several hundred people accompany a Virgin image carried on horseback from Trevélez (1476m) to the top of Mulhacén (3482m).

Romería de la Reina de los Ángeles (8 Sep) All the Sierra de Aracena converges on Alájar for this festive pilgrimage.

Cómpeta Walking Festival (www.walkspain.co.uk; final weekend Sep) Four days of guided group walks in the Axarquía hills around a white village east of Málaga, for a bargain €20.

39

CASTAÑO DEL ROBLEDO & ALÁJAR LOOP

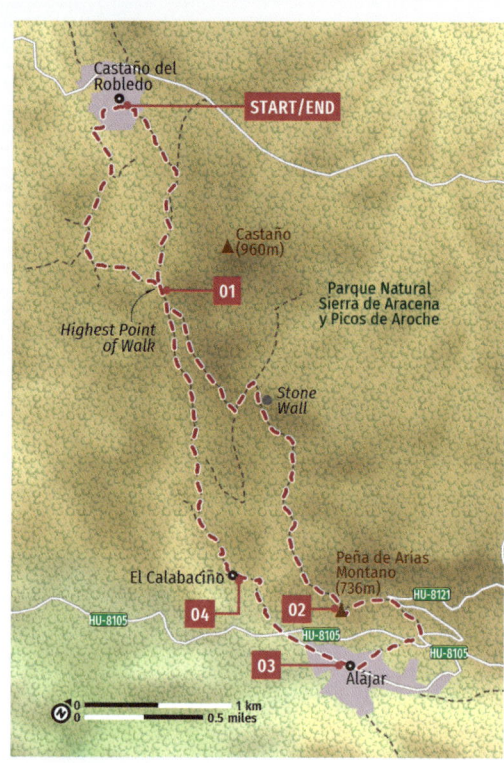

DURATION	DIFFICULTY	DISTANCE	START/END
3½–4hr return	Easy	13km	Castaño del Robledo
TERRAIN	Earth or cobbled paths, unpaved and paved roads		

This walk along centuries-old trails combines two charming villages with dense woodlands, long-distance panoramas and a dab of historical interest. Treat it as the start of a foray into the charms of the Sierra de Aracena, where an extensive web of walking trails winds along river valleys between picturesque villages and over gentle hills covered in thick pelts of cork oak, chestnut and pine, and expanses of *dehesa* (oak-dotted pig pastures).

GETTING HERE

You need your own vehicle to get to Castaño del Robledo (pictured). Alternatively, you could bus it to Alájar then walk Alájar–Castaño–Alájar. Damas (www.damas-sa.es) buses depart Seville (Plaza de Armas) at 4pm Monday to Friday for Alájar (€8.70, two hours), via Aracena. Return buses leave Alájar at 6.45am the same days.

STARTING POINT

Plaza del Álamo, the central plaza of Castaño del Robledo, a village with two very large churches.

01 Head up Calle Arias Montano, turn right along the first lane and follow a fine old cobbled track up between stone walls and earth banks. At a crossroads at the track's **highest point**, 1.5km from the village, go straight on, then fork left about 150m later.

02 After a level 900m with long-distance panoramas, go left on meeting another track, then turn right alongside a stone wall 250m later. Head steadily downhill and through woodlands to a plateau-like area with the NS Reina de los Ángeles chapel and balconies overlooking Alájar. This is the top of the **Peña de Arias Montano** crag, named after a celebrated 16th-century

146/ANDALUCÍA

More Sierra de Aracena Walks

Good accommodation hosts will help with route info.

Navahermosa to Galaroza via Valdelarco An easy and pretty 14km, north through the Talenque valley to Valdelarco, then southwest over cork-oak-covered hills to Galaroza.

Castaño del Robledo to Almonaster la Real A panoramic 14km that crosses Cerro San Cristobal (912m) to Almonaster, where the Mezquita (mosque) is a real gem of Moorish architecture.

Santa Ana la Real to Alájar A dramatic two-gorge walk heads south down the Río Santa Ana then north up the Río Alájar.

Best for
OFF THE BEATEN PATH

polymath – theologian, linguist, poet, Bible translator, librarian and chaplain to Felipe II – who repeatedly came here for retreat and contemplation. There's a small interpretation centre about the man.

03 Head down the road from the chapel; 50m after it joins a bigger road, fork right down a cobbled track. Meeting the road again lower down, go 25m right, then down another path leading into **Alájar**. After a wander round the pretty village (it has shops selling local ham, sausages, jams and honey, and a characteristic brick-and-stone sierra church), head west along Calle Médico Emilio González and cross the HU-8105 onto a roughly paved track.

04 This leads up through **El Calabacino**, a once-abandoned hamlet where an alternative-lifestyle community (*jipis*) has established itself. Fork right at a white house 600m from the road, pass a church, and the beautiful cobbled path winds on uphill. Take the lesser, right-hand fork 600m after the church, and in another 1.4km you meet the track you came down earlier in the day. Continue uphill about 150m then go left at the track crossroads at the highest point (stop 01). You wind westwards then bend northwards downhill to come out on a paved road just below Castaño del Robledo. Turn right for the village.

TAKE A BREAK

There are plenty of bars and restaurants in Alájar: **Mesón El Corcho** (Plaza de España 3; mains €8.50-25; 1.30-4pm) is worth a visit for its amazing cork-based decor alone. In Castaño del Robledo, **La Bodeguita** (www.facebook.com/paumesina; Plaza del Álamo; dishes €3-8; 9am-4pm & 6-10pm or later Tue-Sun) is good for egg dishes, burgers, salads, *bocadillos* and tapas. For the area's famed ham and pork, try **Mesón El Roble** (661 715457; Calle Arias Montano 8; dishes €8-17; noon-5pm & 8pm-midnight Wed-Sun).

40

RÍO BOROSA

DURATION	DIFFICULTY	DISTANCE	START/END
6hr return	Moderate	22km	Aparcamiento Río Borosa
TERRAIN	Unpaved roads, stony paths, tunnels		

Follow the crystal-clear Río Borosa upstream through scenery that progresses from the pretty to the majestic, via a narrow gorge, many waterfalls, two tunnels and a mountain lake. This is one of Spain's most beautiful walks. There's 650m of ascent and descent, but also a lot of shade. Because of the walk's popularity, it's recommendable to go on a weekday.

Drive 34km north from Cazorla town on the A-319, turn east opposite the **Torre del Vinagre visitor centre**, and go 1.5km to the **Río Borosa parking areas**. Walk 150m on up the road, cross the **bridge**, and turn right along the **dirt road** beside the tumbling, beautiful Río Borosa. Where the road starts climbing left after 3km, take a path forking right, signposted 'Cerrada de Elías'. This leads into a very lovely 1.5km section threading the narrow **Cerrada de Elías** gorge. Re-emerging on the dirt road, continue 3km to the **Central Eléctrica**, a small hydroelectric station, where there's a good drinkable fountain.

Past the power station, a 'Nacimiento Aguas Negras, Laguna Valdeazores' sign directs you onwards. You pass a series of **waterfalls** (spectacular after rain, but sometimes dry) as you climb beneath rock crags and towering, black-streaked cliffs. After about 3km, enter the **first tunnel** conducting water towards the power station. It takes about five minutes to walk through (by a narrow path beside the watercourse). The **second tunnel**, a few minutes later, takes about one minute. Fork up left just after the second tunnel to the **Embalse de los Órganos**, a picturesque reservoir surrounded by forested hills. Walk five minutes left to the **Nacimiento de Aguas Negras**, where the infant Río Borosa wells out from under a rock. Picnic beneath the spreading boughs of a large tree here, then head back down.

41

SIERRA DE CAZORLA

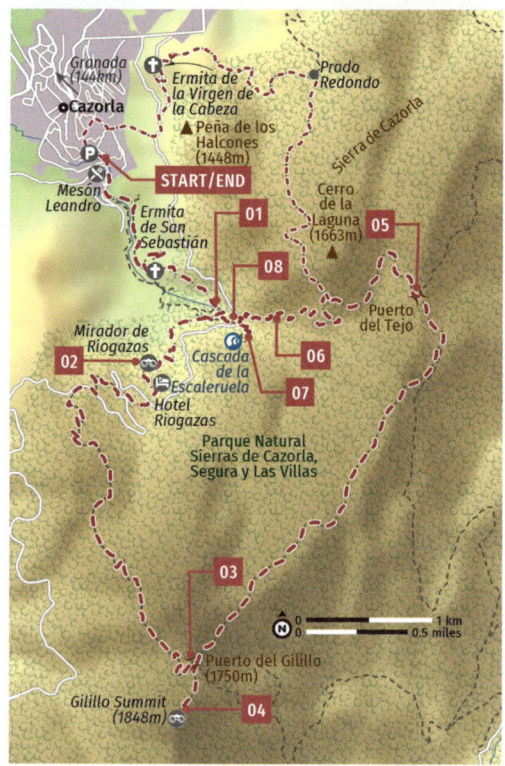

DURATION	DIFFICULTY	DISTANCE	START/END
6½hr return	Moderate	21km	Cazorla
TERRAIN	Earth or stony mountain paths, unpaved roads		

A marvellous circuit through fine mountain scenery from the handsome old town of Cazorla. You head 10km uphill to the Sierra de Cazorla's highest peak, Gilillo (1848m), and return via an exhilarating path called La Escaleruela (The Ladder). The paths are well made, and well signed with varied white and red/yellow/green paint markers.

GETTING HERE
Cazorla is a 144km drive northeast from Granada. Alsa (www.alsa.com) runs three to five daily buses from Granada (€18, 3¾ hours) via Jaén and Úbeda.

STARTING POINT
Plaza de Santa María, Cazorla.

01 Walk up Calle Hoz and fork left after 250m at a PRA313 Gilillo board. Walk up to a concrete road and turn right. Keep following PRA313 Gilillo signs as you wind uphill, with the Río Cerezuelo tumbling away below, then enter **pine woods** and swing southwest.

02 Panoramas over the town, crags and Cazorla's castles just get better as you ascend via the **Mirador de Riogazas** viewpoint.

03 Past the Hotel Riogazas, cross a road onto a footpath, which crosses the same road twice more in the next 800m. Continue climbing and the thinning tree cover reveals long-distance westward views. At the **Puerto del Gilillo** pass (1750m), panoramas over the Cazorla natural park open out.

04 Forty metres down past the pass's highest point, turn right up a minor path. Reaching

Alternative Finish: Prado Redondo

For a gentler alternative to the Escaleruela descent, go straight on (signed Virgen de la Cabeza 3750m) at the fork 1.2km after the Puerto del Tejo. You descend northwards to Prado Redondo, a semi-derelict farmstead. At the bottom left corner of the bucolic clearing here, go left following 'La Iruela GR247' and PRA313 signs. Descend into a gully then bend westwards out of it to pass above the spectacular La Iruela castle and reach the Virgen de la Cabeza chapel. Head down the road to the Mirador Merenderos de Cazorla. A path down to the right of the mirador (viewpoint) takes you down into Cazorla in 20 minutes.

the foot of Gilillo's rocky summit hillock, the path heads along the right-hand side. Find a narrow path climbing left after a few metres. You'll need to use hands a little en route to the tall-cairned **summit** (pictured). On a clear day you can see the Sierra Nevada, 100km south.

05 Head back down and across the Puerto del Gilillo path onto another path, signposted PRA312, passing left of a ruined building. It winds 4km along the Loma de los Castellones ridge to the **Puerto del Tejo**. Fork left here, signed 'SLA267 Cazorla 5200m'.

06 At another fork in 1.2km, go left, signed 'Cazorla 4000m SLA267', to zigzag down through pines. Continuing with Cazorla SLA267 signs, after about 20 minutes, you emerge on an open, rocky area with steep drop-offs. The path turns right across the rocks and then heads downhill beneath cliffs. This is **La Escaleruela**. It's steep and narrow and, initially, there are drops on the left. Take care, especially if it's wet. You zigzag steeply down for another 20 minutes or so, to a paved road.

07 For the best view of the **Cascada de la Escaleruela**, tumbling in stages at least 300m down the cliffs, walk 50m left along the road and then 200m up the path after the bridge.

08 Back at the bottom of the Escaleruela path, take the **downward track** across the road, crossing the river. Within 400m you meet the dirt road you walked up leaving Cazorla. Turn right and walk 2.5km back to town.

TAKE A BREAK

Mesón Leandro (www.meson leandro.com), beside the walk route, is a cut above Cazorla's other dinner options with dishes ranging from *fettuccine a la marinera* to a terrific venison tenderloin.

42

CÓMPETA TO EL ACEBUCHAL

DURATION	DIFFICULTY	DISTANCE	START/END
4½-5hr one-way	Moderate	17km	Cómpeta/El Acebuchal
TERRAIN	Earth or stony footpaths, unpaved roads		

Traverse a panoramic and historic mule trail and some wild mountain country before descending to a great country restaurant. The route is part of the GR249 trail, clearly marked by red-and-white-ringed posts. Cómpeta, a brilliantly white-hill village in the Axarquía district east of Málaga, is a popular walking base, with dozens of routes in the Sierra Tejeda, Sierra Almijara and their foothills.

GETTING HERE

Cómpeta is a 55km drive from Málaga. Loymerbus (http://loymerbus.es) runs two or three daily buses from Málaga (€5, 1¾ hours). Taxis (€30) will come from Cómpeta to take you back there from El Acebuchal. You can ask the staff at Bar-Restaurante El Acebuchal to call one. Note: the approach road to El Acebuchal from Cómpeta is impassable after a lot of rain.

STARTING POINT

The football ground at the top of Cómpeta.

01 Take the uphill path starting just past the stadium gate, then head left along the track above. It winds upwards with huge panoramas spanning from the Mediterranean to Maroma (2069m). Fork right after 400m, then **turn right up a footpath** where the track bends left 750m later.

02 Rejoin the track after 350m. It soon **levels off** and the inland hills come into view, including the almost conical El Lucero (1779m) through a gap ahead.

03 Where the track veers left downhill 2km later, turn right onto a footpath. This delightful trail, the Vereda de Granada, winds 3km, mostly level, in and out of pines, with marvellous mountain and Mediterranean views. It's part of an

El Acebuchal Reborn

Originally a pit stop on a mule trail over the mountains from nearby Frigiliana, this hamlet fell victim to a post-civil-war conflict between the Francoist security forces and anti-Franco guerrillas hiding out in the mountains. Suspected of helping the resistance, El Acebuchal was evacuated in the late 1940s and fell into ruin.

Its resurrection began in 1998 when a former inhabitant, Antonio García, and his family rebuilt one of the derelict houses as a bar. Today, all Acebuchal's 30-plus houses have been renovated, many of them for holiday rentals, and Antonio's Bar-Restaurante El Acebuchal thrives as one of Andalucía's best mountain watering holes.

age-old trade route, frequented until the mid-20th century by mule trains carrying fresh fish and vegetables across the mountains to the valleys of Granada. You immediately pass **Cortijo María Dolores**, the first of three ruined *ventas* (inns) on this stretch.

04 **Venta Los Pradillos**, 2.25km later, has a lovely stone-paved *era* (threshing floor) that positively invites you to make a refreshments stop. Venta de Cándido follows 400m later and the path starts ascending: fork right after 800m, then go right again on meeting another path.

05 Cross the little Collado de las Flores pass to make a steepish **stony descent** to the Arroyo Majadillas stream. Meeting an unpaved road 125m beyond (pictured), go left, passing the **Cortijo del Daire**, a ruined farmstead.

06 The track turns southwest and winds 4km along the flank of a deep valley to the **Puerto Páez Blanca** junction. Continue ahead into the thickly treed valley below.

07 At a fork 200m past the ruined **Venta Cebolleros**, take the footpath down ahead, between the two track branches (briefly deviating from the GR249). The path winds along beside, and sometimes in, a thickly shaded and usually dry stream bed. In 1.5km you emerge on an unpaved road. Walk 150m to the right, into El Acebuchal.

TAKE A BREAK

Book ahead to dine on homestyle country food from venison or boar to some great soups and salads at atmospheric **Bar-Restaurante El Acebuchal** (951 48 08 08; www.facebook.com/bar-el-acebuchal-360441977305565; mains €11-16; 10am-6pm, kitchen 12.30-4pm;). It does superb homemade bread and cakes, too.

43

LAS NEGRAS TO AGUA AMARGA

DURATION	DIFFICULTY	DISTANCE	START/END
4hr one-way	Moderate	13km	Las Negras/ Agua Amarga

TERRAIN	Earth/stony footpaths, dirt roads

The Cabo de Gata peninsula at Spain's southeast corner, the driest area in Europe, is like a chunk of North Africa transplanted across the Mediterranean. Its stark, desert-like, volcanic landscape is fringed by coastal cliffs and capes of surreal grandeur interspersed with mostly uncrowded beaches lapped by blue waters. It's possible to walk 60km on or near the coast right round the peninsula. We reckon the stretch between the villages of Las Negras and Agua Amarga, most of which is unreachable by road, is best of all. Note: there's very little shade on this walk.

GETTING HERE

Las Negras is a 55km drive east from Almería City; Agua Amarga is 62km. Bus M203 departs Almería's Estación Intermodal for Las Negras (€3, 1¼ hours) at 3.15pm Monday to Friday only. Bus M213 departs Agua Amarga for Almería (€3, 1½ hours) at 3pm Monday to Friday, 6.15pm Sunday and 9.15am Monday to Saturday. Check timetables at http://ctal.es. A taxi back from Agua Amarga to Las Negras (24km by road) costs €40.

STARTING POINT

Las Negras beach.

01 Walk north along the beach and continue along the dirt road at its north end. Meeting a paved road 500m inland, go 50m right then continue along a dirt road with a 'Cala de San Pedro' sign. Enjoy views over Las Negras bay (pictured), and the coast beyond, before the track heads inland behind Cerro Negro to a **parking area** (3km from Las Negras), beyond which vehicles cannot go.

San Pedro Village

Cabo de Gata attracts a diverse bunch of visitors and residents, with beach-chic, hippy, camper-van and outdoor-activity vibes melding fairly seamlessly in its low-key villages.

Isolated San Pedro was abandoned by its Spanish inhabitants in the 1960s. For several decades now it has been occupied by an alternative lifestyle community living in rehabilitated ruins, small new stone dwellings, tents and the odd cave – a place of dreadlocks, dogs, marijuana and solar panels. There are a couple of very rustic beach bars selling drinks and *bocadillos* (long-bread sandwiches) and maybe even pizza, if they're open.

Best for

COASTAL VIEWS

02 A path winds high above the sea to **San Pedro** village – a picturesque sight on a deep blue bay with its beach stretched between a ruined castle (founded in the 1570s to fend off pirate attacks) and the cliffs of Punta Javana.

03 The onward path to Agua Amarga starts by a tower on the east side of the valley. You have a stiff 25-minute climb before the path starts to level off. Then you find you're walking along the top of an **inland cliff** – well, a few metres back from it, but take care. Agua Amarga and Mesa Roldán headland (and the top of the Carboneras power-station chimney) come into view.

04 The path descends steadily to the 250m-long sandy beach at **Cala del Plomo**. Take the dirt road inland and after 350m turn right up a path beside some eroded rocks with a blue-and-white paint marker.

05 Wind round the back of a small hill, **Cerro de la Higuera**. At a junction where the right-hand track heads down to little Cala de Enmedio beach, go straight across onto the rocky uphill path ahead. Fork right after some 300m. Blue-and-white paint markers are well in evidence now.

06 Wind across another small hill, Cerro del Cuartel, and down into **Agua Amarga** with its fine 500m beach and plenty of cafes and bars to kick back in.

 **TAKE A BREAK**

Breakfast at **Taka Tuka** (items €3-7; 7.30am-6pm), on Las Negras' main street 50m from the beach, before walking. It has assorted jams, cheeses, sausages, fish or avocado to top your *tostada* (toasted roll), plus croissants and yoghurt-and-fruit bowls.

ANDALUCÍA / 155

44

LA TAHÁ

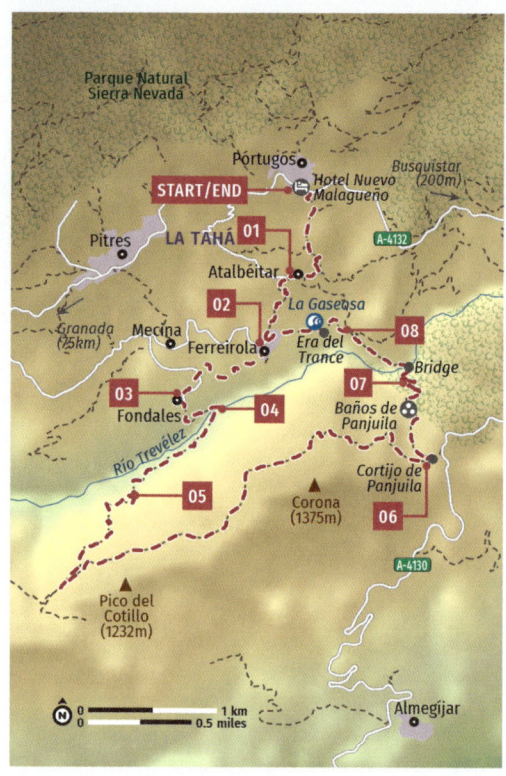

DURATION	DIFFICULTY	DISTANCE	START/END
5¾hr return	Moderate	16km	Pórtugos

TERRAIN	Footpaths up and down hills, unpaved roads

This down-up-down-up walk is a fascinating journey through some wonderfully quaint Alpujarras villages and along beautifully engineered cliffside paths of probable Moorish construction, known as *escarihuelas,* in the plunging valley of the Río Trevélez. Tahá was the name for the districts into which Las Alpujarras was divided in the 14th century under the Emirate of Granada. Today the name survives for a seven-village municipality headquartered at Pitres.

GETTING HERE

Pórtugos is an 11km drive from Capileira, 77km from Granada. Two or three daily Alsa (www.alsa.com) buses come from Granada (€7.20, 2¾ hours), via Capileira.

STARTING POINT

Hotel Nuevo Malagueño on the A4132 in Pórtugos.

01 Walk 150m east along the road, turn down a track just past a roadside balcony area and continue down a stone-paved path. Meeting an unpaved road, continue downhill. At another unpaved road 150m later, go left. The road becomes an earth footpath. Where this emerges onto a footpath, turn right, into diminutive **Atalbéitar**.

02 Wind through Atalbéitar's streets and take the 'Ruta Medieval' path downhill from the church, leading down through fields and orchards to marginally bigger **Ferreirola** (pictured). Again, head downhill from the church.

03 Entering **Fondales**, go left at a street crossing, then left again at the next two forks.

Alpujarras Houses

Best for

BRINGING THE PAST TO LIFE

If you've been to Morocco, you may notice a resemblance between villages in Las Alpujarras and those in the Atlas Mountains. The Alpujarras building style was introduced by Imazighen (Berber) settlers in Moorish times. Most houses have two storeys, the lower one intended for storage and animals. The characteristic flat roofs *(terraos)*, with their protruding chimney pots, consist of a layer of clay packed onto flat stones laid over wood beams. Another typical feature is *tinaos*, passages, porches or patios with rooms or terraces built over them, providing shelter and gathering space. Whitewash is a fairly modern introduction: the villages all used to be stone coloured.

04 Your path winds down and across to the **Puente Romano** ('Roman Bridge' but more likely of Moorish origin), impressively spanning the Río Trevélez ravine.

05 Start up the **Escarihuela de Fondales** (or Campuzano). It runs along high above the river for some 800m, then turns upwards for 800m of steady climbing. The gradient finally eases as you enter pines.

06 Meeting a bigger track, turn sharp left to walk 4km eastwards, with ever better panoramas of the Tahá villages opening up as you go, to a small group of houses, the **Cortijo de Panjuila**. Here turn sharp left downhill.

07 Just past the very ruined **Baños de Panjuila** (probably Moorish-era baths) begins the **Escarihuela de Panjuila**. This time you're going down the spectacular zigzag path, to another bridge across the deep gorge, with a ruined watermill beside it.

08 Take the clear path going left to Ferreirola. You pass the **Era del Trance**, a beautiful old stone-paved threshing floor, and **La Gaseosa**, a natural fountain with a mildly fizzy taste. Fill your water bottle: it will refresh you as you head on into Ferreirola and back up to Atalbéitar and Pórtugos.

TAKE A BREAK

Not quite on the walk route, but well worth booking into for afterwards, French-owned **L'Atelier** (958 85 75 01; www.facebook.com/lateliervegrestaurant; Calle Alberca 21, Mecina; mains €11-14; 1-4pm & 7.30-10pm;), in a 350-year-old village house, unveils a globe-trotting vegetarian feast: spiced couscous, coconut tofu curry and wild-mushroom risotto.

ANDALUCÍA /157

45
MULHACÉN

DURATION	DIFFICULTY	DISTANCE	START/END
5hr return	Moderate	16km	Paraje del Cascajar

TERRAIN	Dirt road, stony mountain paths

This is it. The highest mountain on the Spanish mainland, 3482m above sea level in the Sierra Nevada, southeast of Granada. (Teide on the Canary island of Tenerife beats Mulhacén to the number-one spot for the whole of Spain with its 3718m.) Despite its height, and thanks to a helpful microbus service run by the Parque Nacional Sierra Nevada, Mulhacén is well within the reach of reasonably fit walkers on a day trip.

GETTING HERE

First you need to get to the village of Capileira, more than 1400m high in Las Alpujarras, the picturesque jumble of valleys on the south flank of the Sierra Nevada. Capileira (pictured above) is a 75km drive (about 1½ hours) from Granada, or 135km (two hours) from Málaga. It's served by two or three daily Alsa (www.alsa.com) buses from Granada (€6.35, 2½ hours).

From approximately June to November (exact dates depend on how much snow there is on the mountain tracks), the Sierra Nevada national park's **Servicio de Interpretación de Altas Cumbres** (SIAC, High Summits Interpretation Service; 671 564406; www.reservatuvisita.es; 10am-2pm & 5-8pm approx Easter-early Dec) operates a microbus service from its office beside the main road in Capileira up to a point called Paraje del Cascajar (or Cascajal) at 2574m on the approach to Mulhacén (one-way/return €9/13, 45 minutes each way). Buses make up to four daily return trips and you can book ahead (highly advisable) by email or phone or through the website. Morning departures from Capileira give you ample time to summit Mulhacén and return to Paraje del Cascajar for a bus back down. On the ride up from Capileira, pine woods give way to sparse, scrubby alpine vegetation above about 2300m. Note: the exact location of the bus's upper stop may vary; at times it has gone about 2km further to El Chorrillo (sometimes referred to as Mirador de Trevélez).

STARTING POINT

Paraje del Cascajar. Mulhacén doesn't look terribly impressive when you get out of the bus – a sort of rounded hump up ahead of you. But it's higher than anything else around – and 900m higher than where you are.

01 Walk ahead up the dirt road. As you go you can identify the shark's fin form of Veleta, the Sierra Nevada's second-highest peak (3396m), over to your left. After 1.7km, detour 100m to the right at a 'Trevélez' sign to visit the **Mirador de Trevélez** viewpoint, with views down to Trevélez village in the valley below.

02 Back on the main track, you reach a junction after 450m. Take the right-hand path, with **cairns**, heading steadily uphill. After 750m go left at a fork. The right-hand option here is part of an old, now-abandoned, dirt road – a spur off the old Sierra Nevada road – that reached all the way up to the secondary peak Mulhacén II and which you'll cross or coincide with a few more times as you climb.

03 About 1.25km later, your trail starts up the Loma del Mulhacén (Mulhacén Ridge) proper and steepens. After 200m a Siete Lagunas signpost points along part of the old abandoned road forking off to the right (this leads to another route down to Trevélez); for Mulhacén continue straight on up. You have about 1.75km of upward slog to **Mulhacén II**, marked by a concrete pillar on

The Sierra Nevada Road

A paved road from the north (Granada) side of the Sierra Nevada to the top of Veleta was completed for tourist purposes in 1935, and was touted as the highest road in Europe. In the 1960s this road was joined just below Veleta's summit by a dirt road constructed from Capileira on the range's south side, making it possible to drive right across the range in summer. Concern for the alpine environment and the declaration of the upper Sierra Nevada as a national park in 1999 sounded the road's death knell as a public highway. Since the late 1990s its upper reaches have been closed to motor vehicles without special authorisation.

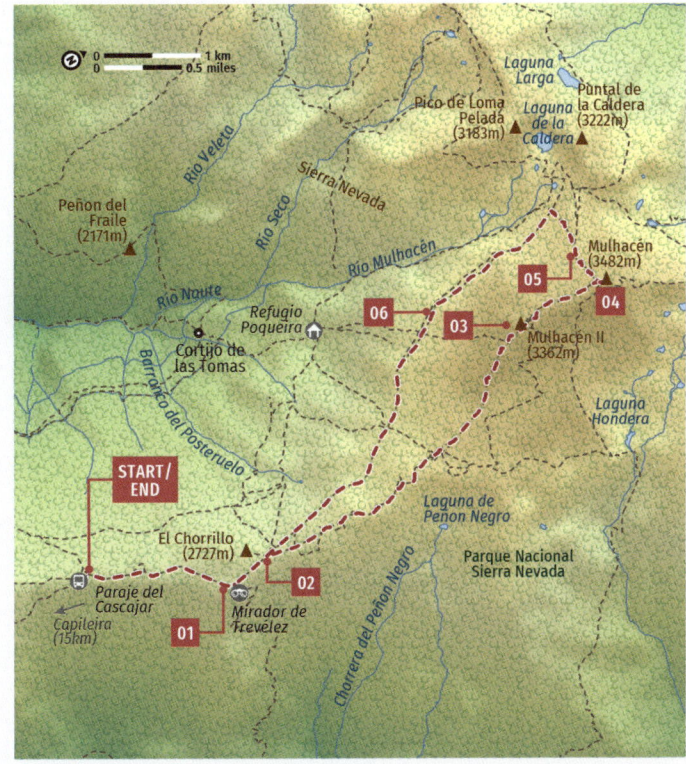

the summit ridge at 3362m. As you climb, vegetation becomes increasingly sparse among the rock.

04 From Mulhacén II the gradient eases off and the path to the peak, across what is now a wilderness of grey rock with almost no vegetation, is clear. In 1km you are taking the last rocky steps to the **highest point on the Iberian Peninsula** (pictured). Beware! Though the ascent you have just made from the south is gradual, the summit stands right on the edge of a sheer precipice plunging 600m down to the Hoya del Mulhacén basin on the mountain's north side. The views are infinite and magnificent, especially down to the Hoya and west along the ridge to Puntal de la Caldera (3222m), the Laguna de la Caldera and Veleta. Ibex often hang around the summit area, seemingly in hopes of sharing walkers' picnics. The remains of ruined buildings around the summit date from a geodesic survey in the 19th century.

05 To descend, you could just go back down the way you came up, but to vary the route, turn down a narrow but clear path to the right just 80m down from the summit. This descends Mulhacén's steep **western slope**, the many zigzags making the gradient much more manageable than might appear from above. A little over halfway down (about 20 minutes) there's a fork, marked by a cairn. Go right here if you want to detour to have a look at Laguna de la Caldera.

06 Otherwise go left, down to the **Sierra Nevada road** (which from above looks like a broad footpath), then walk left along it. Believe it or not, it was once possible to drive a car from Granada to Capileira along this track right over the top of the Sierra Nevada. It's barely recognisable as a road nowadays, with just a narrow single track remaining free of stones and rocks on many stretches. Here and there, piles from rocks prevent anything but walkers and cyclists from passing, and what was a road is slowly returning to rocky wilderness. In 5km, with a little bit of ascent early on, but then gradually descending, you will reach the junction where, on the ascent, you left the road for an uphill footpath. Just continue 2km back to the El Cascajar bus stop.

TAKE A BREAK

Buy supplies in Capileira (it has a supermarket and bakeries) for a picnic on the summit. **Restaurante Moraima** (Carretera de la Sierra; breakfast items €1-4; ⏱from 7am Thu-Tue), across the street from the SIAC office, opens early for fortifying breakfasts (eg omelettes, hot sandwiches, ham/bacon and eggs) before you set out.

Mulhacén Precautions

Take the **weather** seriously. There's no shade and minimal shelter on the route and you're exposed to whatever weather is going. July to mid-September are the best months. Major snowfalls can begin in October and there can be plenty of snow on the ground well into June, making the going difficult and potentially dangerous. Summit temperatures are regularly 10°C to 15°C lower than in Capileira, and the weather can change quickly. Though the trail is easy to follow in clear weather, cloud or mist can easily disorientate walkers.

Altitude sickness is rare on Mulhacén, but it has been known to happen. There is one-third less oxygen in the air at 3500m than at sea level. If you experience mild altitude sickness symptoms such as dizziness, nausea, headache, irritability or exceptional breathlessness or fatigue, stop ascending. If the symptoms don't disappear, descend straight away.

46

ACEQUIAS DEL POQUEIRA

Best for

PRETTY VILLAGES

DURATION	DIFFICULTY	DISTANCE	START/END
6½hr return	Hard	17km	Capileira

TERRAIN	Mountain paths (earth or stony), dirt roads

A great mountain walk that takes you from the Alpujarras village of Capileira up the beautiful Barranco del Poqueira (Poqueira Gorge) onto bare mountainsides above 2100m, and returns by a wonderful high-level path between two *acequias* (human-made water channels) with superb views of the Sierra Nevada's highest peaks. The route (PRA23) is mostly well indicated and the paths clear. There are good chances of sighting ibex, especially on the upper parts of the walk. There's a total of 870m of ascent and descent, and little shade above 1900m.

If you'd prefer a shorter walk that still gives a good feeling for the Barranco del Poqueira, the PRA69 fits the bill nicely. This 7.5km walk (2½ to three hours) follows the same route as the PRA23 as far as the bridge at La Cebadilla, then heads down the west side of the valley, crossing the Río del Poqueira by the Puente Abuchite to return to Capileira.

GETTING HERE

Capileira is a 75km drive (about 1½ hours) from Granada or 135km (two hours) from Málaga. It's served by two or three daily Alsa (www.alsa.com) buses from Granada (€6.35, 2½ hours).

STARTING POINT

Capileira's *ayuntamiento* (town hall).

01 From the *ayuntamiento,* walk 100m up the main road and turn left down the street after Cafe-Bar Rosendo. Ignore a street on the right and take a **stone-paved path**, signed 'Sendero Acequias del Poqueira 125m', up to the right immediately before a car park. Go straight on over a dirt road with signposts and information boards for this walk and the PRA69 at the crossing.

02 The path climbs steadily, with the Río Poqueira deep in its gorge 300m below you. Within a few minutes the Sierra Nevada's two highest peaks, **Mulhacén** and **Veleta**, are in view – Mulhacén (mainland Spain's highest peak at 3482m) a rounded hump up ahead, Veleta visible to its left like a shark's fin just rising above the waves of the sierra. Where your path meets two others coming in from the right, go left following the PRA23 and PRA69 signs. The path levels off. Where a dirt road joins from the right, continue ahead on this, passing left of a large circular structure. After 150m, where the main track bends sharp left downhill, take the lesser track going straight on.

03 In another 800m you join another dirt road coming in from the right and soon start going downhill, with the valley rising to meet you on the left. The road descends gradually to the abandoned hamlet of **La Cebadilla**, built in the 1950s to house the workers of the Poqueira hydroelectric station and their families. Some 200 people once lived here; now nobody does. Have a peep into the abandoned church by the roadside.

04 The Río Poqueira is now almost level with you and you cross it on a bridge. Head up a concrete road to the **Central del Poqueira**, a small hydroelectric station, to the left of which is the confluence of the Ríos Naute and Toril, which is the official start of the Río Poqueira.

Acequias

The people of Las Alpujarras have been channelling the melting snows of the Sierra Nevada for the benefit of their valley villages since at least Moorish, possibly Roman, times.

It was under the Nasrid emirate of Granada in the 13th to 15th centuries that the area's system of *acequias* was extensively developed to carry water from the snowy mountain heights to the springs, wells and *bancales* (cultivation terraces) of villages 2000m below. Cultivation on terraces watered by irrigation channels is widespread across southern and eastern Spain, but Las Alpujarras has a notably ingenious and developed network.

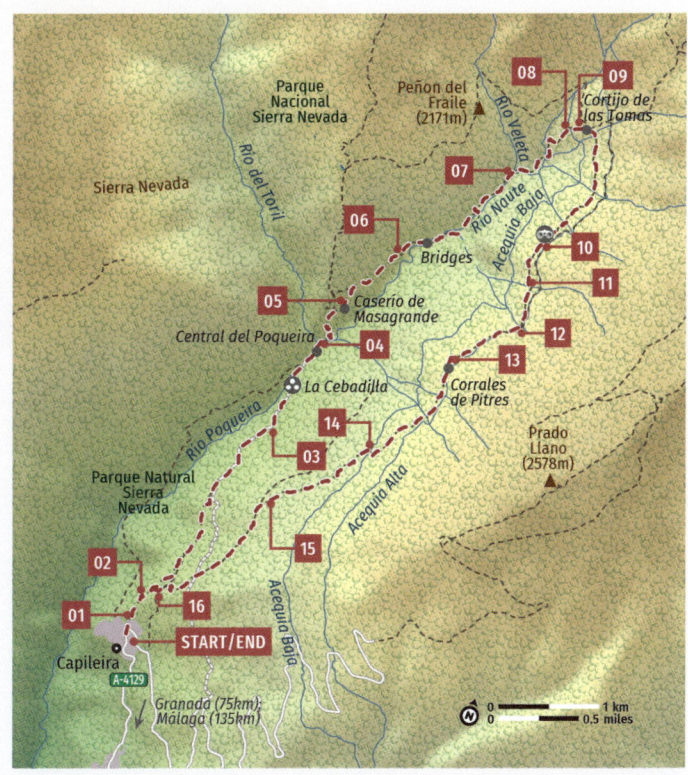

05 Continue up the dirt road past the hydro station, cross a bridge over the Naute and turn right along the path on its far side, which almost immediately starts zigzagging, partly stone-paved, up the steep valley side. It levels off approaching a low stone building, the **Caserío de Masagrande**. Fork left here.

06 The path climbs gently across mountain pastures before descending back to the Naute, which it crosses on two little **stone footbridges**. You cross back to the west bank about 400m further upstream. Wooden posts with yellow and white rings become the main waymarkers as you embark on the hardest part of the walk – ascending 400m in the 2km to the Cortijo de las Tomas.

07 The path negotiates some roughly stone-paved zigzags and a fairly narrow stretch with a tendency to get a bit overgrown before crossing another little stone **footbridge over the Río Veleta** (descending from the snowy heights of Veleta above 3000m). You emerge onto more open hillsides and can now clearly make out the low, dark form of the Cortijo de las Tomas, still a disheartening distance higher.

08 After 20 minutes of upward slog you cross the **Acequia Baja** water channel, one of two *acequias* you'll meet on this walk, channelling water from the Río Mulhacén over to the villages of La Tahá de Pitres, in the next valley east from the Barranco del Poqueira.

JOHN NOBLE / LONELY PLANET ©

09 After five minutes you can deservedly sit down on the grassy areas in front of the **Cortijo de las Tomas** (pictured), a ramshackle, half-abandoned affair but one that many a walker has been very happy to reach. Even at these altitudes, well above 2000m, many of the *cortijos* (farmsteads) were inhabited from spring to autumn until the mid-20th century. People even grew vegetables and grains here. Today most are either abandoned or used for seasonal livestock grazing and shelter.

10 Leaving the *cortijo*, from its top right corner (as you face uphill) head to the right. A path materialises as you approach the stream about 75m away and becomes clear once you're across it. Now it's time to enjoy your just reward for the effort in getting up to these altitudes. The high-level path weaves its way around the eastern side of the valley, crossing a few side streams and with bits of up and down, but overall pretty level. The glistening line of the Acequia Baja snakes across the hillside below you, and a fabulous panorama of **Sierra Nevada high peaks**, from Mulhacén to Veleta to Tajo de los Machos, opens out at the head of and across the valley.

11 The path is pretty clear, if often narrow. Crossing the **Barranco Prado Hondo** (or Barranco Cañavate), 2km from the Cortijo de las Tomas, it winds up to the left after crossing the stream, then bends right (south).

164/ANDALUCÍA

12 Half a kilometre later the path meets the **Acequia Alta** (Upper Acequia). You can walk along the *acequia's* raised bank for 300m until your path veers down to the right just after passing a ruin on the left.

13 Passed an info board identifying the mountain peaks opposite, you reach a rare unruined and white-painted *cortijo,* the **Corrales de Pitres** (or Cortijo del Hornillo). Pick up the onwards path at about the same level on its far side.

14 Go right, downhill, at a fork 800m later to descend to, and hop across, the **Acequia Baja** (Lower Acequia; pictured p162).

15 Continue descending steadily to enter **pine woods** 1km after the *acequia*. Join a dirt road coming from the right, then in another 800m fork right down a footpath with a yellow-and-white-ringed PRA23 post. Coming down onto a wide road, go left then immediately right. Where this dirt road forks after another 400m, take the footpath down opposite, with another yellow-and-white-ringed PRA23 post.

16 Meeting a curve of dirt road on the left, head down towards the **small white building** below, then take the path heading down past the building, signed Capileira 500m, PRA23 and PRA69. You are now back on the path you ascended from Capileira at the start of the walk. It's 700m back to your starting point.

ⓘ The Careo System

The *acequias* of the Sierra Nevada and Alpujarras fall into two basic types.

Acequias de riego (irrigation channels), of which there are over 400km, principally feed water from streams and rivers to *bancales* and to tanks storing water for the same purpose.

Acequias de careo, generally found at higher altitudes, often 2000m or more, conduct water to mountain pastures and to areas known as *simas,* where it percolates into the ground and feeds underground aquifers, re-emerging months later from springs or fountains down in the valleys to help provide a year-round water supply for villages and farms. Developed chiefly during Moorish times 600 to 800 years ago, this ingenious system would have required an astoundingly detailed knowledge of the hydrogeology of the sierra and the valleys.

☕ TAKE A BREAK

Buy supplies at Capileira's bakeries or supermarket for a picnic on the grass enjoying the vistas at the Cortijo de las Tomas. The village has a good selection of cafes and restaurants. Try **El Corral del Castaño** (📞958 76 34 14; Plaza del Calvario 16; mains €8-23; ⏱1-4pm & 8-10pm Thu-Tue; 🍴) for a lovely plaza setting and excellent Andalucian cooking with creative international influences.

ANDALUCÍA /165

Also Try...

JOHN NOBLE/LONELY PLANET ©

JUVILES & FUERTE

This little gem links two quiet Alpujarras villages via a hilltop Moorish fort and a rugged ravine.

From Jamones de Juviles in Juviles, follow 'Fuerte de Juviles' and 'Fuerte' signs leading up the cliff-fringed Fuerte hill. The fort up here was destroyed in the Christian Reconquista but three Moorish cisterns remain. The best preserved is 30m left when you come up between rocks onto the hill's upper part. The others are about 170m southwest. Return along the path along the hill's flank and turn right towards the hamlet of Timar (1.25km). Walk along the road from Timar's church and turn right at the cemetery, passing left of a chimney stack. The path becomes much clearer as it climbs the Rambla de Nieles ravine to return to Juviles.

DURATION 2¾hr return
DIFFICULTY Easy
DISTANCE 6.5km

CAMINITO DEL REY

A boardwalk fixed high up the sheer walls of the Río Guadalhorce's spectacular canyon 60km northwest of Málaga, the 'King's Path' was walked by Alfonso XIII in 1921, and fully renovated in 2014–15. The boardwalks comprise just 1.5km of the route, but the scenery is dramatic all the way (pictured above).

It's very popular: book tickets (unguided/guided €10/18) two weeks or more ahead (www.caminitodelrey.info), selecting your time for entering the boardwalk section, 1.5km or 2.7km from the walk start depending on which route you choose. A shuttle bus (€1.55) connects the route's end at El Chorro station (two or three daily trains to/from Málaga) with the start (which you can drive to). Allow four hours for the full circuit. No children under eight.

DURATION 2½hr one-way
DIFFICULTY Easy
DISTANCE 7.7km

TREVÉLEZ TO CAÑADA DE SIETE LAGUNAS

A long, demanding walk (PRA27) from the Alpujarras' highest village up to (and back down from) a stunning, lake-dotted mountain basin beneath Mulhacén (3482m) and Alcazaba (3366m).

Starting from Calle Horno at the top of Trevélez, you ascend past outlying farmsteads and up mountain pastures to the rocky wilderness of the upper Sierra Nevada. The final ascent beside Chorreras Negras waterfall is particularly steep.

DURATION 7–8hr return
DIFFICULTY Hard
DISTANCE 16km

GARGANTA VERDE

Close-up views of enormous griffon vultures make the descent into the Sierra de Grazalema's Garganta Verde (pictured above) gorge especially dramatic.

The trail starts from the CA-9104, 3.5km south of Zahara de la Sierra. The walk requires a (free) permit. The **Centro de Visitantes El Bosque** (956 70 97 33; cvelbosque@reservatuvisita.es; Calle Federico García Lorca 1, El Bosque; 10am-2pm, closed Mon Jun-Sep) will email permits with a minimum 14 days' notice. Leftover permits are sometimes available for collection on the day. The route is closed from 1 June to 15 October.

DURATION 2½hr return
DIFFICULTY Moderate
DISTANCE 5km

PINSAPAR

The highlight of this lovely Sierra de Grazalema walk is the 4-sq-km *pinsapar*, the largest extant woodland of the rare Spanish fir (*pinsapo*). This dark-green tree has survived only in a few locales in Andalucía and Morocco.

You will need a permit from the Centro de Visitantes El Bosque; going with an experienced activities firm like Horizon (www.horizonaventura.com) can simplify things. The walk starts from the CA-9104, 2.5km from Grazalema town, and ends at Benamahoma. It's partly off limits 1 June to 15 October.

DURATION 4hr one-way
DIFFICULTY Moderate
DISTANCE 11km

MEDITERRANEAN COAST

47 **Montserrat** Catalonia's mystical mountain, a short train ride from Barcelona. **p172**

48 **Camí dels Molins** A short walk in remote Maestrat, starring a medieval hilltop castle. **p174**

49 **Peña Cortada Loop** Follow the water, from Roman aqueduct to medieval village to rushing river. **p176**

50 **Serra de Bèrnia Loop** Get away from city bustle on this circuit around – and through – a mountaintop. **p180**

51 **Cadaqués to Cap de Creus** From one of Spain's most enticing coastal towns to the mainland's easternmost point. **p182**

52 **Volcanoes of Garrotxa** Dense green woodlands cloak dozens of old volcanic cones in a uniquely lovely landscape. **p184**

53 **Costa Brava Magic** Sandy coves, cliff-edge pine woods, white fishing villages, turquoise waters. **p186**

Explore
MEDITERRANEAN COAST

Despite the images of mass tourism that might be conjured by names like Benidorm and Lloret de Mar, Spain's Mediterranean coast is often wild and beautiful, while inland rise rugged mountains with networks of exciting trails almost unknown to non-Spaniards. And all a short drive from two exciting cities, Barcelona and Valencia.

BARCELONA
With boundless culture, fabled architecture and unrivalled drinking and dining options, Catalonia's capital calls for more than a night. And with Spain's second-busiest airport and high-speed trains from Paris, Madrid and Andalucía, it's easy to reach – then it's relatively easy to reach walks from here.

GIRONA
Convenient for most places in northern Catalonia, this medieval walled city makes a smaller (population 100,000), quieter alternative to Barcelona. A jewel box of Gothic churches and Modernista mansions, it nevertheless has a diverse dining and nightlife scene. Girona's airport is a Ryanair hub, with flights around Europe.

VALENCIA
Thanks to a solid network of suburban trains, Valencia is within easy reach of many good trails. It's also a lively city (cut through by a 9km-long park, a quality walk in its own right) with excellent restaurants for refuelling at the end of the day.

MORELLA
The heart of the Maestrat (Maestrazgo) region, with a picturesque mountaintop castle, this town is big enough to cover all your food and gear needs, and many trails start or pass through here. It's on the bus line between the coast and Zaragoza, but a car gives access to even more picturesque villages nearby.

BENIDORM
Whether you're in this seaside party capital or the adjoining towns, you can head up into the hills easily by car, and in some cases hop on local buses that will take you to higher elevations in less than an hour.

WHEN TO GO
Walking is most comfortable from April to mid-June and September and October, though near the coast it's possible to walk year-round (start early in summer). Inland mountains see snow, and can be blustery as late as March, but they're a balmy escape in summer. For swimming on the Costa Brava, sea temperatures reach low 20s (°C) July to September.

TRANSPORT
A train runs along the coast but stops only in cities. For towns in-between, take local

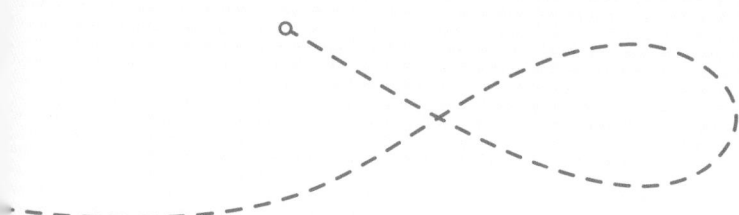

buses or Valencia's suburban rail network. In Valencia, the towns that are not served by commuter rail have buses with schedules geared to townspeople heading to the city for the day, and not so much the other way – so a car can help here and in the whole area of Maestrat and Els Ports. In Catalonia, buses run inland, and to Girona. A taxi can be called in nearly every town.

 **WHERE TO STAY**

Barcelona and Valencia of course give the full range of options; book well ahead in Barcelona. In Catalonia, Montserrat is majestic at night, after day trippers leave. Begur is an attractive base for the Costa Brava Magic walk, with several hotels in 19th-century mansions, and **Casamar** (☎972 30 01 04; www.hotelcasamar.net; Carrer del Nero 3; r incl breakfast €120-160; ⊙mid-Apr-Dec; ❄🛜) in Llafranc is a very good family-run hotel with a top-class restaurant. Staying in charming Cadaqués is part of the appeal of the Cap de Creus walk: **Hostal Vehí** (☎972 25 84 70; www.hostalvehi.com; Carrer de l'Església 6; s/d €65/95; ⊙Mar-Oct; ❄🛜) is

an excellent midrange option. In Garrotxa, Olot's **Can Blanc** (☎972 27 60 20; www.canblanc.es; Passatges de la Deu; s/d/tr incl breakfast €72/114/156; P❄🛜♨) is a country-house delight, and there are more options between the town and Santa Pau village. In the Valencia region, Chelva's old quarter has a few cosy options, and every village has at least one spotless, bargain *hostal*. The Xàtiva Loop (see p190) is a good excuse to stay at the great **Montsant** (☎962 27 50 81; www.mont-sant.com; Subida al Castillo; incl breakfast s €108-144, d €120-168; ⊙Feb-Dec; P❄🛜♨) hotel. Campgrounds are available, but not plentiful.

👍 **WHAT'S ON**

Falles (⊙mid-Mar) Valencia's residents build hundreds of giant papier-mâché puppets and parade them in the streets for five days before setting them on fire.

Cantada d'Havaneres (⊙1st Sat in Jul) Calella de Palafrugell celebrates Catalonia's 19th-century links to Cuba with a festival of melancholy Caribbean sea shanties.

Festival de Cap Roig (⊙mid-Jul–mid-Aug) Top artists of varied musical genres – past headliners have included Lady Gaga and Paco de Lucía – take the stage in the beautiful Cap Roig gardens near Calella de Palafrugell.

La Tomatina (⊙last Wed in Aug) Get messy at Buñol's legendary tomato-throwing festival.

Festes de la Mercè (⊙around 24 Sep) Barcelona's biggest party, which lasts for four days, involves concerts, dancing, parades, street theatre and the building of *castells* (human castles).

Resources

Parcs de Catalunya (http://parcsnaturals.gencat.cat) Detailed information on Catalonia's natural parks, where three of our walks are located, in five languages including English.

Camins de Ronda: The Costa Brava Way (Sergi Lara & Jordi Puig; 2010) Useful companion guide to walking 255km of the Costa Brava from Blanes to Collioure in France.

Casal dels Volcans (http://parcsnaturals.gencat.cat/en/garrotxa) Main information office for the Garrotxa Parc Natural, in Olot, with a volcano museum and pleasant cafe in the same building.

Morella Turística (www.morella.net/morellaturistica) Details on most walks in the Maestrat region.

Parcs Naturals de la Comunitat Valenciana (www.parquesnaturales.gva.es) Detailed maps of all trails.

47

MONTSERRAT

DURATION	DIFFICULTY	DISTANCE	START/END
3hr return	Easy	8km	Monestir de Montserrat

TERRAIN Earth and rock footpaths, steps

An astonishing, 10km-long massif of giant rock pillars, Montserrat ('serrated mountain') rears up from the Catalan countryside 30km northwest of Barcelona. One nook of the mountain holds the historic **Monestir de Montserrat** (pictured; www.abadiamontserrat.cat). You can combine the monastery with an exhilarating mountain walk in a day trip from Barcelona using R5 line trains from Plaça d'Espanya station to Montserrat Aeri (one hour), then the Aeri cable car (http://aerideressat.com).

Many walking trails thread the mountain (see http://muntanyamontserrat.gencat.cat) but it's hard to beat the trip to the highest point, **Sant Jeroni** (1237m). Start by riding the **Funicular de Sant Joan** (www.cremallerademontserrat.cat; one-way/return €9.10/14; every 12min 10am-4.50pm Nov-Mar, to 5.50pm Apr-Jun & mid-Sep-Oct, to 6.50pm Jul-mid-Sep, closed 3 weeks Jan) up from the monastery area. From its top station (971m) a good, well-signed, shady path winds northwest to the Sant Jeroni summit. Take care not to stray from the path in cloud or mist.

Stunning views of awesome rock pillars and turrets unfold almost immediately. Across the valley, the rock **l'Elefant** bears a remarkable resemblance to an elephant's head. As the path steepens, you pass the **Ermita de Sant Jeroni** chapel. In about 20 minutes more, you're at the summit. Terrible precipices drop sheer away from the mountaintop **viewing platform**, surrounded by a reassuring guard-rail.

Returning, take a path to the left signposted 'Monestir de Montserrat pel Pla dels Ocells', 700m after the Ermita de Sant Jeroni. Descend gently through **woodlands** and finally down a narrowing **ravine** back to the monastery complex.

48

CAMÍ DELS MOLINS

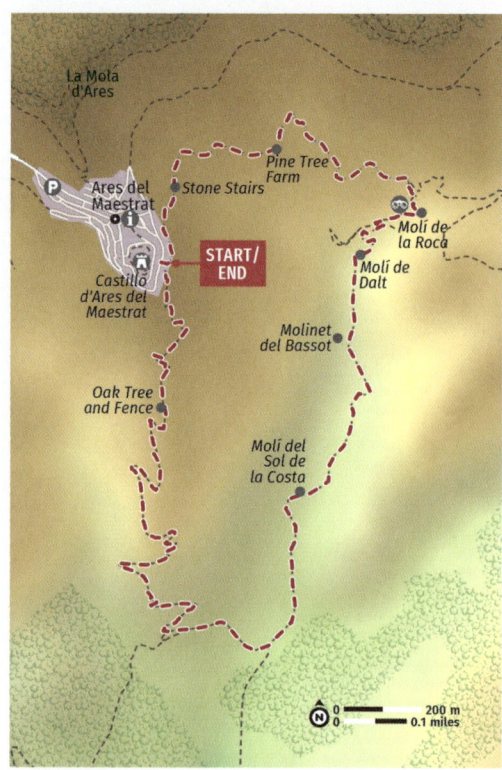

DURATION	DIFFICULTY	DISTANCE	START/END
2hr return	Easy	6.3km	Ares del Maestrat

TERRAIN	Switchbacks, farm roads, shaded ravine

Perched on a pinnacle, the rock-hewn fortress of Ares (pictured) dominates this walk, even as you descend into the valley far below. The trail circles past five 18th-century mills that are now the domain of nimble Pyrenean chamois, wild violets and birds of prey. In spring, the waterfall at the top of the ravine is flowing.

Marked with green-and-white waymarkers, the trail (SL-CV45) starts on the southeast side of the village, just outside the walls. A footpath cuts between farm terraces to the 'prow' of Ares' hill, with a grand view far down the valley. By a **large oak tree**, pass through a wire fence to join a rough stone road.

After zigzagging down the hill, you reach the river valley. Turn left on a narrow road (sealed, then dirt), which passes the lowest of the five mills, **Molí del Sol de la Costa**. Nicely restored, it's occasionally open to demonstrate flour milling and the waterworks system. Even if it's closed, note the impressive bird claw mounted on the door.

Just after the next mill, **Molinet del Bassot**, the trail narrows to a small footpath that slowly ascends through terraces on the hillside opposite Ares. At the third mill, **Molí de Dalt**, start looking – and listening – for chamois. The small wild goats give a birdlike 'cheep' when alarmed. The **fourth mill** is immediately uphill.

At the top of the ravine, **Molí de la Roca** sits astride the water source. This is a good picnic spot, with the view down where you've just walked, as well as up to the ever-visible Ares castle. The gradual climb back to town leads through a shady **pine-tree farm** and up **centuries-old stone stairs**, by the barest remnants of Moorish-era town walls.

Best for
WILDLIFE

49

PEÑA CORTADA LOOP

Best for
BRINGING THE PAST TO LIFE

DURATION	DIFFICULTY	DISTANCE	START/END
3½hr return	Easy	15.5km	Calles

TERRAIN	Clear trail, dirt roads and a town walk

This is one of the most popular day hikes in Valencia, thanks to its combination of easy trails and varied scenery, which includes wooded ravines, the impressive tunnels of a 1st-century Roman aqueduct system, a shaded river stroll and the pretty medieval town of Chelva.

GETTING HERE

Hispano Chelvana (www.hispanochelvana.com) runs infrequent buses from Valencia to Calles and Chelva (about 1½ hours). Year-round it's possible to go out and back by bus on Saturdays; in summer, there's additional service on weekdays. Otherwise, it's an easy drive from Valencia.

STARTING POINT

Park on the north or east bank of the river in Calles, just west of the bridge into town. For coffee or snacks, cross into the village centre.

For the trailhead turn the opposite way, on the paved street running uphill (north and west). Cross the road to Ermita de Santa Quiteria, where yellow-and-white PRCV92 signs mark the way further north.

01 For the first 1.5km or so, the route follows a narrow, intermittently paved road that criss-crosses a thin stream. You very gradually gain altitude while cliffs slowly rise alongside. A **trail sign** marks the point where you leave the road for good, and head on a narrower trail into the Rambla de Alcotas, a deep, dry ravine.

02 A short **stone staircase** takes you up out of the dry stream bed, along the east side of the canyon. (If you take the loop through the rambla as described in the Into the Woods box, this is where it joins the main trail.)

03 You've done most of your climb, and at this **viewpoint** where the ravine turns west, take a minute to look back on your progress.

04 After about 350m, a **second viewpoint** stands just below the aqueduct channel, which runs west to east. Resist the urge to clamber in – this channel is technically (if not thoroughly) fenced off, and there are more interesting tunnels ahead. A 100m detour east, following the watercourse (it would have been covered with terracotta tiles when it was in use), leads to a small round **lime kiln**. The Torre Castro loop (see the Into the Woods box) comes in from the east to join here.

05 To control erosion, follow the newest waymarkers, passing below the aqueduct itself, then dipping into a shallow saddle and turning sharply west. Here is the start of a much longer **section of tunnel**, more than 1m wide but less than 2m high, so watch your head. Two windows are carved out, giving a view down the ravine and of swallows diving – a nice picnic spot if you're here on a quiet day. Look out below the western window – there are footholds cut in the rock, probably made by the people building the tunnel.

06 At the end of the tunnels is an extremely **narrow pass between the stones**: the namesake *peña cortada* (cut rock; pictured).

Into the Woods

Some walkers prefer to spend more time in the woods, especially in summer, when the shadeless walk from the aqueduct to Chelva can be unpleasant. For that, there are two options. The more strenuous one is to turn right (east) off the route a bit less than 1km after the *ermita*, following signs for Torre Castro, the ruins of a watchtower set on a ridgeline. This takes in a good view and then rejoins the main trail near stop 04. Another, easier variation is to follow the main trail up through the tunnels and across the bridge, then, in the parking lot on the north side, take a low trail back, through the bottom of the rambla (ravine).

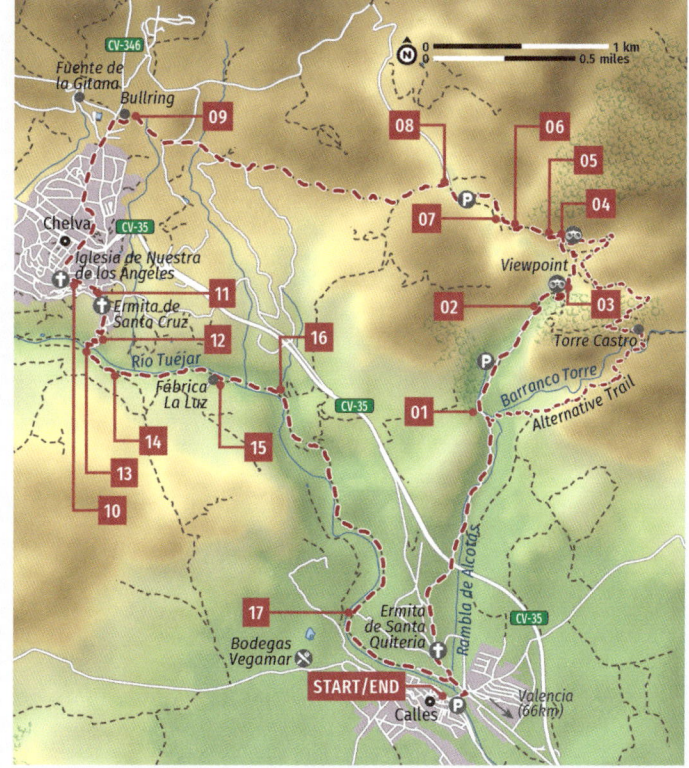

07 The engineering drama continues after the narrow pass, where you emerge at an 18m-high, **triple-arched aqueduct** (pictured) that carried the water across the ravine below. It's likely that the rock cut from the pass was then used to build the bridge.

08 The trail passes through a parking area (the closest car access to the aqueduct), then briefly follows the access road north. After 100m, look for a **dirt path to the west**, identified by waymarkers. This cuts through olive groves and crests a hill. There it joins a dirt road that runs to Chelva in less than 2km.

09 The path leads round the corner of the cemetery and into the parking lot of the **town bullring**. The traces of the aqueduct – now the main channel of the area's *acequia* (canal) system – continue across the road; you can detour a few minutes' walk west, following signs for Fuente de la Gitana, where there is also a low Roman bridge. To continue from the bullring, turn left and walk southwest, gently downhill all the way, into the town centre.

JULIAN BOHORQUEZ/SHUTTERSTOCK ©

10 Chelva's **plaza mayor** features a public tap – refill your water here, or settle at a cafe to enjoy the view of the grand four-tier facade of the **cathedral**. Synchronise your watch with its complex clock, which also marks the days of the week.

11 Exit the *plaza mayor* on the eastern corner, via Calle Caballeros, which leads into Chelva's oldest neighbourhoods. Alternatively, take stairs south to Barrio de Azoque, Chelva's old Jewish district. Your ultimate destination is further east, Barrio del Arrabal, the former Arab quarter, and **Ermita de Santa Cruz**. Built as a mosque (Mezquita de Benaeça) in 1370, it was converted to a small church in the 16th century.

12 From the *ermita*, continue downhill and southeast. When in doubt, take the downwards street, following occasional signs for the Ruta de Agua, as well as the sound of water in the street drains.

You will emerge from the walls at the **town's southeast corner**, at the top of a hill spread with terrace farms – all watered by the old aqueduct, now an *acequia*.

13 Descend to the small **Río Tuéjar**, where there's another water tap if you need it. A detour right (upstream, northwest) takes you to **La Playeta**, a favourite local swimming area at a wide, calm spot in the river, in a little less than 1km.

14 The trail ascends the south bank of the river, yielding a great view of Chelva on the opposite hill. In about 200m, a **set of stairs** leads back down towards the river –

178/MEDITERRANEAN COAST

When Life Gives You Limestone…

The limestone of this area presented both problems and solutions for Roman engineers. Limestone is relatively fragile, and here even more so due to the bedrock's steep slope. Channels carved into a slope are prone to cave-ins – so tunnels were required. As for solutions, limestone makes a versatile building substance. Heated to form the white powder calcium oxide (aka quicklime), it can then be used in plaster and concrete, to seal the channel. A final coat of whitewash also had the benefit of raising the pH level of the water and purifying it. The visible whitewash in the aqueduct is from a 2014 restoration, but the white inside the lime kiln near stop 04 is probably original.

follow this, rather than the PR-CV92 trail waymarkers, which continue up and over the hill. (Following PR-CV92 makes a slightly longer route back to Calles, through more vineyards and olive groves – preferable if you're walking in cool weather and want more sun.)

15 Thanks to its position by the river, Chelva was the first town in the area with electricity, in 1900. The first hydroelectric plant was upstream at La Playeta; the second, **Fábrica La Luz**, was built here in the 1920s. It's in ruins, but the river here is also good for a little dip. A short walk downstream, the path crosses the river.

16 Look carefully for a poorly **waymarked spot** where the trail leads to the right, away from the dirt access road. Head down into the riverside greenery, rather than continuing uphill on the dirt track. After 300m, the trail merges again with another dirt track.

17 Follow black-and-white-stencilled Ruta del Agua signs and generally hug the riverbank for the next 1.3km, until you're on the edge of Calles and the start of a **paved riverside path**. This more maintained park area follows the river around a curve, where there's a bridge across to central Calles. Continue straight to return to the parking area where you started.

TAKE A BREAK

In addition to cafes in Chelva and Calles, and at La Playeta, you can take a more structured break at **Bodegas Vegamar** (962 10 98 13; www.vegamar.es; Camino Garcesa, Calles; 2hr tour & tasting €10; 8am-1pm & 3-6pm Mon-Fri, 10am-2pm Sat), the home winery for a gourmet foods company that distributes all over Spain. Book two days in advance for a two-hour tour and tasting session, and perhaps a meal at the winery restaurant. The vineyards are just west of Calles, and if you follow the full PR-CV92 (rather than the Río Tuéjar route described here), you walk right past it.

50

SERRA DE BÈRNIA LOOP

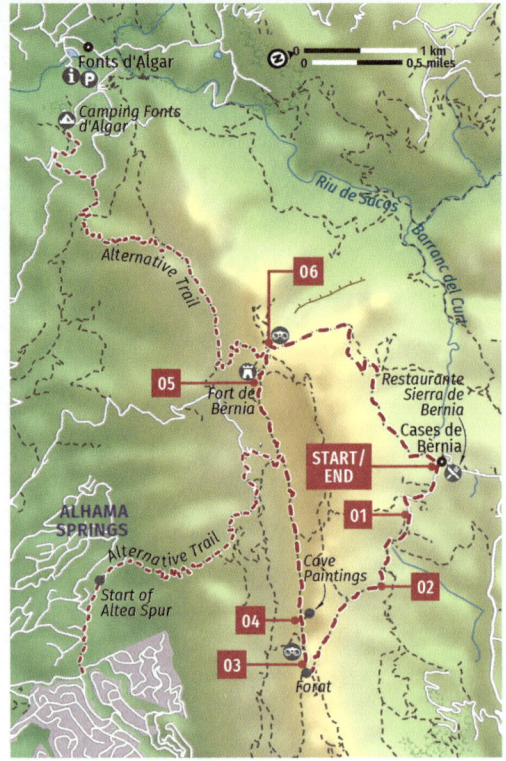

DURATION	DIFFICULTY	DISTANCE	START/END
3½hr return	Moderate	9.5km	Cases de Bèrnia

TERRAIN	Rocky scramble, level footpaths, scree

Get up above the coastal sprawl for dreamy views – as far as Ibiza on a clear day – as well as the ruins of a 16th-century fort, some petroglyphs and a cryptic mountain tunnel. A few steep patches are offset by level paths locals have travelled for centuries. For a longer outing, with easier coastal access, start at one of the spurs on the south face of the mountain.

GETTING HERE
The only way to reach Cases de Bèrnia is by car, on a very scenic route up from Benissa. For alternative, more easily accessible starting points, see the Two Variations box.

STARTING POINT
Cases de Bèrnia is no more than a few farms and a rustic (and not always open) restaurant at the base of the mountain's north slope. There's a parking area by the trailhead.

01 Set out on the loop clockwise (east), as it's far less harrowing to climb the steep slope than it is to descend. Starting on a 4WD track, it's easy at first; the real trail begins about 1.2km along, at a **water tap**.

02 The route up can be a bit of a scramble, and waymarkers are not always clear. About halfway, you cross a steep **scree field**, followed by a few sharp switchbacks.

03 The ridge of the mountain sticks up like stegosaurus spikes – but, fortunately, you don't have to climb over. Instead, you go through: a 20m-long tunnel called a **forat** pierces the stone and you emerge, after an all-fours clamber, on the south side. This is the highest point on the trail (840m), with a breathtaking view of the sea (pictured).

🚶 Two Variations

For less of a drive and more of a walk, join the mountain loop via two spurs on the southern slope. The shorter option, actually the 3.5km start of PRCV7, goes from Altea la Vella, at the top of Calle Colina; the trail has no shade, so start early. (Transit purists could start walking from the tram stop at l'Olla, but it adds another hour, and is fairly steep.)

The longer spur (5.5km, PRCV48) starts above Fonts de l'Algar; park at or taxi to Camping Fonts de l'Algar. If you come back down this way, stop at the *fonts* (waterfalls) for a dip, and buy some *nísperos* (loquats, grown in the plastic-tented orchards here) in season.

Best for
COASTAL VIEWS

ANDREI DASCALU/SHUTTERSTOCK ©

04 About 500m along the south face of the mountain, a short path leads up to Neolithic **cave paintings**. They're not much to see, but you gain some elevation, and a sign here identifies all the visible peaks. Continuing west, the trail is level, but watch your feet, as the drop is severe, and the intermittent scree fields can be slippery.

05 Most hikers stop for a picnic at the ruins of **Fort de Bèrnia**, built by King Felipe II in 1562. Not much later, it was squatted by Muslims escaping persecution, and Felipe III had the place dismantled in 1612 in order to oust the refugees. As a result, few walls remain, but you can still see its four-pointed outline.

06 Near where the spur from Fonts de l'Algar joins, the trail crosses a **saddle** between peaks, and a whole new vista opens up, as you follow a largely level route across a dramatically steep slope. This is a portion of the old footpath used for trade between Xaló and Callosa. Once you come around to the north side of the mountain, this path turns into a dirt track, which descends gradually all the way to the starting point.

☕ TAKE A BREAK

Rustic **Restaurante Sierra de Bèrnia** ( 609 129729, 676 871866; Cases de Bèrnia; mains €10-20; ⏱ noon-6pm Sun-Fri) can sate you with paella cooked as it ought to be, over a wood fire on a giant hearth. Seats outside have a view of the mountain you just came from. Make a reservation before you hike and be prepared to pay in cash. If it's closed, there are two similar restaurants a bit further down the road.

MEDITERRANEAN COAST/**181**

51

CADAQUÉS TO CAP DE CREUS

DURATION	DIFFICULTY	DISTANCE	START/END
5-6hr return	Moderate	15km	Cadaqués

TERRAIN	Footpaths, paved and unpaved roads

Cadaqués, a tumble of white houses ringing a superb natural harbour, is one of the loveliest little towns on the Spanish Mediterranean. Our route runs up the picturesquely contorted coast to mainland Spain's panoramic easternmost point, Cap de Creus. Thorny vegetation encroaches on parts of the path, so good leg-covering is recommended!

GETTING HERE

Moventis/Sarfa (http://compras.moventis.es) runs buses to Cadaqués from Barcelona (€25, 2¾ hours, two or three daily), Figueres (€5.60, one hour, four to eight daily) and elsewhere.

STARTING POINT

The foot of Carrer Miranda on the east side of Cadaqués bay.

01 Walk up Carrer Miranda, which becomes a pedestrian lane, emerging on a paved road. Turn right, passing the **Ermita de Sant Baldiri** chapel, and walk down the road towards Port Lligat.

02 Turn right at Hotel Port Lligat down the steps to the **Casa Museu Dalí** (☎ 972 25 10 15; www.salvador-dali.org; adult/senior & student/child under 14yr €14/8/free; ⏰ 9.30am-9pm mid-Jun–mid-Sep, 10.30am-6pm mid-Sep–early Jan & mid-Feb–mid-Jun, closed early Jan–mid-Feb, plus Mon Nov–mid-Mar), long-time home of surrealist Salvador Dalí (1904–89). Book your visit well ahead if you want to experience the artistic wackiness within.

03 From the far end of Port Lligat beach, follow the road round a U-bend. Fork right 170m later, passing little **S'Alqueria Petita** beach, and take the road ahead uphill at a junction 300m past the beach, then turn right down a path

The Tip of the Cape

A 2km circuit takes you on from Cap de Creus lighthouse to the actual easternmost point of the Spanish mainland. From the 'Itinerari 15' sign just north of the lighthouse, wind round to the right, and go left at a 'Punto de Cap de Creus' signpost. The path runs across jagged volcanic rocks and is poorly marked. Look for occasional diamond-shaped red markers on the ground. Red-paint GR11 arrows on the rocks guide you up the final hump of land to a little shelter at the end of the path. Take care along a short stretch with a sheer drop. Heading back, turn left at the Cova de S'Infern sign to loop round via a deep inlet connected to the sea through an impressive natural archway.

Best for PRETTY VILLAGES

signed Cap de Creus 300m after that. The path winds 500m down and up through scrub and trees. Meeting a road, turn right, then right again after 200m onto another path signed Cap de Creus.

04 Passing between low stone walls and olive trees, you'll reach an unpaved road after 700m. Turn right, passing between a few **houses and pines**, and turn left onto a path signed Cap de Creus after 700m.

05 The stony dirt path winds up and down across scrub-covered hillsides with little shade for 2.7km. Just a few olives and vines remain from the crops that enriched Cadaqués in past centuries. Cap de Creus lighthouse appears ahead. Down to the right are several enticing-looking coves: easiest to reach is **Cala Jugadora**, accessed by a steep, unsigned little path after 2km.

06 At a fork below the lighthouse road, go right, following paint stripes. Reaching the road, head 150m up to the right, then veer right up the clear stone-paved path to the **Far (Lighthouse) del Cap de Creus**. Soak up the panoramas and restore energy at one of the two restaurants, and maybe extend your walk to the tip of the cape. Then return to Cadaqués (pictured) the way you came – or call a **taxi** (606 067015, 626 526832; about €10)!

TAKE A BREAK

At the lighthouse, **Bar Restaurant Cap de Creus** (972 19 90 05; www.facebook.com/restaurante.capdecreus; Cap de Creus; mains €9-24; 10am-7pm Mon-Thu, to midnight Fri-Sun Nov-Apr, 9am-midnight daily May-Oct, hours vary) offers a winning combination of Catalan, Indian and Italian food.

52

VOLCANOES OF GARROTXA

DURATION	DIFFICULTY	DISTANCE	START/END
4hr return	Moderate	12km	Can Serra
TERRAIN	Forest paths, paved and unpaved roads.		

The Garrotxa region in verdant northern Catalonia is home to 40 small extinct volcanoes covered in dense green woodlands – a uniquely beautiful landscape that makes a delightful half-day's walk.

GETTING HERE
Teisa (www.teisa-bus.com) runs buses to Olot, the pleasant main town of La Garrotxa. On April, May, October and November weekends and holidays there's bus service from Olot to Aparcament Fageda d'en Jordà. At other times, you'll need your own wheels or a taxi from Olot (4km).

STARTING POINT
Can Serra information office of the **Parc Natural de la Zona Volcànica de la Garrotxa** (http://old.parcsnaturals. gencat.cat/en/garrotxa), next to the Aparcament Fageda d'en Jordà parking area beside the GI524,

4km southeast of Olot. The walk route follows the park's itinerary 1.

01 Take the underpass beneath the GI-524 and follow signs towards the Volcà de Santa Margarida (sometimes spelt Margarita). The path winds through the wonderful **Fageda d'en Jordà** beech forest. In spring and summer the tall beeches fill the forest with an intense dappled green light; in October and November the forest becomes a riotous autumn palette of reds, browns and yellows.

02 After 2km the path becomes an unpaved road. Meeting a paved road 300m later, turn right and pass the installations of **La Fageda** (www. fageda.com) yoghurt cooperative.

03 The road ends at a private property: turn left along a path with a small 'Volcà de Santa Margarida' sign. After 250m, follow the

184/MEDITERRANEAN COAST

A Little Vulcanology

Garrotxa's volcanoes are between 350,000 and 11,500 years old, the result of movements in the Eurasian tectonic plate that allowed magma to escape through the earth's crust. The youngest is Croscat, whose lava flow extends 6km. It's the humidity of this lava field that has enabled the Fageda d'en Jordà beech forest to develop at the unusually low altitude of 550m. To learn more, visit Olot's **Museu dels Volcans** (https://museus.olot.cat; Parc Nou, Avinguda de Santa Coloma; adult/child €3/free; 10am-1pm & 3-6pm Tue-Fri, 10am-2pm & 3-6pm Sat, 10am-2pm Sun) or find *A Field Guide to La Garrotxa Volcanic Zone* at http://old.parcsnaturals.gencat.cat/en/garrotxa.

Santa Margarida signs to the right and up through woods. Reaching a paved road, go left downhill to the **Església de Sant Miquel de Sacot**, a small Romanesque church rebuilt in the 18th century.

04 Go down to the right of the church and branch right after 60m. Joining a track in 150m, turn right, down to a paved road. Turn right, then at a T-junction after 100m, take the path uphill ahead into the woods. Following Santa Margarida signs, climb steadily for 600m to a sharp left bend, then another 600m to a fork of paths. Head down to the right to walk round the grassy crater of the **Volcà de Santa Margarida**, with the 11th-century **Ermita Santa Margarida** chapel. Returning to the volcano's northern rim, take the downhill path signposted 'Àrea de Santa Margarida'.

05 From the **Àrea de Santa Margarida** parking area, cross the busy road by the zebra crossing and continue along its far side. Fork right after 80m to Bar Santa Margarida. Turn left along a **dirt track** 550m after the bar. The track, almost shadeless, curves round the north side of the **Volcà del Croscat**.

06 Meeting a paved road after 1km, go 30m ahead then left along a track. After 400m turn right onto a path signed 'Fageda d'en Jordà (Aparcament)'. In another 600m turn left at another Aparcament sign. Reaching a concrete road in 200m, turn right to **Can Serra**.

 **TAKE A BREAK**

Stop at **Bar Santa Margarida** (Carretera Gl524 Km 6.4; mains €6-14; 9am-5pm), 300m past the Santa Margarida parking area, for a drink and a snack – or a more substantial salad or grill if you're in the mood.

53
COSTA BRAVA MAGIC

Best for COASTAL VIEWS

DURATION	DIFFICULTY	DISTANCE	START/END
11-12hr one-way (2 days)	Moderate	33km	Palamós/ Begur
TERRAIN	Paved and unpaved roads, footpaths, beaches		

The coastal trails of the central Costa Brava (Rugged Coast) are a journey of mesmerising beauty through clifftop pine woods to little-visited sandy beaches, dozens of rocky coves and still-quaint fishing villages – all lapped by waters of 50 shades of turquoise.

Much of this route follows the well-marked GR92 Catalan coastal footpath, and several stretches are along *camins de ronda,* coastal paths used for centuries by fisherfolk or police patrols looking for smugglers.

GETTING HERE

Moventis/Sarfa (http://compras.moventis.es) runs buses to Palamós from Barcelona (€17, two hours, six to nine daily) and numerous places in northern Catalonia. Its Begur-Palamós service (€1.75, 25 to 50 minutes, three to eight daily) enables you to leave a car at either end of our route and return to it afterwards.

STARTING POINT

The east end of Palamós' main beach, 250m from the Sarfa bus terminal and with a convenient car park (€12 per 24 hours).

01 Walk east through **El Pedró**, the older part of largely modern Palamós, and on to Carretera de la Fosca heading east. Opposite the Port Nautic building (Carretera de la Fosca 9), take the path down to the right. Pass a campground and descend to the stony little beach **Cala Margarida**. Almost immediately, turn left up steps between two stone houses, bringing you up to Carrer del Tamariu. Turn right at the crossroads after 50m, then right again into the pine woods of the **Parc Urbà de Cap Gros**.

02 Drop down to the 400m curve of semi-urban **Platja de La Fosca**. From this beach's far end, the path climbs to the small Sant Esteve de Mar castle then wiggles round through pine woods and past the tiny fishing settlement **S'Alguer** to the glorious 300m sandy sweep of **Platja de Castell**. This is the start of a wonderful, undeveloped, vehicle-free 4km stretch of coast, part of the Espai Natural Protegit de Castell-Cap Roig.

03 Walk up to the headland topped by the remains of the **Poblat Ibèric de Castell**, a pre-Roman village, and continue through pines along the top of steep cliffs above rocky coves, following signs to Cala Estreta and Cap Roig.

04 Reaching an unpaved road 2km from the Poblat Ibèric, go 400m straight on then turn right down the path to Cala Estreta. Go left at the bottom and you emerge on **Cala Estreta** (pictured), the first of four sandy, crescent-moon coves where clothing becomes increasingly optional as you go along. You'll be hard-pressed not to at least kick off your footwear and take a paddle here.

05 Climb the steps at the far end of the fourth cove, **Cala del Crit**, and take the track straight ahead at the top. At a multiple junction after 600m uphill, go right, following the Cap Roig and Calella de Palafrugell sign.

06 In 1km, at a five-way junction of tracks and roads, take the road leading ahead downhill, then turn right down steps after 150m. Go left at the bottom and turn right down more steps after 150m. Go left again at the bottom to wind past rocky coves and through a couple of tunnels and emerge on a paved street after 700m. Walk 200m ahead then round the right side of Hotel Sant Roc and on into **Calella de Palafrugell**, with two popular town beaches.

Begur

Handsome old Begur makes a very appealing place to bed down before or after your walk. Its six surviving watchtowers and the hilltop **Castell de Begur**, dating from 1019, are testament to the strategic role it has played in numerous conflicts for control of Catalan territory down the centuries.

The web of old streets around the castle harbours several good restaurants including contemporary **Catalan Aiguaclara** (972 62 29 05; www.hotelaiguaclarabegur.com; Carrer de Sant Miquel 2; mains €15-22; from 6pm Tue-Sat), in an 1866 mansion, and **Can Torrades** (972 19 91 88; can torrades@gmail.com; Carrer Concepció Pi 'Tató' 5; mains €7-15; 7pm-midnight, with a lovely upstairs terrace for warm evenings.

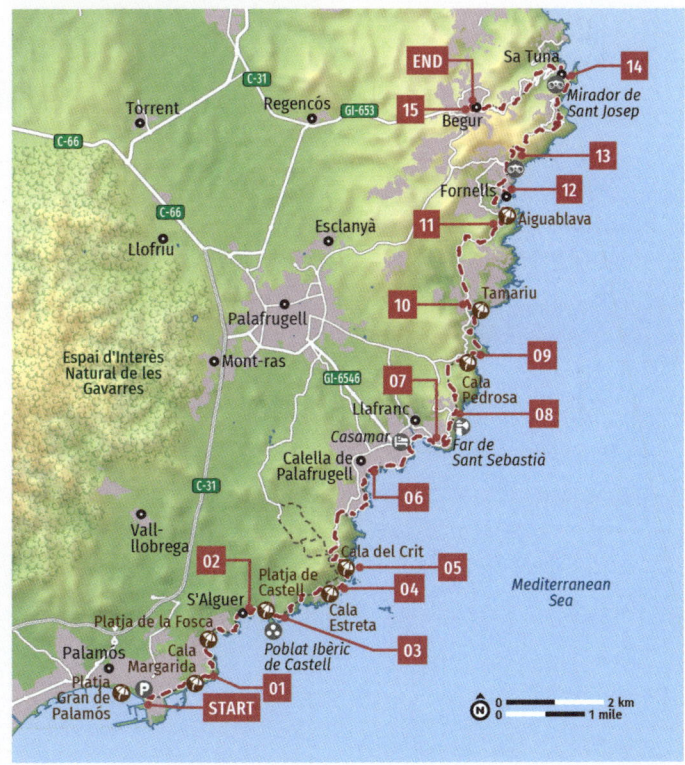

07 Turn right off Passeig Canadell down steps to the excellent Tragamar restaurant, then circle the headland, passing a 400-year-old watchtower. Walk along Carrer Cap de Creus and Passeig Miserachs, then down the steps to the beach of **Llafranc**, the second small fishing-cum-tourism town along this stretch of coast. More tranquil and stylish than Calella, less exclusive than Tamariu, it's a good spot to stop overnight.

08 Leave Llafranc by steps up from the far east end of the beach. Turn right along the street above and wind your way 1km uphill to the **Far de Sant Sebastià** lighthouse. Immediately past the lighthouse take the path to the right and along the seaward side of El Far restaurant, attached to an interesting little complex that includes a 15th-century lookout tower and an 18th-century church. Just beyond, pass along the right side of the excavated remains of the pre-Roman **Poblat Ibèric de Sant Sebastià de la Guarda** and head down a path into the woods.

09 Reaching a path junction within 100m, you briefly head steeply down to the right then level off, heading north. On a left-hand bend take a path to the right, zigzagging through woods. Red-and-white GR markers help show the way. Pass an open field, continue straight at a track crossroads, pass another field and then turn right down a path signposted to the stony but beautiful little beach of **Cala Pedrosa** (500m), on a classic turquoise-watered rocky inlet. Rustic **Barraca de Cala Pedrosa** (entrepans & salads €5-7) is a welcome refreshment stop.

10 Climb the left side of the cove by steps, which become a path with a wooden railing. The trail widens as it winds through pines, then picks its way across rocks for 10 to 15 minutes before the final 200m to **Tamariu** beach.

11 Leaving Tamariu, head north up the main street from the beach. Fork right onto the Begur road, but continue straight at a roundabout after 500m where Begur is signposted to the right. In another 550m, on a left-hand bend, take a path to the right indicated by an Aiguablava signpost that may be half-hidden by vegetation. The path winds up through mixed woodlands for 15 minutes and reaches a GR Aiguablava signpost directing you ahead down a concrete road. Meeting a bigger road, go left downhill for 700m. Turn sharp right down to the Aiguablava car park, and onto **Aiguablava** beach.

12 The steps up from the north end of the Aiguablava sands lead to a pathway along cliffs. Pass a small beach and descend to tiny Cala Malaret beach in **Fornells**. Continue round an even tinier

JOHN NOBLE/LONELY PLANET ©

bay and up the street to a viewpoint over Fornells' little rectangular harbour.

13 Follow Fornells' main street 250m up northwestwards, and turn right along Carrer Platja Fonda in front of Hotel Eetu. After 200m take a narrow path to the left immediately after crossing a tiny stream. Turn right at the top. The street ends after 80m: continue ahead on a footpath, which turns left uphill. Cross a concrete road and continue uphill through trees then up an open hillside. Views back over Aiguablava reward this half-hour of increasingly **steep ascent**. At the top, turn right along the road past Casa Candida, go left at the junction then immediately right along a footpath signposted Sa Tuna.

14 In 500m, after a stretch of high-level Mediterranean panoramas, meet an unpaved road and go 100m left down to a paved road. Turn right and walk 1km. On a right-hand bend turn left down a path (don't follow the gravel road signed Mirador). The path zigzags down to a junction where you follow the paved road straight ahead. This ends after 300m: follow the path up steps ahead. Wind your way up, down, up and along through **clifftop pine woods** then onto a spectacularly panoramic open section leading down to the **Mirador de Sant Josep**, a brick-and-stone monolith overlooking the bays of Sa Tuna (pictured) and Aiguafreda. The path descends, initially steeply, to the pretty village of **Sa Tuna**, where beachfront Hotel Sa Tuna (www.hostalsatuna.com; Passeig de l'Àncora 14; mains €18-38; ◐mid-Feb–mid-Oct; 🛜) is a good refreshment stop.

15 Take the steps up from the northwest corner of Sa Tuna's little beach to the stone-paved street Camí Vell. Follow this up round a U-bend, across a paved road and on uphill. You are now on the **Camí Vell de Sa Tuna**, an old track linking Sa Tuna with Begur. A mix of paved and dirt paths and tracks, it's well indicated by signs with its name, walking-route signposts and GR markers as it makes its way 3km uphill to charming old **Begur**.

 **TAKE A BREAK**

In Llafranc you can pick from a string of appealing beachfront restaurants. **Jani** (www.restaurantjani.com; Passeig de Cipsela 10; mains €11-18; ◐1.15-4.30pm & 8-11pm Tue-Sun) offers a shortish but well-executed Mediterranean menu, with efficient, friendly service. Or book a table at Michelin-starred **Casamar** (📞972 30 01 04; www.hotelcasamar.net; Carrer del Nero 3; mains €21-28, set menus €55-84; ◐1.30-3.30pm & 8.30-10.30pm Tue-Sat, 1.30-3.30pm Sun mid-Apr–Dec), inside the recommended **Casamar** (r incl breakfast €120-160; ◐mid-Apr–Dec; ❄🛜) hotel.

Also Try...

MONT CARO

The rugged, mountainous region Els Ports straddles the southwest corner of Catalonia and neighbouring parts of Aragón and Valencia. The highest peak, Caro (1441m), is a fine introduction and offers a decent chance of seeing ibex and raptors.

A good circular route is listed as walk 25 (Mirador de Caro) of the **Parc Natural dels Ports** (http://parcs naturals.gencat.cat). It starts and ends in little L'Esquirol, also called El Mascar, a 21km drive west from the town of Roquetes. You climb through pine woods to the Coll dels Pallers, then up the steepish rocky ridge, with a few minor scrambles (paint marks and cairns indicate the way), to the summit – which, despite the telecoms towers and the road arriving from the northeast, commands great vistas. The descent track, via the Coll de Vicari, criss-crosses the road several times.

DURATION 3-3½hr return
DIFFICULTY Moderate
DISTANCE 8km

XÀTIVA LOOP

Most visitors to Xàtiva go solely to see its tremendous castle, but it also has a pleasant loop hike through varied terrain, including a lush river valley. Plus you can zip here from Valencia in 40 minutes on the *cercanía* (suburban train).

The trail (PRV78) starts by the Font dels 25 Dolls, a grand fountain with 25 spouts, then passes under a 200m section of an 11th-century aqueduct. The prettiest stretch is along the Río Albaida, a local nature reserve where kingfishers and herons flourish. Palaeolithic remains have been found at Cova Negra near the river. The second half of the hike is a long, gradual climb, with little shade. For an easier trek, you can just hike to the cave and back, and save your energy for the climb up to the **Castillo de Xàtiva** (pictured; 962 27 42 74; www. xativaturismo.com; adult/child €2.40/1.20; 10am-6pm Tue-Sun Nov-Mar, to 7pm Apr-Oct), which has been strung along the summit above town.

DURATION 4½hr return
DIFFICULTY Moderate
DISTANCE 18km

SANGUER/SHUTTERSTOCK ©

COLLSEROLA

The Parc Natural de Collserola (www.parcnaturalcollserola.cat; pictured above) is 83 sq km of forested hills on Barcelona's northwest fringe.

Tibidabo (512m) is the highest and most visited spot, but for a good up-and-down walk through the forest, take the train from Plaça de Catalunya to Baixador de Vallvidrera station and walk 10 minutes to the park's information centre (Carretera de l'Església 92), where the Serra d'en Cardona route starts. You'll have inland views as far as Montserrat and the Montseny massif.

DURATION 2½hr return
DIFFICULTY Easy
DISTANCE 7km

MATAGALLS

The Catalan Pre-Coastal Range, about 30km inland, reaches some surprising heights, especially in the Montseny massif north of Barcelona. The ascent of Matagalls (1698m) makes a fine day out.

You need a vehicle: the route starts at the Coll de Sant Marçal (1100m), 30km north of Sant Celoni on the BV-5114 (80km, 1½ to two hours from Barcelona). The clearly marked path (part of the GR5.2 trail) runs up through lovely beech and oak woods and is steepest in the first 1.5km. Great panoramas from the top.

DURATION 2½-3hr return
DIFFICULTY Moderate
DISTANCE 8km

DESERT DE LES PALMES

The hill behind Benicàssim is a lush terrain of red rocks, tall pines and panoramic views up and down the coastline.

There are several trails criss-crossing the reserve. One good route is a loop from its info centre to Alt del Bartolo (728m). It's not remote but it does put you (relatively) on top of the world. A nice add-on is the 1km level walk to Castell de Montornès, a 10th-century fortification – the path is level, out on a ridgeline to the tower. You can also pick up a trail booklet from the Benicàssim tourist office.

DURATION 4hr return
DIFFICULTY Moderate
DISTANCE 7.7km

MALLORCA & MENORCA

54 **Platja de Cavalleria to Platja de Binimel·là** Family-friendly ramble along breezy bluffs and beaches. **p196**

55 **Cala Morell to Ciutadella** Pyramids, ancient tombs and cliffs along Menorca's wild northeast corner. **p198**

56 **Sant Tomàs to Son Xoriguer** Comprehensive tour of southern Menorca's unspoiled coves, promontories and woodland. **p200**

57 **La Trapa Monastery** Hike rugged coastal paths to scenic viewpoints and a monastery ruin. **p204**

58 **Valldemossa to Deià** Challenging climb and gorgeous descent from one arty village to another. **p206**

59 **Mirador de Ses Barques to Sa Calobra** Classic day hike comprising olive groves, cliffside trails and coves. **p208**

60 **Alcúdia Peninsula** Loop encompassing rocky crags, a remote beach, valleys and a forested ravine. **p212**

Explore MALLORCA & MENORCA

Mallorca and Menorca welcome visitors with a varied kaleidoscope of landscapes: pristine coves with turquoise waters, forested ravines, rocky canyons, precipitous cliffs, pine and holm-oak forests, remnants of ancient cultures and long stretches of white-sand beach. Though some trails are well-trodden, you may have the rest entirely to yourself.

CIUTADELLA

Contrasting with the brasher, more modern capital of Maó on the east end of the island, Ciutadella (aka Vella i Bella – 'Old and Beautiful'), Menorca's second city, is an attractive, distinctly Spanish west-coast settlement with a marina and an evocative old quarter lined with colonial-era architecture. Founded by the Carthaginians and known under the Moors as Medina Minurqa, it has a lively dining scene and excellent public transport connections to trailheads and main towns around the island.

VALLDEMOSSA

Picturesquely situated amid Tramuntana's wooded slopes, Valldemossa is one of Mallorca's most appealing villages. It's partly the setting and partly the tree-lined, cobbled lanes, stone houses, a smattering of attractive landmarks and a respectable dining scene. There are good public transport connections to Palma, Deià and Sóller, and it's a great base for exploring central Tramuntana, with a number of hikes departing directly from the village. Trails in the southwest corner of Mallorca are within easy driving reach.

SÓLLER

If you're planning on doing much hiking in central and northern Serra de Tramuntana or wish to explore Mallorca's west coast, Sóller is a fine jumping-off spot. With its graceful modernist architecture, galleries showcasing Picasso and Miró, picturesque surroundings in the form of mountains and fruit orchards, and decent dining, it's an easy drive from numerous trailheads. If beach time is a must, consider staying in nearby Port de Sóller, connected to Sóller by a vintage tram. Also, Sóller's location halfway along the west coast means that north-coast hikes are only an hour's drive away.

WHEN TO GO

The cooler months (March to May, September to October) are the best time to hit the trails in the Balearics, with mild weather and fewer tourists overall. Winter months bring rain and fog (at higher altitudes), while the summer months are peak tourist season on the islands, meaning high accommodation prices, roads clogged with traffic and weather generally being too hot to hike comfortably.

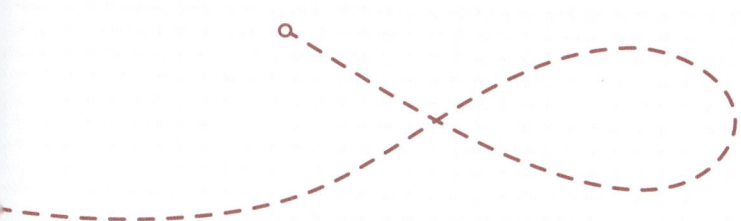

 TRANSPORT

International airports in Palma (Mallorca) and Maó (Menorca) are connected to the Spanish mainland and to international destinations like the UK and Germany by frequent flights. Menorca is easy enough to navigate by bus (though outside peak season you may need a taxi to get to some trailheads). In Mallorca, while the main towns and villages such as Valldemossa and Sóller are served by frequent buses from Palma, remoter trailheads are harder to reach. To make the most of the islands, you ideally need your own wheels.

 WHERE TO STAY

Accommodation on the islands goes from all-inclusive beach resorts and seaside hotels (mostly midrange) to family-run guesthouses, hostels, a few boutique hotels, plus self-catering apart-hotels. Your best bet is to base yourself in a town or village near your desired trailhead and/or with good public transport links. Book accommodation well ahead between May and October.

 WHAT'S ON

Semana Santa Between Monday of Easter week and Easter Sunday parades of *carapunats* (hooded penitents) take place all around Mallorca, with the biggest processions on Maundy Thursday, including solemn parades through the streets at night.

Festa de Sant Joan Taking place in Ciutadella around midsummer's eve, the week-long festivities comprise processions, jousting and horse parades, mock battles with hazelnut shells instead of ammunition, and a huge fireworks display to finish.

Nit de Foc (eve 22 Jun) In Palma de Mallorca, the night before the midsummer feast of St John is celebrated with abandon. The *correfoc* (fire running) begins in the Parc de la Mar, as costumed demons leap and dance in an infernal procession. To finish, the city's beaches host musical groups, bonfires and a crowd that parties until dawn.

Festival Chopin (Aug; www.festivalchopin.com) Classical-music performances are held in Valldemossa's Real Cartuja; most of the works are by Chopin, although music by other composers also features.

Resources

Camí de Cavalls (www.descobreixmenorca.com/es/cami-de-cavalls-2) Detailed breakdown of every stage of the hiking trail that encircles Menorca.

Camí de Cavalls 360° (www.camidecavalls360.com) Info on Menorca's epic hiking trail, complete with tips for hikers, trail runners and mountain bikers.

abcMallorca (www.abc-mallorca.com/hiking-in-mallorca) Tips for trekking in Mallorca, plus hiking trails arranged by theme.

Aemet (www.aemet.es) Weather forecasts for Spain's regions, including the Balearics.

Mallorca (www.infomallorca.net) Mallorca's official tourism website.

Menorca (www.menorca.es) Menorca's official tourism website.

Festa de Sant Bartolomeu (eve 24 Aug) Sóller's patron saint is celebrated in exuberant fashion the third week in August, culminating in a spectacular fire show featuring *esclabutzes* (demons).

Mare de Deu de Gracia (early Sep) Celebrating its patron saint, Our Lady of Grace, this exuberant festival in Maó, Menorca's capital, occurs over two days. A pilgrimage to her chapel is followed by horse processions through the streets, with professional riders showing off their skills. Music and dancing in the Plaça de la Conquesta follow.

54
PLATJA DE CAVALLERIA TO PLATJA DE BINIMEL·LÀ

DURATION	DIFFICULTY	DISTANCE	START/END
2½hr return	Easy	7km	Platja de Cavalleria

TERRAIN	Well-defined coastal trail, gentle uphill sections, no shade

Easily one of north Menorca's most spectacular short walks, this gently undulating cliff trail ends at a remote sandy beach, with panoramic views of two more glorious stretches of sand and a couple of sheltered coves along the way.

The trail begins at the Platja de Cavalleria car park, descending to a promontory, with the Cala Roja cove to the right, and wooden stairs leading down to the golden crescent of **Platja de Cavalleria**, popular with sunbathers and surfers. A gentle ascent behind the dunes affords a wonderful panoramic view of both this beach and the adjoining **Platja de Ferragut**, the latter popular with naturists.

From here, the dirt path skirts the coast, close to the waterline, passing the rocky spur of **Ses Pesqueres**, which surfers use as a jumping-off point, and coming to a Menorcan gate through a stone wall. You then descend gently to the pristine **Cala Mica** cove, with a rural house to one side, before the trail ascends a steep, grass-covered slope, passing two flotsam-and-jetsam-strewn coves, turning sharply inland and arriving at a panoramic **viewpoint**.

Shortly joining the unpaved Camí son Nadal, the trail then passes by a couple of houses before leading down to the golden sand of **Platja de Binimel·là**, complete with a popular seasonal restaurant. Return the same way.

If you have the energy, it is worth detouring from the Platja de Cavalleria car park to the Roman ruins of **Sanicera** and 18th-century **Torre de Sanitja** (4km return, one hour) beyond, signposted off the road to the Cavalleria promontory and lighthouse.

55

CALA MORELL TO CIUTADELLA

DURATION	DIFFICULTY	DISTANCE	START/END
6hr one-way	Easy	19km	Cala Morell/ Ciutadella
TERRAIN	Well-defined dirt trail, some paved sections, gentle inclines, no shade		

Comprising sea-battered cliffs, ancient cave dwellings, picturesque rock arches, a lighthouse and mysterious pyramids, this walk is a wonderful introduction to Menorca's uninhabited northeast coast. There's an almost primeval quality to this unique part of the island, where the rugged calcareous terrain and precipices plunging steeply into the sea contrast sharply with the pine and holm-oak forests, pastureland and white-sand coves that define much of Menorca.

GETTING HERE

From May to mid-September, bus route 62 runs from the north end of Ciutadella's Plaça des Pins to the bus stop by the Cala Morell roundabout.

STARTING POINT

From the bus stop, walk to the roundabout and turn left, passing the necropolis. The trail begins where the street bends uphill.

01 The trail leads towards the coast before turning westwards. It turns inland at the **Punta de s'Escullar** promontory (Km 1.5), with a fine view of Cala Morell.

02 The trail passes the first of many **stepped pyramids** and a turn-off towards an airstrip. Unlike Menorca's ancient remains – *navetes*, *talaiots* and *taulas* – the pyramids are *barraques de bestiar* (animal shelters), built in the 1800s.

03 Turning westwards at Km 2.5, the trail winds its way towards the coast and passes over another stone wall before crossing a **ravine**. At Km 5.5, a **viewpoint** overlooks the cliffs of **Codolar de Torre Nova**.

Necrópolis de Cala Morell

Dating back to the Late Talaiotic period (500–1st century BCE), this **necropolis** (Carrer Lira; 24hr) comprises 15 caves. It was used for several centuries after the Roman conquest of Menorca in 123 BCE. Look out for architectural details, including the remains of original stone passageways in the two oldest caves. Typical late prehistoric burial grounds in Menorca consisted of hypogea (human-made caves), dug out in cliffs and rocky outcrops near villages. The dead were placed on funeral pyres with limestone on top; the heat converted the stones and the soft tissue into quicklime, and the hardened remains were interred in the caves.

Best for

OFF THE BEATEN PATH

04 At Km 6, a short turn-off leads you to a **memorial** for the victims of the *Général Chanzy* shipwreck in 1910.

05 A paved road detours towards the **Punta Nati lighthouse** (Km 7.3; 1.5km return), where you can admire the 1913 lighthouse and old **bunkers**. From the turn-off, the trail continues across a mix of calcareous rock and scrubland, hugging a stone wall.

06 At Km 9.4, you skirt a fine example of a **barraque de bestiar**, followed by two more.

07 Another 20 minutes on, dip into small ravines before ascending the **Turó de Bajolí** hill (Km 11).

08 Descending gently, the trail passes a **water treatment plant** before joining a paved road. Cross the ravine after 500m to reach **Pont d'en Gil** (Km 12.4), an amazing rock arch.

09 A short way south, the path joins Avinguda des Pont d'en Gil; follow it to the end, turn right, and then follow Avinguda dels Delfins to the **Cala en Blanes** cove turn-off (Km 15).

10 From the cove, take the cycle path to the **Sa Farola lighthouse** (Km 16.3), past the Cala des Frares swimming spots.

11 The final stretch to Ciutadella's **yacht marina** lies along the Camí Sa Farola and Passeig des Moll.

TAKE A BREAK

Near the marina in Ciutadella, a meal at the classic seafood haunt **Café Balear** (971 38 00 05; www.cafebalear.com; Plaça de Sant Joan 15; mains €17-45; 1-4pm & 8pm-midnight Mon-Sat mid-Jun–mid-Oct, Tue-Sun mid-Oct–mid-Jun, closed Nov) marks a triumphant end to your walk, though there's often a queue for tables. You can eat outside on the quayside while tucking into Menorcan specialities such as *caldereta de llagosta* (Menorcan lobster stew) and *arròs caldoso* (soupy seafood rice).

MALLORCA & MENORCA/199

56
SANT TOMÀS TO SON XORIGUER

Best for

COASTAL VIEWS

DURATION	DIFFICULTY	DISTANCE	START/END
10hr one-way	Moderate	24.9km	Platja de Binicodrell/ Platja de Son Xoriguer
TERRAIN	Mostly dirt trail along cliffs, beaches and through woods; steep in sections		

Encompassing white-sand coves with turquoise waters, precipitous cliffs and rambles through pine and holm-oak wood, this hike showcases the best of Menorca's south coast. Easy and gentle enough in terms of terrain to be family-friendly (especially if you split it into two halves), it introduces you to surprisingly varied scenery and keeps you in happy anticipation of fresh discoveries around the next bend of the coast.

GETTING HERE
Take bus 72 from Ciutadella or bus 71 from Maó to Sant Tomàs (several daily, May to mid-September). Bus route 65 connects Son Xoriguer to Ciutadella and bus 1 Ciutadella to Maó year-round.

STARTING POINT
The trail begins at the west end of Platja de Binicodrell in Sant Tomàs, next to the Es Bruc restaurant.

01 From the holiday resort of Sant Tomàs, take the level dirt trail west along the coast from next to the Es Bruc restaurant. At Km 1, overlooking the white-sand **Platjes de Binigaus**, there's a **picnic area**.

02 Here you can turn inland to detour to the Cova des Coloms cave. You also have two choices. You may either follow a section of the official Camí dels Cavalls trail that encircles the island, as it rises steadily uphill through dense woods, along the confluence of two limestone rock **ravines** (Barranc de Torrevella and Barranc de Binigaus), before descending a winding road alongside the Barranc Cala Escorxada, past a small

stone hut used as an emergency shelter, to the **Cala Escorxada**. Alternatively, you may opt for the flatter (and shorter by 1km) route along the cliffs (less shade). Assuming you've chosen the longer, more interesting route, at Km 4.4 you find yourself at a pristine, frequently deserted **white-sand cove**.

03 Running uphill from Cala Escorxada, the cliffside track joins an unpaved road that snakes its way to another sheltered sandy cove, the lovely **Cala Fustam**, 700m later. Passing it by, another 20-minute walk along the cliffs brings you to the white-sand **Cala de Trebalúger** (Km 6.7), with the calm bay, framed by densely wooded cliffs, a favourite with yachties.

04 At Cala de Trebalúger, you again have two options. One: you pass through several Menorca gates bordering the enclosures of some cultivated fields of the **Barranc de Sa Cova** before joining the official Camí dels Cavalls route inland and proceeding west through dense holm-oak and pine forest then descending gently to the unspoiled **Cala Mitjana**. Alternatively, let's assume that you climb the steps at the west end of the beach and follow the wooden arrows along the shorter coastal trail as it meanders through the greenery along the calcareous cliffs to the aforementioned cove.

05 West of and above Cala Mitjana (Km 8.4) there are some **old sandstone quarries** from where you get a great view of the beach before a short and largely flat walk through the woods brings you to a wall with a gate. You then come to a junction in the Avinguda de la Punta in Cala Galdana (10.3km). It's worth strolling for three minutes to the west for a wonderful view of Cala Galdana beach before descending to the **beach** and making your way to the canal that bisects the little town.

⮕ Detour: Cova des Coloms

From the picnic area overlooking the Platjes de Binigaus, a worthwhile 2km detour inland (40 minutes each way) leads you to the **Cova des Coloms**, Menorca's largest and most impressive cave. Nicknamed 'the Cathedral', it's 110m long and 25m high. The reverence you feel when you step inside and are dwarfed by it may explain why it was used for religious ceremonies by the Talaiotic culture (Menorca's earliest known inhabitants), which dates back to around 1000 BCE.

Ten minutes before you reach the Cova dels Coloms, you'll pass the turn-off for the **Cova de na Polida**, a smaller cave with impressive stalactite and stalagmite formations.

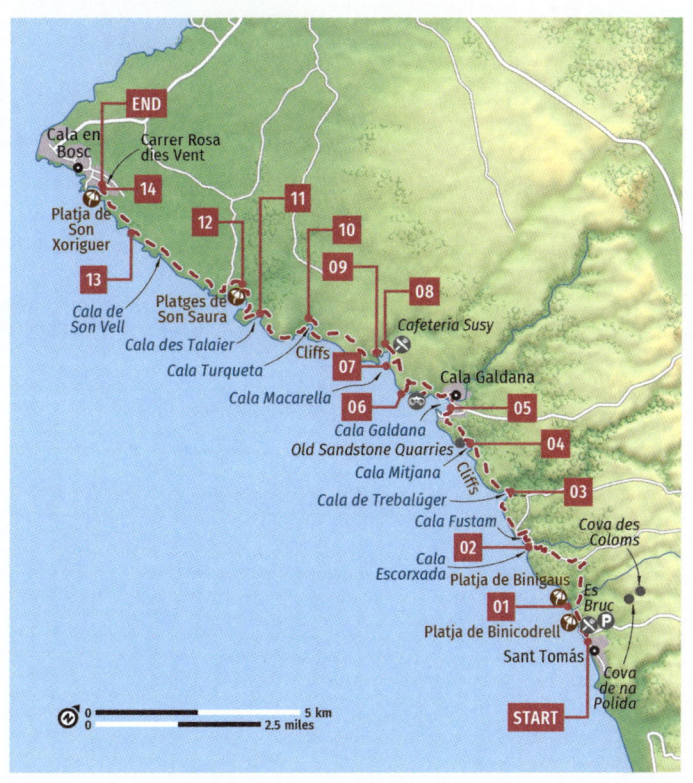

(Incidentally, if you'd rather do a shorter walk than the full Sant Tomàs to Son Xoriguer hike, then you may consider the 13km stretch from Cala Galdana to Son Xoriguer instead, particularly if you want to hit southern Menorca's most celebrated beaches. Or, for paths less trodden and varied scenery, opt for just the 9km between Sant Tomàs and Cala Galdana.)

06 Take the bridge over the canal, turn left, and follow the street to the base of the cliff, where the trail picks up. It climbs up the side of the cliff for a few minutes before flattening out into a broad dirt track that runs through pine and holm-oak forest much of the way to Cala Macarella. You'll pass four **turn-offs** along the way; each leads to a **clifftop viewpoint** overlooking the sea. The first two are missable, but the third one is a worthwhile little detour, as it presents you with gorgeous vistas of the bay and of boats approaching the cove.

07 From the third viewpoint to the fourth one, it's a quick 600m ramble. The **final viewpoint** overlooks the mouth of the cove, the teal waters frequently dotted with small pleasure craft.

08 It's a 10-minute walk down to **Cala Macarella** (Km 13.3), with its restaurant and lifeguard in season; you descend some wooden stairs for the last part. Lunch beckons. The waters are usually calm and very swimmable. Pack your snorkelling gear, too.

09 The official Camí dels Cavalls trail runs inland, but it's much more rewarding to take the steep, narrow and, at times precipitous, path along the side of the cliff on the west side of the beach, past the **caves** used as a necropolis by Menorca's earliest inhabitants. Make your way around the headland, with a backward glance at the beach you've just left from a **viewpoint**. Then descend steeply to **Cala Macarelleta** (Km 13.8), another wonderful place for a break and a swim if Cala Macarella is too crowded.

10 The signposted trail continues along a broad dirt track from Cala Macarelleta, running inland through the woods before emerging on top of some more calcareous cliffs, then descending to the broad sweep of white sand that is **Cala Turqueta** (Km 15.9). There's a **water wheel** at the back of the cove, but no facilities. If you're here in low season, you may have this delightful swimming spot all to yourself.

11 It's a shadeless but flat and easy 25-minute walk along the low, scrubland-covered cliffs of the headland to the next beach, the small **Cala des Talaier** (Km 18), hemmed in by rocks and woodland.

 Walk Dos & Don'ts

Start your hike early. Menorca's southern coves get very busy during the day, particularly during summer. The shoulder months of May or September are best.

Take plenty of water with you. The Cala Macarella to Son Xoriguer section of the trail is mostly shadeless, and there's nowhere to fill up beyond Cala Macarella. Outside peak season, take enough water to cover the entire Cala Galdana–Son Xoriguer stretch (13km).

Consider the practicalities of hiking in low season. Pros: few people. Cons: few facilities open along the way and no public transport to Sant Tomàs outside May to mid-September. Either catch bus 1 from Ciutadella to El Mercadal, or bus 74 from Maó to Es Migjorn, and then take a taxi.

12 Passing through a gate in a stone wall and rounding another headland, you're greeted with the sight of twin stretches of sand that make up the popular twin **Platges de Son Saura** (Km 19.4). Only the nearest one is good for swimming; the one further west tends to be clogged with epic amounts of *posidonia* sea grass.

13 From the far Son Saura beach, the flat trail runs right by the water, and you may find yourself surprising some naturists as you pass a couple of tiny coves. Proceed along the bare cliffs. You'll pass **Cala de Son Vell**, where there's an old underground bunker and another sheltered swimming spot, before you reach **Cova des Pardals** (Km 23.4), with a jetty below, dug out of sheer rock, alongside a small white cottage.

14 The final 25-minute stroll to your destination of **Platja Son Xoriguer** (Km 24.9) is completely flat and follows a stone wall on your right along the low and rocky coast, carpeted with sparse vegetation, before you find yourself at a small sand-and-pebble beach. The bus stop where you catch your ride back to Ciutadella is two blocks north of the beach along a pedestrianised street.

 TAKE A BREAK

Halfway into your hike, Cala Macarella is an ideal place to stop for lunch. It's an exquisite, sheltered white-sand cove, with unbelievably clear turquoise water, the seasonal **Cafetería Susy** (971 35 94 67; www.cafeteriasusy.com; mains €6-13; 10am-6.30pm mid-Apr–mid-Oct) restaurant set back from the sand, beneath the trees, and cliffs cloaked in pine and holm-oak. Swimming and snorkelling are both excellent here, and at the smaller Cala Macarelleta, a five-minute walk along a cliffside path. Note the caves in the cliff that were once used as a necropolis by the Talaiotic culture.

57

LA TRAPA MONASTERY

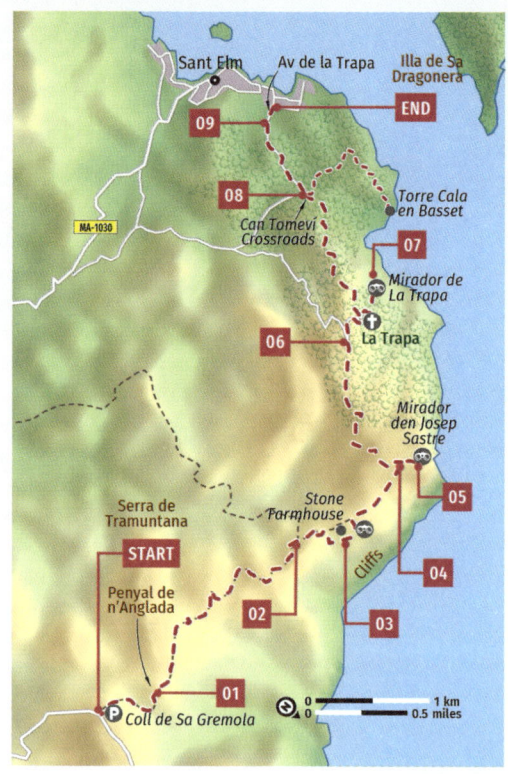

DURATION	DIFFICULTY	DISTANCE	START/END
4hr one-way	Moderate	9km	Coll de Sa Gremola/ Sant Elm
TERRAIN	Well-marked dirt trail, short steep section, little shade		

This path over the coastal cliffs of Ses Serres to the La Trapa monastery ruin showcases Mallorca's dramatic west coast, with stellar views of Illa de Sa Dragonera en route. Combining a gentle wander past olive groves and arid hills with precipice-top trails and an energetic scramble down through pine forest, this is the best that southwest Mallorca has to offer.

GETTING HERE
The trailhead is located off the A-10, 6km north of Andratx and 12km northeast of Sant Elm. It's not reachable by public transport, so you'll need a taxi.

STARTING POINT
The trailhead is located next to the small Coll de Sa Gremola car park. There's an information board here and several picnic tables, but no other facilities.

01 From the car park, take the well-signposted trail running gently uphill, passing a fenced-off farmstead on the right. Around the corner, terraced fields come into view, descending towards the Mediterranean. On your left looms the **Penyal de n'Anglada** rock face and you may spot Mallorca's wild mountain goats around here. The largely shadeless trail loops around the **valley of Gorg d'en Bersis**, with rocky slopes rising on the right...

02 ...before reaching a **signposted junction** at Km 3. At the junction, where the main trail continues left towards s'Arracó, keep right. After five minutes, you reach a **farmhouse**. The trail divides.

03 Take the right fork, with **fantastic views of the bay** from high above the coastline. Parts of the trail are overgrown, but it's easy to follow. Keeping left, you rejoin the main trail after 500m.

Detour: Torre Cala en Basset

Roughly halfway down between the La Trapa monastery and Sant Elm, you reach the Can Tomeví crossroads. Take a right along the forest path, past the Can Pepe property, and follow the cairns as the trail climbs through pine forest before emerging from the trees.

The solitary Torre Cala en Basset watchtower sits on a clifftop crag, some 750m from the crossroads. From here, there are wonderful views of the Illa de Sa Dragonera.

04 The path ascends a rocky plateau, where you find a large **stone cairn** at Km 4.5.

05 Here, a 100m detour leads right to the **Mirador d'en Josep Sastre**, where there's a vertical drop and excellent views of **Illa de Sa Dragonera**.

06 From the cairn, the path narrows and descends into the La Trapa valley. At Km 6, you climb over a stile, walking the remaining 500m to the **monastery** (pictured) along a wide unpaved road.

07 A short trail leads from the monastery to the **Mirador de La Trapa**.

08 The zigzagging and steep 1.5km descent from the monastery involves some scrambling down from a rocky ridge and then follows a faint, cairn-dotted trail to the **Can Tomeví crossroads** in the pine woods, where you can detour to the **Torre Cala en Basset**.

09 Alternatively, press on straight ahead at the crossroads. After 700m, the wide dirt trail becomes the paved **Avinguda de la Trapa**, and you emerge in **Sant Elm**.

☕ TAKE A BREAK

There is no finer place to picnic than the **Mirador de La Trapa**, a clifftop viewpoint near the remains of La Trapa, a monastery founded by Trappist monks in 1820. Located two-thirds of the way into your walk, the abandoned terraces, cloister and the restored mill are overseen by a local environmental group. You may spot some ospreys, black vultures and numerous orchids that are among Mallorca's protected species. There is little shade here, but the panoramic views of Illa de Sa Dragonera are jaw-dropping: the cliff falls away vertically, and you can also see the sheltered Cala en Basset cove.

58

VALLDEMOSSA TO DEIÀ

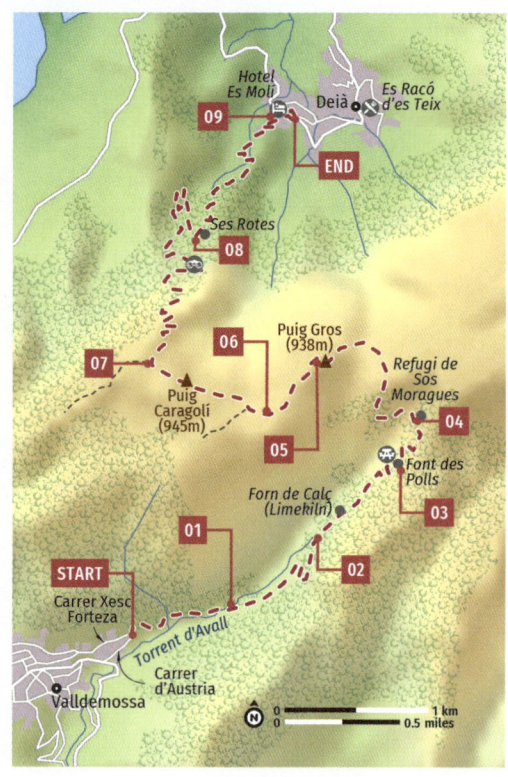

DURATION	DIFFICULTY	DISTANCE	START/END
3½hr one-way	Moderate	10km	Valldemossa/ Deià
TERRAIN	Well-defined dirt trail, some paved sections, long and steep descent		

This spectacular hike leads you high up into the Serra de son Moragues mountains between the picturesque villages of Valldemossa and Deià. Experiencing the varied scenery of the Cairats valley en route, you get a bird's-eye view of your destination on descent.

GETTING HERE

Valldemossa is 20km north of Palma de Mallorca along the MA-1110. It's reachable via bus route 210, which runs from Palma to Sóller via Deià.

STARTING POINT

Follow Valldemossa's main street eastwards. Just before it departs the village, turn left and uphill along Carrer d'Austria. The signposted trailhead is around the corner on Carrer Xesc Forteza.

01 From the trailhead take the gravel road, pass through a **side gate**, cross a **cattle grid** and walk past a ruined house. When the trail loops around to the right; climb over a **wooden gate**...

02 ...before arriving at a **signpost** (Km 1.7). Take the right-hand **'Camí des Cairats'** trail. Shortly after, you pass a **stone limekiln**, from where the rocky path snakes steeply up through holm-oak forest.

03 Arriving at the **Font des Polls** (Km 2.7) spring and picnic tables, ignore the right-hand trail and continue uphill for another 500m.

04 You'll reach the **Refugi de Sos Moragues** (mountain hut). A steep and rocky stretch later, the trail emerges from the woods and gently traverses a stony plateau.

Valldemossa: An Arty Enclave

Sitting on the slopes of the Serra de Tramuntana, Valldemossa's cobbled streets, flower-festooned stone houses, and handsome palace and cathedral have been attracting creative types for centuries. One of Valldemossa's most famous residents, composer Frédéric Chopin, spent the winter here in 1838 with his lover, writer George Sand; you can visit the **Real Cartuja de Valldemossa** (www.cartujadevalldemossa.com; Plaça Cartoixa; adult/child €10/6.50; 10am-4.30pm Mon-Sat Feb-Oct) where they stayed. Piano concerts are held here five times daily (Monday to Saturday) during peak season.

Best for

BRINGING THE PAST TO LIFE

05 Passing two stone cairns and a viewpoint, at Km 4.7, you come to **Puig Gros** (938m), and your first glimpse of Deià below (pictured). Continuing along a broad ridge, you have the Bay of Palma on one side and the north coast on the other.

06 At Km 5.8, the trail reaches the Pla des Aritges (908m) **crossroads** next to some pine trees. Take the right fork, past **Puig Caragolí** (945m)…

07 …until you reach the **turn-off for Deià**, next to a large stone cairn, 10 minutes later. The impressive descent begins close to the precipice. A narrow, scree-covered mule track switchbacks steeply through holm-oak woods, passing two **charcoal burners' sites**, and flattening out as holm-oak gives way to pine and wild olive.

08 Follow the cairns through the abandoned olive terraces to the **Ses Rotes spring** (Km 9.5).

09 From here, the partially overgrown path bisects a green valley, passing through a gap in a stone wall, past some buildings on your left, and onto a roadway with houses and **Hotel Es Molí**. Finally, you emerge on the MA-10 (Carrer des Molí) in Deià.

 TAKE A BREAK

A wonderful way to end your hike in Deià is at the Michelin-starred **Es Racó d'es Teix** (971 63 95 01; www.esracodesteix.es; Carrer de Sa Vinya Vella 6; mains €35-40, 3-course lunch menú €38, with wine €52, 4-/6-course tasting menú €78/115; 1-3pm & 7.30-10.30pm Wed-Sun Feb-Oct;), run by chef Josef Sauerschell, an island legend. Expect immaculately presented classic flavours (beef carpaccio with Manchego cheese) and interesting pairings of ingredients (lobster ravioli with white peach). The mountain backdrop from the terrace is sublime. Reservations essential.

MALLORCA & MENORCA/207

59
MIRADOR DE SES BARQUES TO SA CALOBRA

DURATION	DIFFICULTY	DISTANCE	START/END
6hr one-way	Moderate	15.3km	Mirador de ses Barques
TERRAIN	Dirt trail, some paved road, steep sections, limited shade		

This classic one-way hike takes you from a lofty viewpoint overlooking Port de Sóller to the waters of Sa Calobra, taking in olive groves, rugged cliffs and sea views in-between. Cala Sa Calobra (Snake Bay) takes its name from this zigzagging trail that winds its sinuous way towards the coast, opening up the varied terrain of the Tramuntana and western Mallorca to those who enjoy exploration at a leisurely pace.

GETTING HERE
The trailhead is on the MA-10, 10km northeast of Sóller. The L354 bus connects Port de Sóller to the Mirador de ses Barques during summer; otherwise, take a taxi from Sóller (€20).

STARTING POINT
The trail departs from the car park at the Mirador de ses Barques, where there's a seasonal restaurant and bathroom. Look for the 'Tuent/Sa Costera/Bàlitx' signpost.

01 Head up the **steps from the trailhead**. The wide dirt path is first flanked by stone walls; it meets a cart track, carries on over the hill, and then passes through a metal gate. Narrowing, it runs through an olive tree grove, reaching a **junction** some 800m into the walk, where you ignore the turn-off for Sóller/Port de Sóller and carry straight on. Widening again, and traversing another olive grove, the trail passes by the turn-off for the **Finca Bàlitx d'Amunt** (farmhouse) at Km 1.5, swinging to the right through a gap in the stone wall.

02 Soon after, you reach a **signpost for 'Tuent/Sa Calobra'**. With scenic views of olive terraces straight ahead and to your right, the paved path runs straight on, acting as a shortcut, and allowing you to bypass several looping bends of the dirt road. Soon you pass the **Font de Bàlitx** (spring) on your right, fed via a stone tunnel. Descending fairly steeply through a copse of pines and then some olive groves…

03 …the paved path then runs right past the **Finca Bàlitx d'Enmig** (Km 2.3), joining a wide dirt road. A welcome stretch of flat walking follows, with the rocky Coll de Binamar pass that you'll be climbing shortly visible in the distance straight ahead of you.

04 You reach a small farmhouse, a junction where three trails meet, and another **signpost** at Km 3.2. Press on towards 'Bàlitx d'Avall/Tuent/Sa Calobra'. The trail soon becomes a series of stone steps, leading gently down through woodland, before emerging from the trees and zigzagging down a hill slope dotted with olive trees…

05 …towards the **Bàlitx d'Avall defence tower**, a farmhouse that offers farm stays and a small chapel (Km 4.1). Near the farmhouse, cross the dry stream bed beneath a defunct stone bridge. Ignore the cart track at the **junction** where the trail splits in two, and take the waymarked trail…

06 …that ascends smoothly to the **Coll de Binamar pass** (365m) along a stone wall. The trail widens and emerges in a forest at the top of the pass (Km 5). You may well see some of Menorca's wild goats here among the trees and giant boulders; they were introduced to the island in ancient times and have inhabited the Tramuntana ever since. They are distinguishable from local goats recently gone feral: the wild goats are smaller than domestic goats, are reddish-brown in colour with a black

Return Journey by Boat & Train

Time your hike right in order to get back to Port de Sóller, since Sa Calobra is not served by public transport. **Barcos Azules** (971 63 01 70; www.barcos azules.com; Passeig Es Travès 3; adult/child one-way €21/8, return €30/15; hours vary;) makes several daily journeys between Port de Sóller and Sa Calobra (April to October), with twice-weekly departures in February, March and November.

If you wish to do a shorter version of the hike, it's possible to arrange pick-up from Cala Tuent instead. In Port de Sóller, the **Tren de Sóller** (http://trendesoller.com; one-way €4; 7am-8pm) – Mallorca's wonderful heritage tram – rattles along the waterfront before chugging uphill through fruit orchards, to the Sóller railway station.

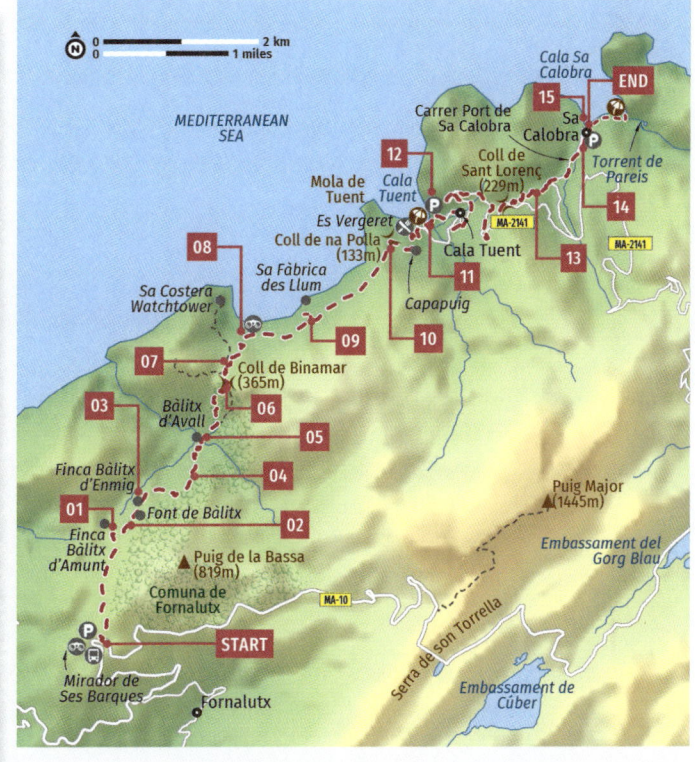

MALLORCA & MENORCA/209

belly, and both the males and the females have horns (though the males' horns are curved and more impressive).

07 Some 600m below the pass, you come to another **junction**. The left-hand trail is a dead end, where the **Sa Costera watchtower** sits high up on a cliff. Take the right-hand fork.

08 Some 50m later you reach a **cluster of boulders** beneath the trees – a good rest stop, with fine views of the rugged coastline. From here, it's a gentle up-and-down ramble along a well-constructed stone path that winds its way among spruce trees, high above the sea, in the direction of the **Mola de Tuent promontory** up ahead.

09 At Km 6.5 you pass the turn-off leading down to the old electricity works of **Sa Fàbrica des Llum** by the sea, a worthwhile detour (1km return) if you have the time and energy.

10 It's an easy ascent from the turn-off to the **Coll de na Polla** (133m) at Km 8.1. You pass through a gap in the stone wall and, five minutes from the top of the pass, the dirt trail joins a gravel track before the **Capapuig farmstead**. Just to the left of the farmstead, take the **stone steps** down, and then head immediately left again where the trail splits, in the direction of 'Cala Tuent/Es Vergeret'. Above a house, you hit the dirt road again. Keeping left, descend along some steps.

11 Five minutes later, you'll emerge in the car park of the Es Vergeret restaurant, from where it's another 150m down to the **Cala Tuent** beach (pictured; Km 9.2), along the access road and then some steps down to the water.

12 From the small parking area on the north side of Cala Tuent, up some steps from the beach, a very lightly used, narrow road snakes its way uphill past some isolated houses, looping up the mountain ridge that separates Cala Tuent from your destination of Sa Calobra. It takes around an hour of largely shadeless walking (ignore the steps that appear to be shortcuts across some bends) to get up to the **Coll de Sant Lorenç** (229m) and its namesake **church** at the top of the pass (Km 12.9).

13 Beside the church, pass through a metal gate and descend relatively steeply along a narrow, zigzagging stone path that's rather overgrown in places to **Cases sa Calobra**, a clutch of holiday homes sitting in an olive grove. Passing them, you shortly reach the main tarmac road, the MA-2141. (If you don't wish to finish the hike looking as if you've been to Custer's Last Stand, you may consider descending from the pass the long way, via the paved road that joins the MA-2141 after 2km, though that adds an extra 1.5km to your hike.)

14 A final kilometre along the narrow MA-2141 (watch out for cars!) leads you past two enormous **car parks**…

15 …to the **Sa Calobra** cove, a sheltered and popular pebble beach, flanked by three mediocre restaurants. The boat back to Port de Sóller departs from the **pier**.

Detour: Torrent de Pareis

Since you've already come all this way, what's another 10-minute walk? From the Sa Calobra cove, take the steps up and then follow the waterfront promenade. At the far end, there's a tunnel in sheer rock that you have to pass through before emerging at the mouth of the Torrent de Pareis gorge. Besides the striking beauty of the gorge itself, the main attraction here is a small, pebbly beach and some of the clearest, coolest and calmest waters in Mallorca for swimming. The word is out, though: it's best to come here during shoulder seasons, since during peak months the waters teem with yachts and every inch of the small beach tends to be taken up by coach parties.

TAKE A BREAK

Around 3½ hours into the hike, Cala Tuent is a wonderful place to break your journey. Here you'll find a broad, pebble-and-shingle beach with calm cerulean waters. Also, given Sa Calobra's mediocre dining options, it's worth grabbing lunch at **Es Vergeret** (971 51 71 05; www.esvergeret.com; Camí de Sa Figuera Vial 21; mains €16-22; 12.30am-4.30pm Mar-Oct), on the hillside above the beach. The restaurant specialises in Mallorcan classics, such as soupy seafood rice, grilled fish and lamb chops, and its shaded terrace takes in the full sweep of the bay below and the surrounding mountains.

60

ALCÚDIA PENINSULA

DURATION	DIFFICULTY	DISTANCE	START/END
5-6hr return	Moderate	12.7km	Ermita de la Victòria

TERRAIN	Well-maintained dirt trail, some steep rocky sections, limited shade

This wonderful circular walk gives you the best of the Alcúdia peninsula: panoramic views from rocky crags, a splendid remote beach, pine forest, inquisitive wild goats and gentle rambles through valleys with sea views. This less-trodden part of northeast Mallorca has appeal for summit-baggers and beachgoers alike, with a great variety of scenery throughout, and a vertigo-defying, optional detour overlooking the peninsula's northernmost tip.

GETTING HERE

Ermita de la Victòria is 6km northeast of Alcúdia. While Alcúdia is well-connected by bus to other Mallorcan towns, you'll need your own wheels or taxi to get up to the hermitage.

STARTING POINT

From the Ermita de la Victòria car park, take the well-defined dirt trail marked 'Ses Tres Creus'.

01 From the car park, a broad dirt track runs uphill through the woods. Some 250m up, a **turn-off** marked 'Ses Tres Creus' leads to the eponymous **viewpoint** with three crosses.

02 Ten minutes later you reach the junction for the **Penya des Migdia detour**.

03 From the junction, the gentle uphill track emerges from the trees, with **Talaia d'Alcúdia** (446m) visible ahead. Climb the zigzagging stony path uphill. Below the summit, there's a signposted **stone cairn**.

04 It's a short scramble to the **summit**, where you're rewarded with 360-degree views of the peninsula. There's shade beneath the pines, plus

212/MALLORCA & MENORCA

Detour: Penya des Migdia

Some 750m from the Ermita de la Victòria car park, this precipitous (2km return) trail leads you to the **Penya des Migdia viewpoint** for one of the best panoramic views in northeast Mallorca. You need a good head for heights: after climbing gently beside a handrail, the narrow trail hugs the cliffside. Slipping through a narrow rock passage, hold on to a metal chain to navigate your way past the sheer drop. You then find yourself next to a bunker and cistern, with the northern tip of the Alcúdia peninsula spread out below you. Peak baggers may wish to do a 10-minute scramble to the top of the Penya des Migdia hill (358m) for somewhat loftier views.

the ruins of a watchtower and mountain shelter.

05 Descending again, head for 'Collet des Coll Baix'. The surfaced path descends steadily, with fine views of the coast. At Km 3.4, you reach a **viewpoint** overlooking the Platja des Coll Baix (pictured).

06 Another kilometre of steep switchbacks brings you to the **Collet des Coll Baix** (Km 4.5), a shaded rest area with picnic tables.

07 A narrow path snakes down through pine forest until you emerge on top of low cliffs. Scramble to the sheltered **beach**.

08 Back at Collet des Coll Baix, head downhill along the broad forest path. Passing a parking area, turn right onto the **path** signposted 'Campament de la Victòria' 10 minutes later.

09 The trail follows a stony, dry riverbed, with cairns marking the overgrown sections, before climbing steeply up to the **Coll de na Benet** pass (Km 9.2).

10 Rest beneath the olive trees before descending a stony path through the **Fontanelles valley** towards the Badia de Pollença. The path eventually swings to the right, before reaching a **signposted junction** (Km 11.2).

11 Head right and uphill at the next **junction**, towards the **Ermita de la Victòria**, then cross a clearing and a dry stream bed into a pine-filled valley. The trail ascends steeply to your starting point.

TAKE A BREAK

Lapped by turquoise waters and sheltered beneath greenery-clad cliffs, the pristine pebble Platja des Coll Baix beach is reachable only on foot (or by boat), and is hugely worth the effort. Halfway into your hike, it's an ideal place to break for a picnic lunch or swim, and meet the resident wild goats – who are unafraid of humans and may take an active interest in your food.

MALLORCA & MENORCA/213

Also Try...

PUIG DE MASSANELLA

Taking you up to the twin summit of the island's second-highest peak, this demanding ascent is one of the Mallorca's classic hikes.

Starting from the Coll de sa Batalla, 22km southwest of Pollença, the trail runs past the fruit tree terraces of Finca Comafreda, follows a cart track into the woods, and climbs uphill, reaching the Coll de sa Línea pass at the 3km point. Here, the trail departs from the roadway and leads uphill from between two waymarker stones to Avenc des Camí at 4km. At this point, you choose between two trails: 'Puig y Font' (summit then spring) or 'Font y Puig' (spring then summit); the former is less steep, with a flatter section of the cairn-dotted high plateau, the Pla de sa Neu. The last 30 minutes up to Puig de Massanella (1365m) is very steep and involves scrambling up a rocky slope. Your reward? Stupendous Tramuntana views (pictured).

DURATION 4½hr return
DIFFICULTY Hard
DISTANCE 12km

ES GRAU TO CAP DE FAVÀRITX

A striking and remote section of Menorca's Camí de Cavalls, this trail takes in dramatic rock formations, pristine coves and wetlands.

Departing near the white-sand Platja des Grau, the trail ascends the top of a natural balcony, with panoramic views of the coast's bays and points. Descending to the Cala des Tamarells, it passes by the Torre de Rambla (1802), a defence tower built by the British, and crosses a small wetland. The trail then runs through pine forest and crosses the headland to Cala de sa Torreta, before traversing fields and woodlands further inland. Passing through pastureland, you emerge at the pebbly Cala en Cavaller. Beyond, the trail climbs alongside a dry stone wall and passes through more pine forest before coming to Cala Morella. You then climb over a headland to the dune-backed Platja d'en Tortuga, beyond which the trail joins the road to the dramatically situated Favàritx lighthouse.

DURATION 3½hr one-way
DIFFICULTY Moderate
DISTANCE 9.2km

VALL DE BÒQUER

Reaching the Cala Bòquer cove, this valley walk is superb for early-morning birdwatchers.

Starting from a car park near a roundabout in Port de Pollença, follow the unsurfaced road to the Finca Bòquer, cross the courtyard and take the trail through the broad Bòquer valley, with the Serra Cavall Bernat mountains on either side and ospreys soaring overhead. The trail meanders gently between dwarf palms until you reach Coll del Moro (3km), where you either descend to the cove or press on ahead to the viewpoint above the turquoise sea. Return the same way.

DURATION 2hr return
DIFFICULTY Easy
DISTANCE 7km

TORRENT DE PAREIS

A natural obstacle course and gorge hike through Mallorca's 'Grand Canyon', this is a must for super-fit adventurers.

Starting at Escorca restaurant at Km 25.2 on the MA-10 between Sóller and Pollença, this descent takes you between rocks as tall as houses to s'Entreforc (2.5km), where two canyons meet. Walk along the main canyon's river-bed, passing a cave. Here the gorge narrows to a crevice; squeeze through a groove to get past a boulder, then slide down a huge 'cannon ball' boulder. Reaching the Font des Degotís spring, bypass a large pool before emerging at Cala Sa Calobra beach (pictured).

DURATION 5hr one-way
DIFFICULTY Hard
DISTANCE 7.4km

SANT TOMÀS TO BASÍLICA DE SON BOU

Taking in coastal views, dune-backed white-sand beaches and birdlife-rich wetlands, this is Menorca's quintessential seaside walk.

Start at the car park at the west end of the Sant Tomàs beach resort. The trail runs along the waterfront then gently climbs up the Punta de Talis and crosses the pine-covered headland, before emerging at the Platjes de Son Bou, a 2.5km string of beaches. You can either walk along the sand, follow the wooden boardwalks behind the dunes, or take the longer official trail past the wetlands. Finish at the Basílica de Son Bou.

DURATION 2hr one-way
DIFFICULTY Easy
DISTANCE 7km

Language

Spanish (español) – or Castilian (castellano), as it is also called – is spoken throughout Spain, but there are also three co-official, regional languages: Catalan (català), spoken in Catalonia, the Balearic Islands and Valencia; Galician (galego), spoken in Galicia; and Basque (euskara), which is spoken in the Basque Country and Navarra.

The pronunciation of most Spanish sounds is very similar to that of their English counterparts. If you read our coloured pronunciation guides as if they were English, you'll be understood. Note that kh is a throaty sound (like the 'ch' in the Scottish loch), r is strongly rolled, ly is pronounced as the 'lli' in 'million' and ny as the 'ni' in 'onion'. You may also notice that the 'lisped' th sound is pronounced as s in Andalucía. In our pronunciation guides, the stressed syllables are in italics.

Where necessary in this chapter, masculine and feminine forms are marked with 'm/f', while polite and informal options are indicated by the abbreviations 'pol' and 'inf'.

BASICS

Hello.	Hola.	o·la
Goodbye.	Adiós.	a·dyos
Yes./No.	Sí./No.	see/no
Excuse me.	Perdón.	per·don
Sorry.	Lo siento.	lo syen·to
Please.	Por favor.	por fa·vor
Thank you.	Gracias.	gra·thyas
You're welcome.	De nada.	de na·da
How are you?	¿Qué tal?	ke tal
Fine, thanks.		
Bien, gracias.		byen gra·thyas
Do you speak English?		
¿Habla inglés?	a·bla een·gles (pol)	
¿Hablas inglés?	a·blas een·gles (inf)	
I don't understand.		
No entiendo.	no en·tyen·do	

ON THE TRAIL

hiking	senderismo	sen·de·ris·mo
trail	sendero	sen·de·ro
summit	cumbre	kum·bre
mountain hut		
refugio de montaña		re·fux·hio de mon·ta·nya

I'd like to buy/hire...
Me gustaría comprar/contratar...   meh goos·ta·ri·a kom·prar/kon·tra·tar...

hiking poles		
bastones de senderismo		bas·to·nes de sen·de·ris·mo
hiking boots		
botas de montaña		bo·tas de mon·ta·nya
raincoat		
impermeable		im·per·me·a ble
backpack		
mochila		mo·chi·la

How is the weather today?
¿Cómo está el clima hoy?   ko·mo es·ta el klee·ma oy?

EATING & DRINKING

What would you recommend?
¿Qué recomienda?   ke re·ko·myen·da

What's in that dish?
¿Que lleva ese plato?   ke lye·va e·se pla·to

I don't eat...
No como...   no ko·mo...

Cheers!
¡Salud!   sa·loo

That was delicious!
¡Estaba buenísimo!   es·ta·ba bwe·nee·see·mo

Please bring us the bill.
Por favor, nos trae la cuenta.   por fa·vor nos tra·e la kwen·ta

I'd like to	Quisiera	kee·sye·ra
book a table		
reservar una		re·ser·var oo·na
for ...		
mesa para ...		me·sa pa·ra ...
(eight) o'clock		
las (ocho)		las (o·cho)
(two) people		
(dos) personas		(dos) per·so·nas

KEY WORDS

bottle	botella	bo·te·lya
breakfast	desayuno	de·sa·yoo·no
(too) cold	(muy) frío	(mooy) free·o
dinner	cena	the·na
food	comida	ko·mee·da
fork	tenedor	te·ne·dor
glass	vaso	va·so
highchair	trona	tro·na
hot (warm)	caliente	ka·lyen·te
knife	cuchillo	koo·chee·lyo
lunch	comida	ko·mee·da
market	mercado	mer·ka·do
(children's) menu	menú (infantil)	me·noo (een·fan·teel)
plate	plato	pla·to
restaurant	restaurante	res·tow·ran·te
spoon	cuchara	koo·cha·ra
vegetarian		
vegetariana		ve·khe·ta·rya·na

EMERGENCIES

Help!	¡Socorro!	so·ko·ro
Go away!	¡Vete!	ve·te
Call ...!	¡Llame a ...!	lya·me a ...
a doctor	un médico	oon me·dee·ko
the police	la policía	la po·lee·thee·a
I'm lost.		
Estoy perdido/a.		es·toy per·dee·do/a (m/f)

Signs

Abierto	Open
Cerrado	Closed
Entrada	Entrance
Hombres	Men
Mujeres	Women
Prohibido	Prohibited
Salida	Exit
Servicios/Aseos	Toilets

I'm ill.
Estoy enfermo/a.   es·toy en·fer·mo/a (m/f)

It hurts here.
Me duele aquí.   me dwe·le a·kee

I'm allergic to (antibiotics).
Soy alérgico/a   soy a·ler·khee·ko/a
a (los   a (los
antibióticos).   an·tee·byo·tee·kos) (m/f)

Where are the toilets?
¿Dónde están los   don·de es·tan los
servicios?   ser·vee·thyos

DIRECTIONS

Where's …?
¿Dónde está …?   don·de es·ta …

What's the address?
¿Cuál es la   kwal es la
dirección?   dee·rek·thyon

Can you please write it down?
¿Puede escribirlo,   pwe·de es·kree·beer·lo
por favor?   por fa·vor

Can you show me (on the map)?
¿Me lo puede   me lo pwe·de
indicar (en   een·dee·kar en
(el mapa)?   (el ma·pa)

at the corner
en la esquina   en la es·kee·na

at the traffic lights
en el semáforo   en el se·ma·fo·ro

behind …
detrás de …   de·tras de …

in front of …
enfrente de …   en·fren·te de …

left   izquierda   eeth·kyer·da

next to …	al lado de …	al la·do de
opposite …	frente a …	fren·te a
right	derecha	de·re·cha
straight ahead	todo recto	to·do rek·to

TRANSPORT

boat	barco	bar·ko
bus	autobús	ow·to·boos
plane	avión	a·vyon
train	tren	tren
first	primer	pree·mer
last	último	ool·tee·mo
next	próximo	prok·see·mo

a … ticket
un billete de …   oon bee·lye·te de …

1st-class	primera clase	pree·me·ra kla·se
2nd-class	segunda clase	se·goon·da kla·se
one-way	ida	ee·da
return	ida y vuelta	ee·da ee vwel·ta
aisle seat	asiento de pasillo	a·syen·to de pa·see·lyo
station	estación	es·ta·thyon
ticket office	taquilla	ta·kee·lya
timetable	horario	o·ra·ryo
window seat	asiento junto a la ventana	a·syen·to khoon·to a la ven·ta·na

I want to go to …
Quisiera ir a …   kee·sye·ra eer a

At what time does it arrive/leave?
¿A qué hora   a ke o·ra
llega/sale?   lye·ga/sa·le

Does it stop at (Madrid)?
¿Para en (Madrid)?   pa·ra en (ma·dree)

Which stop is this?
¿Cuál es esta   kwal es es·ta
parada?   pa·ra·da

Please tell me when we get to (Seville).
¿Puede avisarme   pwe·de a·vee·sar·me
cuando lleguemos   kwan·do lye·ge·mos
a (Sevilla)?   a (se·vee·lya)

I want to get off here.
Quiero bajarme   kye·ro ba·khar·me
aquí.   a·kee

How much is it per day/hour?
¿Cuánto cuesta   kwan·to kwes·ta
por día/hora?   por dee·a/o·ra

I'd like to hire…
Me gustaría   meh goos·ta·ri·a
contratar…   kon·tra·tar

4WD	un todo-terreno	oon to·do-te·re·no
car	un coche	oon ko·che
child seat	asiento de seguridad para niños	a·syen·to de se·goo·ree·da pa·ra nee·nyos
motorcycle	una moto	oo·na mo·to
bicycle	una bicicleta	oo·na bee·thee·kle·ta
helmet	casco	kas·ko
mechanic	mecánico	me·ka·nee·ko
petrol	gasolina	ga·so·lee·na
service station	gasolinera	ga·so·lee·ne·ra

Is this the road to (Barcelona)?
¿Se va a   se va a
(Barcelona)   (bar·the·lo·na)
por esta carretera?   por es·ta ka·re·te·ra

(How long) Can I park here?
¿(Por cuánto   (por kwan·to
tiempo) Puedo   tyem·po) pwe·do
aparcar aquí?   a·par·kar a·kee

The car has broken down (at Valencia).
El coche se   el ko·che se
ha averiado   a a·ve·rya·do
(en Valencia).   (en va·len·thya)

Want More?

For in-depth language information (including Catalan and Basque) and handy phrases check out Lonely Planet's *Spanish Phrasebook*. You'll find it at **shop.lonelyplanet.com**, or you can buy Lonely Planet's iPhone phrasebooks at the Apple App Store.

Behind the Scenes

Send us your feedback

We love to hear from travellers – your comments help make our books better. We read every word, and we guarantee that your feedback goes straight to the authors. Visit **lonelyplanet.com/contact** to submit your updates and suggestions. We may edit, reproduce and incorporate your comments in Lonely Planet products such as guidebooks, websites and digital products, so let us know if you don't want your comments reproduced or your name acknowledged. For a copy of our privacy policy visit lonelyplanet.com/privacy.

ACKNOWLEDGEMENTS

Cover photograph Senda de los Cazadores (Hunters Trail), Ordesa Canyon via the Faja de Pelay, Pyrenees, Hemis/Alamy Stock Photo ©

Digital Model Elevation Data U.S. Geological Survey Department of the Interior/USGS U.S. Geological Survey

Photographs (pp6-11) MoLarjung, Enrique Alaez Perez, Rolf G Wackenberg, Wolfgang Jargstorff, Jose Ramiro Laguna, Pablesku, TMP – An Instant of Time, Philip Reeve/shutterstock ©; Stuart Butler, John Noble/lonelyplanet ©

WRITER THANKS

STUART BUTLER

I've written for Lonely Planet for 15 years and covered destinations as tricky as Chad, Yemen, Congo and Iraq, so a book dedicated to the best walks in Spain should have been a breeze. Thanks to COVID-19, this turned out to be the most complicated book I have ever worked on and I would like to thank my fellow writers and everyone in-house at Lonely Planet – especially Darren O'Connell and Sandie Kestell – for keeping the project afloat when so many hurdles were thrown at us. But as logistically complicated as it was, it was a sheer pleasure to be out walking when the world appeared to be collapsing. For sharing so many of my walks with me and making the experience even better, I would like to thank my wife Heather and children Jake and Grace. I would also like to thank Simon Mahomo for companionship on many a mountain trail.

ANNA KAMINSKI

I would like to thank Sandie Kestell for entrusting me with Mallorca and Menorca – some of my favourite walking destinations, and also everyone who's assisted me along the way, including Keith in Palmanova for assisting with hike planning, Diego in Ciutadella, Xavi in Valldemossa, Patricia in Sant Elm, Veronica in Alcúdia, the good people of Alpina for their excellent trekking maps of Mallorca and Sergi Lara i Garcia for the fantastic *El Camí de Cavalls* book.

JOHN NOBLE

Many people helped in many ways. Special thanks, for companionship on the trails, meals, transport, tips, advice and other vital support, to Isabella and Jack Noble, Andrew Brannan, Phil Lawler, Nigel Burch, Mari Carmen Leis Calo, Eliseo Leis Calo, Susanne Neven, Adolfo González Alvarez, Craig Balmain, and Sasha McFadyean.

ZORA O'NEILL

Thanks to Robert Landon and the anonymous attendant at Camping Fonts de l'Algar who left the gate open for me.

THIS BOOK

This Lonely Planet guidebook was researched and written by Stuart Butler, Anna Kaminski, John Noble and Zora O'Neill.

This guidebook was produced by:

Senior Product Editor Sandie Kestell

Product Editor Claire Rourke

Book Designer Virginia Moreno

Assisting Editors Michelle Bennett, Anne Mulvaney

Cartographers Anthony Phelan, Hunor Csutoros

Cover Researcher & Design Ania Bartoszek

Product Development Imogen Bannister, Liz Heynes, Anne Mason, Dianne Schallmeiner, John Taufa, Juan Winata

Design Development Virginia Moreno

Cartographic Series Designer Wayne Murphy

Thanks to Imogen Bannister, Karen Henderson, Darren O'Connell, Genna Patterson

By Difficulty

EASY

Punta del Pacino..................................30
Alto & Bajo Sestrales 32
Plan de Aiguallluts 34
Puertos de Áliva..................................68
San Sebastián to Pasai Donibane........70
Illas Cíes..100
Laguna Grande de Gredos................120
Castaño del Robledo &
 Alájar Loop 146
Montserrat..172
Camí dels Molins 174
Peña Cortada Loop 176
Platja de Cavalleria to
 Platja de Binimel·là.....................196
Cala Morell to Ciutadella..................198

MODERATE

Ibón de Anayet...................................36
Valle de Otal 38
Cañón de Añisclo................................40
Circo de Gurrundué............................42
Ibón Gran de Baticielles......................46
Estanh de Rius &
 Estanh Tort de Rius.......................48
Estanys de Siscaró Loop......................50
Ruta del Cares 72
Vega de Ario 74
Mirador de Ordiales 76
Horcados Rojos 78
Picu Pierzu 80
Costa Naviega 82
Parada de Sil Circuit..........................102
Castro Caldelas Magical Forests........104
O Vicedo to Porto de Espasante........106
San Lorenzo de El Escorial to
 Machota Baja 122
Peñalara 124
Siete Picos 126
Río Borosa 148
Sierra de Cazorla 150
Cómpeta to El Acebuchal 152
Las Negras to Agua Amarga 154
La Tahá 156
Mulhacén 158
Serra de Bèrnia Loop........................180
Cadaqués to Cap de Creus 182
Volcanoes of Garrotxa......................184

Costa Brava Magic 186
Sant Tomàs to Son Xoriguer 200
La Trapa Monastery..........................204
Valldemossa a Deià 206
Mirador de ses Barques to
 Sa Calobra 208
Alcúdia Peninsula 212

HARD

Ordesa Canyon via
 the Faja de Pelay 52
Puerto de Barrosa 56
Circ de Colomèrs 58
Picu Urriellu 84
Somiedo Lakes...................................86
Arantzazu, Aizkorri, San Adrián 90
Anboto..92
Muxía to Lires..................................108
Lires to Cabo Fisterra.......................110
La Mira 130
El Morezón 134
Ruta de Carlos V 136
Acequias del Poqueira 162

Index

A

accessible travel 16-17
Acequias del Poqueira 11, 162-5
Alcúdia Peninsula 212-13
Alto & Bajo Sestrales 32-3
Anboto 92-3
Andalucía 22, 143-67
    planning 144-5
Andorra 28, 50-1
Arantzazu, Aizkorri, San Adrián 90-1

B

Balcón de Pineta & Lago Marboré 62
Barcelona 170
beaches 83, 106-7, 108-9, 110-13, 187-8, 203
bears 24, 89
Benasque 28
Benidorm 170
Begur 187, 189
Bielsa 28
Bilbao 66
birdwatching 42-3, 101, 215

C

cable cars
    Funicular de Sant Joan 172-3
    Teleférico de Fuente Dé 68-9, 78-9
Cabo Ortegal 115
Cadaqués to Cap de Creus 182-3
Cala Morell to Ciutadella 198-9
Camí dels Molins 174-5
Caminito del Rey 166
Camino de Faros 110-13
Camino de Santiago 23, 94, 111
Cangas de Onís 66
Cañón de Añisclo 40-1
Capileira 144
Castaño del Robledo & Alájar Loop 146-7
castles 190
Castro Caldelas Magical Forests 104-5
Cazorla 144
Central Spain 22, 117-41
    planning 118-19
children, travel with 14-15
Circ de Colomèrs 6, 58-61
Circo de Gurrundué 42-3
Ciutadella 194
climate 18, 19, *see also individual locations*
coastal trails 13
    Alcúdia Peninsula 212-13
    Cabo Ortegal 115
    Cadaqués to Cap de Creus 182-3
    Cala Morell to Ciutadella 198-9
    Costa Brava Magic 9, 186-9
    Costa Naviega 82-3
    Desert de les Palmes 191
    Es Grau to Cap de Favàritx 214
    Gaztelugatxe 95
    Illas Cíes 100-1
    La Tahá 156-7
    La Trapa Monastery 204-5
    Las Negras to Agua Amarga 154-5
    Lires to Cabo Fisterra 7, 110-13
    Mirador de ses Barques to Sa Calobra 8, 208-11
    Monte de Santa Trega 115
    Muxía to Lires 108-9
    O Vicedo to Porto de Espasante 106-7
    Platja de Cavalleria to Platja de Binimel·là 196-7
    Ribadesella to La Espasa 94
    Ruta Cañón do Río Mao 114
    Ruta Costa da Morte 115
    San Sebastián to Pasai Donibane 70-1
    Sant Tomàs to Basílica de Son Bou 215
    Sant Tomàs to Son Xoriguer 200-3
    Serra de Bèrnia Loop 180-1
    Torrent de Pareis 215
Collserola 191
Cómpeta to El Acebuchal 152-3
Costa Brava Magic 9, 186-9
Costa Naviega 82-3
Cuerda Larga 141

D

Desert de les Palmes 191
disabilities, travellers with 16-17

E

El Morezón 8, 134-5
Es Grau to Cap de Favàritx 214
Estanh de Rius & Estanh Tort de Rius 48-9
Estanys de Juclàr 51
Estanys de Siscaró Loop 50-1

F

Faja Tormosa 62
family-friendly trails 15
    Alto & Bajo Sestrales 32-3
    Cañón de Añisclo 40-1
    Circ de Colomèrs 6, 58-61
    Circo de Gurrundué 42-3
    Estanys de Juclàr 51
    Ibón de Anayet 36-7
    Parada de Sil Circuit 102-3
    Plan de Aigualluts 34-5
    Puerto de Barrosa 56-7
    Punta del Pacino 30-1
    Refugio de Armeña 63
    Valle de Otal 38-9
family travel 14-15
Fisterra 98
forest trails
    Alcúdia Peninsula 212-13
    Arantzazu, Aizkorri, San Adrián 90-1
    Cala Morell to Ciutadella 198-9
    Cañón de Añisclo 40-1
    Castaño del Robledo & Alájar Loop 146-7
    Castro Caldelas Magical Forests 104-5
    Circo de Gurrundué 42-3
    Collserola 191
    Cómpeta to El Acebuchal 152-3
    Es Grau to Cap de Favàritx 214
    Garganta de Navamediana 141
    Lago de Cregüeña 63
    Matagalls 191
    Ordesa Canyon via la Faja de Pelay 10, 52-5
    Peña Cortada Loop 176-9
    Pinsapar 167
    Puerto de Barrosa 56-7
    Puertos de Áliva 68-9
    Punta del Pacino 30-1
    Ruta Cañón do Río Mao 114
    Ruta Garganta de los Infiernos 141
    Ruta Macizo de Ándara 95
    San Sebastián to Pasai Donibane 70-1

Sant Tomàs to Son Xoriguer 200-3
Siete Picos 126-9
Valle de Otal 38-9
Vega de Liordes 95
Volcanoes of Garrotxa 184-5
Xàtiva Loop 190

G

Galicia 22, 97-115
  planning 98-9
Garganta de Navamediana 141
Garganta Verde 167
Gaztelugatxe 95
Girona 170
Granada 144

H

historical sites 199
historical trails 13
  Arantzazu, Aizkorri, San Adrián 90-1
  Camí dels Molins 174-5
  Castaño del Robledo & Alájar Loop 146-7
  Juviles & Fuerte 166
  La Tahá 156-7
  La Trapa Monastery 204-5
  Montserrat 172-3
  Parada de Sil Circuit 102-3
  Peña Cortada Loop 176-7
  Platja de Cavalleria to Platja de Binimel·là 196-7
  Ruta de Carlos V 136-39, 140, 141
  Ruta del Emperador 140
  San Lorenzo de El Escorial to Machota Baja 122-3
  Valldemossa to Deià 206-7
  Xàtiva Loop 190
Horcados Rojos 78-9
Hoya Moros 140
Hoyos del Espino 118

I

ibex 24, 132, 160,
Ibón de Anayet 36-7
Ibón Gran de Batisielles 46-7
Illa de Ons 114
Illas Cíes 100-1
islands
  Gaztelugatxe 95
  Illa de Ons 114
  Illas Cíes 100-1

J

Jarandilla de la Vera 118
Juviles & Fuerte 166

L

La Mira 130-3
La Peral to Villar de Vildas 94
La Tahá 156-7
La Trapa Monastery 204-5
Lago de Cregüeña 63
Laguna Grande de Gredos 120-1, 135
lake trails
  Balcón de Pineta & Lago Marboré 62
  Circ de Colomèrs 6, 58-61
  El Morezón 8, 134-5
  Estanh de Rius & Estanh Tort de Rius 48-9
  Estanys de Siscaró Loop 50-1
  Hoya Moros 140
  Ibón de Anayet 36-7
  Lago de Cregüeña 63
  Laguna Grande de Gredos 120-1, 135
  Mirador de Ordiales 76-7
  Peñalara 124-5
  Plan de Aiguallut 34-5
  Port de Ratera d'Espot Loop 63
  Río Borosa 10, 148-9
  Somiedo Lakes 86-9
  Trevélez to Cañada de Siete Lagunas 167
  Vega de Ario 74-5
lammergeiers 43, 44, 54
language 216-17
Las Negras to Agua Amarga 154-5
lighthouses
  Cabo Touriñán 109
  Cap de Creus 183
  Far de Sant Sebastià 188
  Far del Cap de Creus 183
  Faro de Fisterra 113
  Faro de la Plata 71
  Sa Farola 199
  Senokozulua 71
Lires to Cabo Fisterra 7, 110-13

M

Madrid 118
Mallorca 22, 193-215
  planning 194-5, 203
Matagalls 191
Mediterranean Coast 22, 169-91
  planning 170-1

Menorca 22, 193-215
  planning 194-5, 203
Mirador de Ordiales 76-7
Mirador de ses Barques to Sa Calobra 8, 208-11
monasteries
  La Trapa Monastery 204-5
  Monasterio de Yuste 140
  Monestir de Montserrat 172-3
  Mosteiro de San Paio de Abeleda 104
  Mosteiro de San Pedro de Rocas 103
  Mosteiro de Santa Cristina de Ribas de Sil 103
  Mosteiro de Santo Estevo 103
  Real Monasterio de San Lorenzo 123
  Santuario de Arantzazu 91
Mont Caro 190
Monte de Santa Trega 115
Montserrat 172-3
Morella 170
mountain trails
  Acequias del Poqueira 11, 162-5
  Anboto 92-3
  Balcón de Pineta & Lago Marboré 62
  Cañón de Añisclo 40
  Circ de Colomèrs 6, 58-61
  Circo de Gurrundué 42-3
  Cómpeta to El Acebuchal 152-3
  Cuerda Larga 141
  El Morezón 8, 134-5
  Estanh de Rius & Estanh Tort de Rius 48-9
  Estanys de Siscaró Loop 50-1
  Faja Tormosa 62
  Garganta de Navamediana 141
  Horcados Rojos 78-9
  Hoya Moros 140
  Ibón de Anayet 36-7
  Ibón Gran de Batisielles 46-7
  La Peral to Villar de Vildas 94
  Laguna Grande de Gredos 120-1, 135
  Mirador de Ordiales 76-7
  Mont Caro 190
  Montserrat 172-3
  Mulhacén 158-61
  Ordesa Canyon via the Faja de Pelay 10, 52-5
  Peñalara 124-5
  Picu Pierzu 80-1
  Picu Urriellu 7, 84-5
  Plan de Aiguallut 34-5
  Port de Ratera d'Espot Loop 63
  Puerto de Barrosa 56-7

Puig de Massanella 214
Punta del Pacino 30-1
Refugio de Armeña 63
Ruta del Cares 11, 72-3
Ruta Macizo de Ándara 95
Serra de Bèrnia Loop 180-1
Sierra de Cazorla 150-1
Siete Picos 126-9
Somiedo Lakes 86-9
Valldemossa to Deià 206-7
Xàtiva Loop 190
Mulhacén 158-61
museums
  Casa Museu Dalí 182
  Museu dels Volcans 185
Muxía to Lires 108-9

N

national parks 25, 28-9, 42, 63, 125, 158
natural parks 25, 34, 86, 184
Navia 83
Necrópolis de Cala Morell 199
Northern Spain, *see* Picos de Europa

O

O Vicedo to Porto de Espasante 106-7
off-the-beaten-path trails 12
  Alto & Bajo Sestrales 32-3
  Cala Morell to Ciutadella 198-9
  Castaño del Robledo & Alájar Loop 146-7
  Castro Caldelas Magical Forests 104-5
  Ibón Gran de Batisielles 46-7
Ordesa Canyon via la Faja de Pelay 10, 52-5
Ourense 98

P

Parada de Sil Circuit 102-3
Peña Cortada Loop 176-9
Peñalara 124-5
Picos de Europa 22, 65-95
  planning 66-7
  wildlife 75
Picu Pierzu 80-1
Picu Urriellu 7, 84-5
Pinsapar 167
Plan de Aiguallusts 34-5
planning 20-5, *see also individual locations*
  accessible travel 16-17
  essentials 18-19
  highlights 6-11
  children, travel with 14-15

Platja de Cavalleria to Platja de Binimel·là 196-7
Pola de Somiedo 66
Port de Ratera d'Espot Loop 63
Potes 66
Puerto de Barrosa 56-7
Puertos de Áliva 68-9
Puig de Massanella 214
Punta del Pacino 30-1
Pyrenees, the 20-2, 27-63
  planning 28-9

R

Refugio de Armeña 63
refugios 23-4
resources 19
  accessible travel 16
  Andalucía 145
  Central Spain 119
  Galicia 99
  Mallorca 195
  Mediterranean Coast 171
  Menorca 195
  Picos de Europa 67
  Pyrenees, the 29
  wildlife 25, 89
responsible travel 18
Ribadesella to La Espasa 94
Río Borosa 10, 148-9
rock climbing 23
Ruta Cañón do Río Mao 114
Ruta Costa da Morte 115
Ruta de Carlos V 136-39, 140, 141
Ruta del Cares 11, 72-3
Ruta del Emperador 140
Ruta Garganta de los Infiernos 141
Ruta Macizo de Ándara 95

S

safety 19, 81, 160, 203
Sallent de Gállego 28
San Lorenzo de El Escorial 118
San Lorenzo de El Escorial to Machota Baja 122-3
San Pedro 155
San Sebastián to Pasai Donibane 70-1
Sant Tomàs to Basílica de Son Bou 215
Sant Tomàs to Son Xoriguer 200-3
Santiago de Compostela 98
Serra de Bèrnia Loop 180-1
Sierra de Cazorla 150-1
Siete Picos 126-9

snow shoeing 23
Soldeu 28
Sóller 194
Somiedo Lakes 86-9
Spanish language 216-17

T

Torla 28
Tornavacas 139
Torrent de Pareis 215
trashumancia 131
Trevélez to Cañada de Siete Lagunas 167

V

Valencia 170
Vall de Bòquer 215
Valldemossa 194, 207
Valldemossa to Deià 206-7
Valle de Otal 38-9
Vega de Ario 74-5
Vega de Liordes 95
Vielha 28
Vigo 98
village trails 13
  Acequias del Poqueira 11, 162-5
  Cadaqués to Cap de Creus 182-3
  Camí dels Molins 174-5
  Juviles & Fuerte 166
  Picu Urriellu 7, 84-5
  Valldemossa to Deià 206-7
Volcanoes of Garrotxa 184-5

W

waterfalls 35, 37, 39
waymarkers 19
weather 18, 19, *see also indivyudual locations*
wildlife 24-5, 75, 81, 89
wildlife trails 12
  Camí dels Molins 174-5
  Circo de Gurrundué 42-3
  Garganta Verde 167
  Illas Cíes 100-1
  Laguna Grande de Gredos 120-1, 135
  Mont Caro 190
  Picu Urriellu 7, 84-5
  Vall de Bòquer 215
wineries 105
wolves 24, 75

X

Xàtiva Loop 190

ANNA KAMINSKI
Mallorca & Menorca

Anna Kaminski has contributed to over 30 Lonely Planet titles across six continents, including Borneo, Mexico, Jamaica, Russia, Canada, West Coast Australia and Australia's Best Walks. She is an avid trekker who's hiked the Inca Trail, and to the Everest Base Camp, and her favourite pastimes include exploring the Sierra de Almijara mountains around her home base of Cómpeta, Andalusia, and the more far-flung hiking trails on Spain's islands.

My favourite walk Mirador Ses Barques to Sa Calobra because it showcases the best of Mallorca, from olive groves, mountains and clifftop trails to pristine sandy coves.

JOHN NOBLE
Andalucía, Mediterannean Coast (Catalonia walks), Central Spain, Galicia & Picos & Northern Spain

Originally from England's Pennines, John moved to an Andalucian hill village in the 1990s and has since explored most parts of Spain. He particularly loves places you can only get to on foot. Researching walks for this book took him to all four corners of the country (and the middle); he walked 920km of trails and ascended 31,950 metres, the equivalent of 3½ Mt Everests. Find more of his photos on Instagram @johnnoble11. He is co-author of approximately 150 Lonely Planet editions covering 20-odd countries, including all 13 editions of Spain.

My favourite walk Is…Morezón. The panorama of the wild Gredos cirque and the Laguna Grande 450m below my feet just took my breath away. And a friendly ibex practically sat down beside me while I picnicked.

ZORA O'NEILL
Mediterannean Coast (Valencia walks)

Zora has been writing guidebooks since 2002, and taking walks in the woods for decades before that. For Lonely Planet, she has previously covered Andalucía, where she discovered the pleasure of village-to-village walking, as well as Morocco, Egypt, Greece and Amsterdam and other destinations. She is the author of All Strangers Are Kin: Adventures in Arabic and the Arab World, a travel memoir about studying Arabic. Find her on Twitter @zora.

My favourite walk The Peña Cortada Loop outside Valencia – just a great, varied day out, and I'd never seen aqueduct tunnels like those.

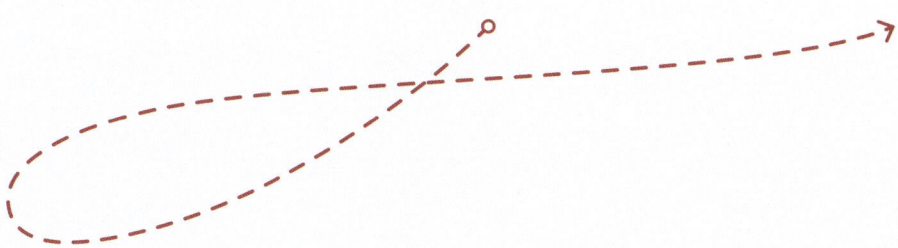

Our Story

A beat-up old car, a few dollars in the pocket and a sense of adventure. In 1972 that's all Tony and Maureen Wheeler needed for the trip of a lifetime – across Europe and Asia overland to Australia. It took several months, and at the end – broke but inspired – they sat at their kitchen table writing and stapling together their first travel guide, Across Asia on the Cheap. Within a week they'd sold 1500 copies. Lonely Planet was born.

Today, Lonely Planet has offices in the US, Ireland and China with a network of over 2000 contributors in every corner of the globe. We share Tony's belief that 'a great guidebook should do three things: inform, educate and amuse'.

Our Writers

STUART BUTLER
Pyrenees & Plan chapters

Stuart has been writing for Lonely Planet for a decade and, during this time, he's come eye to eye with gorillas in the Congolese jungles, met a man with horns on his head who could lie in fire, huffed and puffed over snow bound Himalayan mountain passes, interviewed a king who could turn into a tree, and had his fortune told by a parrot. When not on the road for Lonely Planet he lives on the beautiful beaches of Southwest France with his wife and two young children.

Today, as well as guidebook writing work, Stuart writes about conservation and environmental issues (mainly in eastern and southern Africa), wildlife watching and hiking. He also works as a photographer and was a finalist in both the 2015 and 2016 Travel Photographer of the Year Awards. In 2015 he walked for six weeks with a Maasai friend across a part of Kenya's Maasai lands in order to gather material for a book he is writing (see: www.walkingwiththemaasai.com). His website is www.stuartbutlerjournalist.com.

My favourite walk Living at the foot of the western (French) Pyrenees these mountains have a special place in my heart. For me, no walk showcases the beauty of the Pyrenees quite like the Circ de Colomèrs.

 MORE WRITERS

STAY IN TOUCH LONELYPLANET.COM/CONTACT

IRELAND Digital Depot, Roe Lane (off Thomas St), Digital Hub, Dublin 8, D08 TCV4, Ireland

Although the authors and Lonely Planet have taken all reasonable care in preparing this book, we make no warranty about the accuracy or completeness of its content and, to the maximum extent permitted, disclaim all liability arising from its use.

All rights reserved. No part of this publication may be copied, stored in a retrieval system, or transmitted in any form by any means, electronic, mechanical, recording or otherwise, except brief extracts for the purpose of review, and no part of this publication may be sold or hired, without the written permission of the publisher. Lonely Planet and the Lonely Planet logo are trademarks of Lonely Planet and are registered in the US Patent and Trademark Office and in other countries. Lonely Planet does not allow its name or logo to be appropriated by commercial establishments, such as retailers, restaurants or hotels. Please let us know of any misuses: lonelyplanet.com/ip.

 twitter.com/lonelyplanet

 facebook.com/lonelyplanet

 instagram.com/lonelyplanet

 youtube.com/lonelyplanet

 lonelyplanet.com/newsletter